SEARCHING
FOR HEROES

SEARCHING FOR HEROES

Fifty Year of Sporting Encounters

IAN WOOLDRIDGE

HODDER &
STOUGHTON

The *Daily Mail* are marking publication of *Searching For Heroes* with a donation to the Trust run by the Saints and Sinners Club in London, of which Ian Wooldridge was a member. The Trust has already received the proceeds from the collection at IW's memorial service, and these have been passed to the Chance to Shine project, run by the Cricket Foundation.

First published in Great Britain in 2007 by
Hodder & Stoughton
An Hachette Livre UK company

1

Copyright © Associated Newspapers Limited 2007

A CIP catalogue record for this title is available from the British Library

ISBN 978 0 340 96087 5

Typeset in Sabon by Hewer Text UK Ltd,

Printed and bound by Mackays of Chatham Ltd, Chatham, Kent

Hodder & Stoughton policy is to use papers that are natural, renewable and recyclable products and made from wood grown in sustainable forests. The logging and manufacturing processes are expected to conform to the environmental regulations of the country of origin.

Hodder & Stoughton Ltd
338 Euston Road
London NW1 3BH

www.hodder.co.uk

CONTENTS

CONTENTS

CONTENTS

CONTENTS

Photographic Acknowledgements

The publisher would like to thank the following for their permission to reproduce photographs:

Alan Davidson, Colorsport, Getty Images, PA Photos.

Particular thanks go to the *Daily Mail* for their help picture researching and for supplying the majority of images in *Searching for Heroes*.

All other pictures are from private collections.

TRIBUTE
by Paul Dacre

Just a few journalists are both great reporters and great writers and even fewer are great reporters, great writers *and* great thinkers. Then, at the very top of the pyramid, through the genius of their writing and perception, a golden handful almost transcend the subject they write about. Ian Wooldridge was one such person. Not that he would ever accept that of himself – he was far too self-deprecating.

In the days immediately after he died, an outpouring of words were published about Ian. His rivals in the highly competitive newspaper industry rose to salute the sports journalist whom they acknowledged as the master craftsman. These tributes, more than routinely fulsome and admiring, were filled with a very deep affection for the man. As the *Mail on Sunday*'s Patrick Collins noted in his column:

'A small comfort to Woollers' friends is the thought of him propping up a celestial cocktail bar while reading his own obituaries and spluttering, "Good lord! Quite extraordinary . . . far too generous."'

In that exquisite image, Collins captured just what it was that made Wooldridge unique.

Although he was the best sportswriter of his generation – arguably, of any generation – whom others strove to equal, he was never resented for it. To understand why, you only had to spend time in Ian's company, preferably in a bar. It soon became clear that this man of passion and conviction was also a figure of innate and very real modesty. When joining the *Mail* in 1961, he was uncertain about taking the job because, he said, he didn't know much about sport except for cricket and golf, and didn't think he was a good enough writer!

This self-doubt was both endearing and enduring. The ultimate professional, Wooldridge was a perfectionist. Although he made his craft look so easy, he agonized over his writing. The precision and care taken to perfect each column occupied countless hours and demanded an endless supply of Scotch and cigarettes – cynics have suggested (quite disgracefully!) that this may have encouraged him to take even longer than necessary – but the result was a column, published twice a week in the *Mail* for the best part of three decades, that was required reading not only for sports enthusiasts but for many people who had little interest in sport. These people read Wooldridge simply for the glory of his words and his ability to turn sport into a metaphor for life.

This was a man who left Brockenhurst Grammar School in Hampshire aged 16 with a mere two O-levels – in English and Art – and who, after National Service in the Royal Navy, began his journalistic career on the *New Milton Advertiser*. His first two assignments were covering the funeral of a local 'bigwig', coal-merchant Charlie Browning, in the morning – and, incidentally, Ian was so laborious in taking down mourners' names that he made the service half an hour late – followed, in the afternoon, by reporting on one Les Tomkins taking 9 wickets for 21 runs in the local derby against Brockenhurst.

It's pretty obvious which story raised his excitement more because the young Ian was a good enough batsman to have ambitions to play for his county. The path of his life seems to have been decided when batting at number four for Hampshire Schoolboys against the county second eleven. Facing the leg-breaks of Tom Dean, he missed the first three deliveries and was then clean bowled. More than 30 years later, while reporting an England tour to South Africa, he bumped into Tom Dean at Port Elizabeth.

'You totally altered my life,' Ian told Tom Dean. 'If I'd been able to pick your googly, I'd now be a fifty-year-old ex-pro running a crumbling pub and, I daresay, contemplating suicide.'

So cricket's loss was journalism's gain. And I'd like to think that when the 29-year-old Ian arrived – via the lamented *News Chronicle* – at the *Daily Mail*, he had found his natural home.

Ian Wooldridge would become, in the words of another sports-writing giant, the *Guardian*'s Frank Keating, 'a man whose mere presence enhanced any sporting occasion . . . from Las Vegas to Melbourne you knew the great man had logged the phone-boxes that worked, booked the best restaurant, told the barman about shaking (not stirring), and that the crucial contacts were already beating a path to his door.'

In fact, there was another – and, I think – more important side to Ian. Yes, he was inspired by the great sporting occasions, but he also cared about the welfare of the unsung majority of sportsmen and women, people who never reach the heights nor earn the multi-millions of the superstars.

He cared about the diminishing Corinthian spirit, which he saw as the very essence of every youngster's sporting dreams and without which, he feared, sport was being reduced to just another business arrangement.

And he cared about, in fact he deplored, the widespread use of drugs which, he believed, was reducing the Olympics almost to pointlessness.

His indignation vibrated on the page. Entire generations of corrupt officials, football thugs and opportunists were cut down by his elegantly damning phrases. He never chose easy targets. He attacked the villains, cheats and imposters who dragged down the sporting arena he loved, as well as those preposterously self-important, plumped up parasites who paraded the world as administrators – people such as Juan Antonio Samaranch, whose endless years as Olympic president Wooldridge corruscatingly, and brilliantly, ridiculed as 'his self-styled Excellency's exploitation of the Games as his personal court, a shadowy chamber of furtive sycophants, dubious grace and dodgy favours'.

So while Ian revered the 'greats' he had even more admiration for the also-rans, the triers. And no one tried harder, in his view, than Eddie 'The Eagle' Edwards – 'the worst ski jumper in the world' – who finished last in the Winter Olympics in Calgary in 1988.

As Ian wrote: 'Since the sport was invented in Norway in 1886, Britain's contribution to it until Eddie came along was roughly the equivalent of Samoa's impact on Wagnerian opera. At least Eddie had a go – he had the sheer guts needed to swoop off a vertiginous hypotenuse the height of St Paul's and fly in mid-air without wings, brakes or parachute.'

Wooldridge never lectured his readers, never hectored them, never preached and, certainly, never bored them. To understand what I mean, and capture the essence of his column, let's go back to May 1996 and the eve of the final three being chosen by the public for a TV series about the Greatest Ever Sportsmen.

'It is just conceivable,' Ian wrote in his *Mail* column, 'that next Monday George Best will be named as the greatest British sportsman this century. Anyway, it's between him, Ian Botham and Daley Thompson.

'It is all subjective, of course. Personally I would have Denis Compton in the first three, probably as the winner.

'I also retain a huge regard for Douglas Jardine, of whom many of the present generation will never have heard.

'Jardine invented "bodyline bowling", blasted the seemingly invincible Australians to humiliating defeat and then uttered the immortal phrase: "I don't speak to the Press and I never speak to Australians." Lord, how we could do with such verbal austerity these days.'

Ian then noted the irony that these three men had been chosen despite having very chequered backgrounds – Best with his booze and harem of Miss Worlds, Botham with an exotic hemp by-product found in his house, and Thompson acting the fool on the victory rostrum.

'Paragons,' Ian wrote, 'they were not.' Naughty they could be. Roughly as naughty, that is, as some of us in the world of journalism have been in our distant pasts. Clearly the public were not affronted. They were not judging recidivist child abusers, IRA terrorists, pederast priests, road-rage killers, drug barons or high-flying embezzlers who leave old folk penniless.

'George wouldn't harm a kitten. He is a gentle man. He, along with Pelé and Alfredo Di Stefano, were the last footballers I would have crossed oceans, let alone roads, to see in action. George Best was a genius whose talent lifted the human spirit. So were Mozart and Picasso and a right couple of larrikins they were also.'

Wooldridge was nothing if not loyal. His friendship with Lord Archer was unaffected by Jeffrey's period in prison for perjury. And Ian refused to believe for a moment that another friend, the former football manager Ron Atkinson, who was sacked from his television job over an unguarded aside about a black footballer, had a racist bone in his body.

Of course, all journalists have contacts, but not all have contacts that turn into the closest of friends. Ian did. You build that kind of relationship through trust, loyalty and not betraying confidence, and in Ian's case, providing great company too.

In Ian's obituaries, story after story was told about his love of food and drink, but what they don't capture is that his real nourishment was comradeship – the integrity, the genuineness, the sense of fun, the curiosity that is fundamental to good journalism and the power of story-telling.

When Ian celebrated his 65th birthday a decade ago, with a lunch at Simpson's in the Strand, a surprise guest was his old friend and drinking partner Denis Compton. The great England batsman was dying, but when the invitation arrived he said, 'For Woollers, anything.'

No one who was there will ever forget his unsteady but smiling arrival, supporting himself on sticks. The two men embraced. Compton drank a toast to his old friend, and a few more, before being taken home in a taxi. His salute to Woollers was the last time he left home.

Ian's own terrible illness had been with him for so long it was all too easy for us, his colleagues, to forget his heroic and never-voiced battle with pain and discomfort.

It was almost four years ago that he came to see me – he was then 72 – to say he could no longer do two columns a week and while he desperately wanted to carry on writing, he would understand if I did not want him to continue.

I wrote back to him – in fact, I still have a copy of the letter – 'Dear Ian, As long as I remain Editor of the *Daily Mail*, there will be a place in this paper for your peerless words.'

So Ian continued writing his now once-weekly column, often dictating it from his hospital bed, and never a word was out of place. At his side throughout this long and difficult period was his second wife, Sarah, whose son Jorge adored Ian, and to whom Ian was such a loving step-father.

Sarah was Ian's secret weapon. Through the awesome powers of love and willpower, it was she, I have absolutely no doubt, who literally kept Ian going. She would often take down his column and dictate it for him, old style, to the copytakers in the office. What a team!

Ian's first wife, Veronica, had also encouraged him selflessly in all his ambitions, and bore him three fine sons, Kevin, Simon and Max, of whom he was immensely proud. When Ian was awarded an OBE back in 1991, how typical it was of him to take both wives, Veronica and Sarah, to the investiture at Buckingham Palace.

Ian's last column for the *Mail* appeared on 24 February 2007. His main item alerted readers to a charity evening being held in aid of a boxer – not a famous name – for whom, as he put it, 'the lights had gone out on two thirds of his life' after the final round of a fierce bout 12 years ago. Since then, the ex-fighter had been helped by his two sisters, both working women. But he really needed round-the-clock attention, and that required a lot of money. With the simplicity that was his hallmark, Ian wrote: 'This column does not frequently support charity appeals, especially when allied to boxing, about which it remains ambiguous. But it's a free world, though I do wish, as a profession, boxing would pay more attention to its fallen.'

In the end, of course, Ian himself had to be carried out. 'Retire?' he would say. 'NEVER.'

The day after he died, we wrote these words about Ian in the *Mail* leader column. 'He was a life enhancer with a passionate belief in loyalty, integrity and the little man – not just a sports-writer of genius and a magnificent ambassador for journalism, but a man with a rare understanding of the human condition, at its best and its worst.'

Those words seem strangely inadequate today. Ian's are much better. He summed up his life with the simple epitaph: 'It's been fun.'

For us, it has been a privilege.

Paul Dacre, Editor in Chief
Associated Newspapers

FOREWORD
by Richie Benaud

One of the great things about sport is taking part. In cricket this activity can be at the very top level or in one of the lowly teams where the skill is relative, but the competition and enjoyment is just as fierce as in a Test match. Bringing to life the characters taking part in these and other contests is not easy. Some journalists have the task of doing that in newspapers, others through the medium of television where what is happening is brought to the watchers exactly as it happens on the field. Wireless commentators, now radio commentators, paint the picture for listeners and an accurate one it is too, although these days, with television also available, there is a little more pressure on those in the Test Match Special box who describe the game with a television set alongside their microphones.

Very occasionally these members of the sporting media are unfortunate in that they are condemned to watch a poor football match, a boring game of rugby, a slovenly exhibition from two cricket teams where even their nearest and dearest would be disappointed.

Then the job for the journalist is to select something, or someone, to write about so the reader will be captivated and wonder at the creativity that has brought about something from nowhere.

Two of Wooldridge's great friends were Denis Compton and Keith Miller. If that tends to suggest there was a love of cricket lurking near his typewriter, it is not far from the truth but, in fact, he had a great love of artists of any sport and characters in any game. Compton, of England, was a genius as a batsman. Miller was an Australian all-rounder of whom it was said that whether with bat or ball, or just standing languidly at slip, he could make cricket glow.

Wooldridge was one of the greatest sportswriters of all time. He wrote his copy with pencil on to foolscap pad or by tapping the keys of an old-fashioned typewriter. He did this with such brilliance and skill he made his pages glow.

I have carefully avoided referring to any individual article included in *Searching for Heroes*. The book covers many aspects of sport, how it has been played well or how there has been disappointment at the end of the day or night. The pages are full of memories, some good, some falling short of that accolade, some revealing the slight or major weaknesses of character possessed by a few of those who have moved over the playing fields of the world, or even controlled sport by being what are loosely described as administrators. 'Woollers' knew them all; he also wrote about fellow journalists in all media areas.

All of us search for heroes as we start in life and often we are lucky enough to find them. I first met Wooldridge in 1962 and have been an avid reader through all those years, and I hope you too derive great enjoyment from the collection.

PUBLISHER'S NOTE

It is now over 30 years since I first had the pleasure of working with Ian Wooldridge, when he was the co-author of Mary Peters' most readable autobiography. He was the most engaging of men and wonderful company, whose warm personality and passion shone through his writing. It was a particular pleasure therefore to be invited by the *Daily Mail* to produce a selection of his work for publication by Hodder & Stoughton.

As I knew it would, it proved a deeply rewarding though daunting task, for Ian was a prolific journalist – some seven million published words over 50 years – and his standards were uniformly high.

In preparing this book I have enjoyed the help of John Ford, a close friend from university days. A huge fan of Ian's, he has a wide knowledge of all sport and wrote a highly acclaimed social history of early cricket. Together we sifted through trunk loads of cuttings and were in remarkably close agreement about what we felt should be included.

What we have tried to do is to reflect the wide range of Ian Wooldridge's interests in a variety of sporting endeavours from the international arena to his personal pursuit of the adrenalin rush that gave his life an extra spice. He loved style, originality, courage, honesty and a sense of fun in his sporting heroes, the self-same qualities that mark his journalism. We believe that the pieces we have chosen reflect the range of his gifts and also provide the story of sport over half a century.

Sarah Wooldridge, who was such a tower of strength to Ian over the last few years when he was so ill, has still found the time and energy to come forward with ideas for the book, and give valuable advice, for which I am deeply grateful. Ian's son Max has provided a fitting and moving Final Word.

The various departments at the *Daily Mail* were quick to offer help whenever it was needed and thanks go to my conduit, Charles Garside.

When short introductions were required for various articles to put them in context, they have been included in italics. Where Ian had already written introductions they are in plain type. His initials have been inserted where necessary, rather than 'Woollers', the name by which he was affectionately known.

Roddy Bloomfield, Editor
Hodder & Stoughton
October 2007

THE OVERSEAS MEMBER

I have never been able to establish whether the following story is accurate. I include it because, if it is, one of its perpetrators may yet come forward to receive the acclaim he deserves.

Dateline: **Australia 1982**

Tales from the Australian outback have room for embellishment by the time they reach the watering holes of Fleet Street but I am assured that the story of how the exclusive Marylebone Cricket Club – waiting list four years at least – recruited its latest member is true.

Last month a London banker and his MCC-member friend played a few club matches in Australia and then decided to hire a car and explore the vast expanses of silent nothingness that lie out there beyond Melbourne and Adelaide.

The vehicle had two unfamiliar steel bars above the front fender. 'These,' explained the car-hire man, 'are to prevent the bonnet being smashed in when those daft kangaroos leap out straight in front of you.'

Some days later with the banker touching 60 mph down a dirt road, a kangaroo seeking nothing more than companionship did precisely that. He was struck by the car and killed instantly.

The MCC member, armed with a camera and a public school sense of humour, had a terrific idea. While his banker friend hauled the late mad marsupial to its feet the MCC member pulled his cricket bag from the car and proceeded to knot an

MCC tie round its throat, place an MCC cap on its head and drag an MCC blazer over its front legs and shoulders.

The motive, of course, was to take a photograph which would raise a hell of a laugh back at Lord's and, if sufficiently good, even make the centre-page spread in a newspaper like the *Daily Mail*.

A jubilant thing then happened. The kangaroo, merely heavily stunned and not killed by the impact, shook its thick head a few times, broke from the banker's grasp and raced off.

It shook off the MCC cap but presumably is the only kangaroo now strolling around wearing an MCC tie and blazer. If so it is only poetic justice that the blazer still has the MCC member's passport in the left-hand inside pocket.

I was hoping to prove the veracity of this strange encounter by publishing a photograph. Unfortunately, inquiries reveal that the MCC member is now in South Africa on a temporary passport, probably doing terrible things with a rhinoceros.

Chapter One

PERSONAL

HOW TO ADDRESS
A TYPEWRITER

A RANDOM survey of the famous bars along Fleet Street between noon and closing time any day except Saturday would do little to dispel an ugly rumour. It is that if a career in sportswriting demanded academic qualifications beyond an accidental O-level in metalwork, most British newspapers would end with four blank pages.

British sportswriters, almost to a man, live by the Hemingway creed that movement should never be confused with action. Thus the archetypal sportswriter's working day tends to start with field research over several glasses of lunch in either El Vino's or Scribes' Cellar and end in heated debate about Geoffrey Boycott's patriotism in the Press Club some 14 hours later.

This, of course, is provided you are not in Australia with England's cricketers or New York for a big fight. In that case the same argument will be going on in either the Sydney Press Club or Costello's Bar on East 44th Street. Sportswriters are frequently uncomfortable in the presence of outsiders, particularly those with views about sport.

From time to time the sportswriter is required to address a typewriter. This is mostly to fill out expenses forms itemizing the horrendous amounts of largesse that have to be invested in restaurants and nightclubs these days in order to extract from sportsmen, referees, mistresses, politicians and former Sports Council employees the kind of information that makes a sports page worth reading.

The university has yet to be founded which offers graduate courses in these matters. Only in America is it possible for earnest young men to major in journalism, whatever that means. This explains why much American sportswriting, with a few formidable exceptions, reads as though it has been computed in a word-processing machine.

One of the exceptions was Red Smith, of the *New York Times*, who was once asked whether sportswriting was a difficult trade. 'There's nothing to it,' Mr Smith replied. 'You merely sit there at a typewriter and think until the blood seeps out of the pores on your forehead.' I once saw him seeping blood at the end of a golf tournament in Ireland. His chair was ankle-deep in crushed balls of paper. These were the introductory paragraphs he had fought with and discarded before hitting on one that would grab the reader by the throat and pin him down for the next 1,200 words.

Work, however, is the unspoken area of a business whose main credentials are swift two-finger typing, knowing how coin-telephones operate in Kiev, having the wisdom to leave semicolons to those who believe they know how to use them, and a metabolism that can cope with jet-lag, Indian sanitation, Australian hospitality, and hangovers. Anyone with the remotest understanding of what happens inside fuse boxes or internal combustion engines is unlikely ever to make a sportswriter. Anyone who prefers to sit down and write for three hours and then pay someone *else* to paint the bathroom is at least morally equipped for the struggle.

Most English sportswriters started out desperately wanting to play for England at anything, failed, and then pestered their way on to local weekly newspapers with names like *The Bugle* or *Sentinel*. Mine, in Hampshire, was called the *New Milton*

Advertiser and was run by a proprietor-editor who had a roll-top desk, candlestick telephone and, while writing powerful leader columns, hawked and spat into the waste-paper basket at seven-minute intervals between November and March. He was a benevolent bully, a brilliant journalist and was convinced that Lenin had personally founded the National Union of Journalists. Most of the apprentice reporters he employed on Dickensian salaries were in Fleet Street inside four years.

The editorial offices were a prefabricated bungalow heated by paraffin stoves that made noises like irritated cobras. The paper did not run to a specialist sportswriter. It employed young men with acne and bicycles who were expected to report local cricket, football and darts on Saturdays as a relaxation after a week at magistrates' courts, council meetings, inquests, weddings and flower shows.

Its big circulation-booster, however, was funerals. Funerals attracted mourners. Mourners who got their names into the *Advertiser* always bought one copy and frequently three.

My first assignment in journalism, apart from scuttling off to fetch 20 Senior Service for the chief reporter, was the funeral of Charles Browning, coal merchant and wealthy pillar of rectitude of the parish, God rest his soul.

Charles Browning has lain at peace these past 30 years in a lovely New Forest churchyard but getting him there was a less tranquil business altogether. No one had advised me that the trick was to get to the church, which was a mile from the graveside, an hour before the kick-off to collect the names, full initials and, in some cases, former service ranks plus decorations of those attending – on their way *in*. They just gave you a spiral-bound notebook and a 4B pencil and assumed everything would be OK.

It was. But not before a fledgling reporter had blocked the church doorway to scribble the names, full initials, former service ranks and decorations of the mourners – on their way *out*. None passed unrecorded but the half-hour of strain on the sagging pall-bearers waiting to slide the coffin of the coal-tycoon into the hatch-back hearse for his last terrestrial journey was not quickly forgotten.

It was nothing to do with sport, but it was incomparable training for hijacking important witnesses, on their way out after disciplinary hearings against naughty footballers, and real little anarchists like John McEnroe, many years later. Foot-in-the-door techniques now meet with the disapproval of the Press Council but by a fortuitous oversight the Press Council has no sportswriters sitting on it.

No reporter will ever work harder than during his seven-day, 6,000-word week on a highly disciplined local rag. You learn about fire engines, how rates are levied, suicides, head-on car collisions, what corpses look like, how to cheat in husbanding prize-winning root vegetables, perjury, how the scoring works at lawn bowls and that local sports club officials are frequently close personal relatives of Adolf Hitler.

SEVENTY-ONE BEDS
PER ANNUM

THERE are mornings when you wake up and cannot believe they pay you for it. By nightfall you will have seen another Test match day in Sydney or Port of Spain, a Grand Prix in Brazil or Monaco, a world heavyweight title fight in Las Vegas or darkest Africa, a tennis match in Wimbledon or Melbourne, a wrestling contest in Tokyo, a chess think-in in Iceland, the 100-metres or 1500-metres Olympic final in Rome or Moscow or maybe just the Cup final at Wembley. It adds up, in a good year, to about 150,000 miles, 70 hotels, 3,500 telephone calls and between 200,000 and 210,000 words. There are times, struggling with the words, when you would cheerfully chuck it all for some quiet index-linked pension life at the Ministry of Anything but it is surprising how swiftly a good dinner at the Algonquin in New York or the Peninsula, Hong Kong, will bring you to your senses.

The Peninsula management send an olive-green Rolls-Royce to meet you at the airport. Two minutes after you reach your room a servant enters bearing a tray and invites you to choose from any of the world's dozen most luxurious toilet soaps. An expansive friend of mine from the *Daily Express* said: 'Yes, that will do very nicely, thank you.' He grabbed the tray and hurled all twelve soaps into his case. You meet all kinds of people and learn many recondite things along the sportswriting road.

You learn that jet propulsion, motorways, six-hour laundries, penicillin, plastic credit cards, secretaries who can actually write shorthand, and whisky are the seven real wonders of the world. The whisky is to brush your teeth with in India where some taps drip pure hemlock. You learn the truth of a phrase that Cliff Michelmore once coined or quoted: take half the clothes and twice the money. You learn to cram suits, shirts and shoes into your hand-baggage to save hanging around at airports. You learn to eat only one meal in three on long-haul trips to Australia to prevent feeling like death when you get off. You learn, if you are right-handed and propose to work on the plane, to choose a right-hand window seat. If you don't your neighbour, however well bred, will inhibit you by glancing at your last sentence. You learn that first-class airline travel is frequently a waste of your money or your firm's. The free champagne comes quite expensive when, quite often, you could stretch out across three seats back in tourist class and get a good night's sleep. You learn that jet-lag is a term invented by second-division salesmen who come home with an empty order-book. What you do on arrival is adjust your watch to local time, carry on and go to bed as usual. You learn when travelling between Britain and the United States to fly Concorde on every occasion you can induce someone else to pay the fare.

For a lark we once used Concorde for an unusual golf match. On the eve of New Year's Eve, and thus on almost the shortest day of the year, we played the first nine holes at Royal Mid-Surrey, took a taxi to London Airport, recharged our batteries with Dom Perignon '69 on the 3,778-mile, 3-hour 56-minute crossing to Washington on Concorde Alpha Delta, drove out past the Pentagon to the Army and Navy Country Club and there played the second nine holes. The five-hour time difference allowed us to complete the contest in a single span of daylight. In the bar that evening we met an American lady of indeterminate age, much plastic surgery and several marriages, the latest of which apparently allowed her to call herself the Countess von Essen. 'How have you spent your day?' inquired the Countess. 'Playing golf,' we replied. 'Oh,' huffed the lady, 'how stupendously boring.'

On the homeward journey, 2,000 miles out over the Atlantic and at an altitude almost twice the height of Mount Everest, my opponent, Trevor Nash, struck an undeviating putt down the aisle of Concorde into a wine glass. Since the plane was travelling at 1,400 miles an hour at the time, the flight-deck computer soon calculated that the putt had actually travelled 5,111 feet, a distance from which even the great Jack Nicklaus has occasionally been known to miss. What was even more stupendously boring was that the *Guinness Book of Records* subsequently refused to deem it worthy of inclusion.

Thankfully the *Daily Mail* has a long track-record of encouraging its reporters to renounce the comforts of a Press-box and join in. One of the more esoteric discoveries of my sports editor, Tom Clarke, was a 1,110-mile dog-sled race across the same outer wastes of Alaska that 80 years previously had claimed the lives of hundreds of ill-fed and wrongly clothed men in their avaricious rush for gold.

It was a sleepy Sunday evening when Clarke telephoned and inquired: 'How are you feeling, baby?' This solicitous approach invariably means you can cancel all engagements for the next fortnight. In this case it was almost a month. A few days later photographer Monty Fresco and I were flying low along the Iditarod Trail that winds out west from Anchorage, crosses the broken molars of the Alaska Range, swoops down to the Yukon, turns up the Norton Sound and ends in Nome, a wild town that stares straight up the wrong end of Siberia. An equivalent distance is from London to Naples but the analogy is a bad one. It implies warmth and civilization, both of which are conspicuous by their absence through the Eskimo and Indian territories of Jack London's old Alaska.

Below us, padding onwards at eight miles an hour and 5,000 canine strides to the mile, the huskies were dragging their mushers on what the *Daily Mail* was billing as The Last Great Race on Earth. It was, too, but the real race was to find somewhere to sleep. Delusions of comfort disappeared first night out. Fresco's ingenuity found us a double bed-frame in a log cabin which, by 4 a.m. was occupied by 28 mushers who came in stamping snow from their feet and thus contributing to the inch-deep pool of water on the floor. This we fell into when the bed broke. On a corner stove the mushers were boiling up huge chunks of horse flesh to feed to their dogs for breakfast. The cabin was so blue with fetid fumes that you could almost cut solid cubes of the atmosphere to keep as grisly souvenirs. No dawn would have ever been more beautiful had the temperature outside not been 45° Fahrenheit below. This dropped to 80° below on the unsheltered side of the Alaska Range when the cruel winds off Siberia brought the chill factor into play. On a soft European face it felt as though the skin was being scoured right down to the nerve ends with steel wool.

Our bush pilot, Serge Amundson, flew us up four valleys of the Alaska Range before he finally lifted his 31-year-old Piper aircraft clear of the swirling cloud and got us to the other side. We were luckier than the Spanish television crew who came to film the race two years later, struck a mountain face and died.

The huskies are the heroes. They have indomitable hearts and will run on till they drop. The Iditarod that year was won by 800 yards in 16 hours 27 minutes and 13 seconds by Rick Swenson. Next morning, resurrected by the opulence of bed sheets, a shower and a loo that actually flushed, I breakfasted with Rick.

'I'd like a large glass of milk,' he said to a waitress who gave every impression of having known not only Jack London but also 5,000 other gold-rushers intimately. She screwed up her eyes against the smarting irritation of her own cigarette smoke and delivered an immortal line: 'You kiddin' or somethin', all we serve here is whisky, gin or vodka.' Rick explained, unnecessarily, that Nome is not quite like other towns.

Discomfort, though, is rarely a factor in the sportswriting life. Even cricket tours of India, once rated by reporters as a four-month prison sentence without remission, are no longer the white man's burden. There are now hotels where you can get a passable dry martini though, while enjoying it, you have to cope with a conscience that reminds you that you have just spent more on a single drink than many Indians earn in a month. You despair that a country of such untapped intelligence and charm can be so gutted by terminal bureaucracy and corruption. It is one of cricket's more hilarious stories that the entire profits of an Indian tour to England, allegedly lost in mysterious circumstances, later turned up in bricks and mortar in the form of a brand new house for one of the senior officials who had handled the funds.

On my first and last lengthy visit there I was surprised to be asked to close the door behind me when going to settle my not-inconsiderable bill for accommodation, meals and entertainment at a famous residential club. Eventually the secretary stopped beating around a thicket of bushes. 'I see no reason to inconvenience you by paying now,' he said. 'When you get back to England just make out your cheque and send it off to this man at this address.' The address was that of a well-known seat of English learning and what I was being asked to do was contribute to the school fees of the secretary's son. Appropriately the secretary is now dead and there is little doubt that his festering country is a better place for that.

One of the few good reasons for ever visiting India again would be to catch up with the Nawab of Pataudi, a superb Test batsman and captain in the 1960s, who hardly sustains the contention that modern sport is so grim and humourless that it has killed off the great characters and eccentrics.

Batting better than ever after losing an eye when catapulting through his own windscreen in a car crash, Pataudi returned to England as captain where his handicap eventually came to the attention of a BBC radio programme whose producer realized that it was far too important a story to entrust to a mere sports reporter. He assigned instead to conduct the interview at Lord's a young gentleman with leather elbow-patches and an entire honours' board of academic qualifications.

The learned interviewer tapped on the dressing-room door and asked if it would be possible to speak to Mr Pataudi. The Nawab arrived. 'Tell me,' demanded the interviewer, 'do you speak English?'

'Yiss,' stuttered Pataudi, 'I spik English little. I try for you very hard make good talk. Now, pliss, enter sir.'

When the interview was broadcast next day it tended, for a few moments, to bemuse Pataudi's closest friends. The sublime Peter Sellers Hindi sounded rather unfamiliar from a man who had spent six years at Winchester, three at Oxford and whose accent, at other times, was pure Brigade of Guards.

Almost as unpopular as India on the sportswriting itinerary

are the Eastern European countries. Anyone ideologically attracted to their system should prepare himself for a lifetime of hotel furniture scarred with cigarette burns, ill-cut synthetic fibre clothes, long queues for everything except ice-cream and a chilling lack of any form of humour. Their extreme efforts to dissuade Western journalists from noticing these shortcomings can occasionally be embarrassing.

Arriving at Varna, on the Black Sea coast of Bulgaria, for an Olympic Congress, I was amazed to be shown to a hotel room quite up to Trust House Forte standards. It even had a telephone, which shortly rang. 'Look,' said someone from my London news desk, 'there's quite a good story near you. Apparently hundreds of British package-deal tourists have been flung out of their hotels. They've got nowhere to go. They're sleeping on park benches and on the sands.'

A brief stroll around the town confirmed the truth of it. My fellow-countrymen, some enraged but more bewildered, looked like refugees. A firm interview with the hotel manager was clearly in order. He arrived, all smiles and urbanity.

'You are comfortable in your room?' he asked solicitously.

'Extremely,' I replied.

'I am so glad,' he said. 'We had to ask a lot of holidaymakers to leave in order to make room for all you journalists.'

Even Moscow was never as callous as that, although the contrast between the bare shelves of the food stores and the lavish supplies of caviar and imported meat and butter in the restaurants set aside for the 9,000 visiting reporters at the 1980 Olympics did spear the conscience. The Games, of course, were a massive propaganda exercise for Soviet prosperity and happiness and the lengths to which the commissars were prepared to go to promote this illusion and keep visiting journalists in a contented frame of mind went far beyond five-star food and cut-price tickets for the Bolshoi Ballet.

14

The most amusing, because of the subtlety of its psychology, involved the sudden arrival in Moscow of many attractive women from all over the western Soviet Union. By extraordinary coincidence if you phoned to book a table for six at one of the city's expensive tourist restaurants and spoke in English, you found on arrival a neighbouring table occupied by six English-speaking Russian ladies. If you booked in German or French then they all spoke German or French. They were mostly between 20 and 35, extremely friendly and intelligent and, despite giving the impression they had not known one another very long, were unanimously ready to engage guests at nearby tables in relaxing conversation.

Frequently, I understand, one thing led to another and quite a few journalists left Moscow's Sheremetyevo Airport with nostalgic backward glances and a much greater understanding of Russian social mores. The ladies, I must add, were all considerably more amateur than most of the Olympic athletes. Their professional counterparts had long since been rounded up and packed off to the woods.

WHY MUST I BE A TEENAGER IN LOVE?

UNIVERSITY never entered into it, even if I'd had the brains. The only yearning was to get out of those bloody classrooms where every week was as long as the years now are short. There was a terrific world out there somewhere, I knew that from Hemingway, James Hadley Chase and *Picture Post*, and it was full of newspapers, adventure, bars, promiscuous women and men who lit cigarettes like Humphrey Bogart.

It wasn't in the genes. My dad hardly ever drank and the only time he went abroad he was shot on the Somme. He thought rather well of Oswald Mosley and we fought like polecats, particularly during my Marxist period. My mother was a lovely lady, the peacemaker who made marmalade instead of buying it and voted the way my dad told her to. On the morning of my first marriage she came into my bedroom to explain the facts of life and I hadn't the heart to tell her she was about ten years too late.

It probably never crossed their minds that teenagers might have problems. In his teens my father was a fighting soldier in a hellish war. In her teens, my mother was already a cook in a highly disciplined country house. So how could their teenage offspring, with his smart school uniform, racing bike, lots of books, sufficient pocket money and a warm, protective home, conceivably have problems?

Well, I did have a couple. The first was to get out of that school before anyone had any bright ideas about further education and the second, as Mr Hadley Chase so enticingly put it, was getting laid. These days they're all sexual veterans at 16, but then the best you could hope for was elementary net practice behind the pavilion and the chance of staving off a bout of acne.

I'd won a scholarship to a co-ed grammar school where they also had women teachers. Miss Harrison, a young trainee history mistress with sensational legs, was the prize fantasy of all of us throughout the Napoleonic Wars, and a wave of furious jealousy ran through the school when it was rumoured she'd been walking hand-in-hand with that bastard sixth-form prefect, Rigby. It must say something about my state of mind then that I can still remember his name.

In lieu of the unattainable Miss Harrison I fell passionately in love with a pretty blonde named Janet Baker, though not the one destined to become an ethereal soprano. This, tragically, was unrequited. Monica, Bunty, Madeleine and a few others were marginally more responsive but, at 16, what James Hadley Chase had been describing so graphically was still at the end of some distant rainbow.

Sublimation was the only answer, and by luck it wasn't difficult to find. Futile dreams of becoming a professional cricketer were jettisoned and I joined my local newspaper as a dogsbody cub reporter. Within the week I was standing alongside grim-faced policemen as they hauled from a deep well the body of a small lady, bullied by a brute of a husband, who'd chosen this tragic route to suicide. She came from my own small village and my parents knew her well.

I was still 16 but out in the world. At no time since my teens have I worked so hard: seven days a week covering courts, inquests and council meetings, chasing the fire engine to the latest blaze, listing mourners at funerals, drinking with cops and pompous councillors, covering football, rugger, cricket and flower shows at weekends.

My parents were probably alarmed that I was now smoking 20 Senior Service a day, and some nights would have been hard pressed to have passed the breathalyser on a bicycle, had such contraptions been invented. But they never remonstrated. My social circle was widening, from our Tory MP to petty thieves, and they knew I was happy aiming, one day, to make it to Fleet Street.

At home, sex was never mentioned so there seemed no point enlightening my parents when I eventually broke my duck on a river bank with a girl who now has two grandchildren. Nor was a word ever breathed about an unnerving but thrilling encounter that occurred a few months later.

One afternoon, a strong-voiced lady telephoned our little

newspaper and announced she was an American racing driver who was prepared to be interviewed at her holiday home. We didn't see too many American women racing drivers in the New Forest around then, so I caught the evening bus.

Dinner was set for two. It didn't last long and nor did the subsequent action. She was 42 and I was 18. She wrote me a charming letter later thanking me for my effusive write-up.

Anyway, it was all good training for the immediate future. My teens ran out square-bashing around Royal Naval Barracks, Portsmouth, and then learning Russian, of which I now speak hardly a word. They posted us to Cushaven, Germany, not far from the sin city of Hamburg, and, yes, I do believe that National Service contributed to an all-round education.

The point was that there were never enough hours in the day. And there never have been since.

LEST WE FORGET

It was the year we indulged in a small personal campaign. One month separated the following two pieces and I include both here to encourage others to fight the good fight.

Dateline: **New Milton 1987**

SHORTLY after dawn on 1 July 1916, my father Private Edmund Wooldridge endured a great stroke of luck. He was shot through the legs by a German machine-gunner. On that insane morning on the Somme more than half the 120 men of his unit were killed. My father was hauled off the battlefield after nightfall and lived for a further 56 years.

Thus by a matter of inches he avoided becoming the 66th

name on the simple war memorial that on summer evenings casts a poignant shadow across the football pitch on the town-centre Recreation Ground at New Milton in Hampshire.

Among the 65 men it commemorates – plus many more who fell in World War II – several were his boyhood mates. They died on the Somme, at Gallipoli, Passchendaele and Jutland.

In their memory the grateful villagers of New Milton did more than erect a cross. They collected £850 and bought the land that was to become the Recreation Ground. In a deed registered with the Charity Commission on 16 April 1920, they stipulated that the space was 'exclusively for the sporting amusements or pleasures of the inhabitants of the parish and for no other purpose.'

New Milton is my home town and I am but one of several generations of urchins who benefited from their foresight.

We learned our cricket and our soccer there, smoked our first Woodbine behind the pavilion, attempted to kiss our first girl-friends on its benches and collected a headful of stitches trying to ride a bicycle down the children's slide.

Mostly we managed to keep out of the juvenile courts and, since there was so much else to do, I don't think we went around gratuitously smashing up people or property.

Paragons we were certainly not but each Remembrance Sunday, in our best clothes, we used to line up in front of the war memorial in our playground and stand very still for precisely two minutes. It was small enough tribute to the men who had died to preserve our freedom and give us such fun.

I direct these thoughts to the boards of directors of a property development company called Trencherwood and the Gateway supermarket chain who are proposing to rip up New Milton's Recreation Ground and transform it into a £6½ million community asset which sells cut-price shampoo and has parking space for 250 cars.

True, they propose to compensate the inhabitants by providing alternative sporting facilities on the fringe of the town and, with a suitable show of piety, pledge that their temple of commerce will be so tastefully landscaped that the war memorial cross won't even have to be moved. All this appeared to be going quietly ahead until it came to the ears of two remarkable urban resistance fighters: 79-year-old pensioner Bob Gates and 52-year-old widow Doreen Fernie.

Gates tramped 64 miles of the parish streets to collect 5,170 signatures of protest and Mrs Fernie's petition is currently 4,000 signatures long and growing.

The Trencherwood-Gateway axis are smoothly countering this by proposing to finance a parish referendum proving that the majority of New Milton's 20,000 population would prefer cut-priced shampoo to a tree-ringed town-centre park where the elderly may doze while the kids play their sport and get up to innocent mischief.

The kids there yesterday were quite relishing the prospect of a fight. 'We shall,' declared their spokeschild, 'lie down in front of their bulldozers.'

What may seem like a parochial hassle in a dot on the map between Southampton and Bournemouth is, of course, nothing of the sort.

Down the length of Britain the developers have rapacious fingers in dozens of pies.

They rely on community apathy to give them their breaks. Playing fields, sports clubs, open spaces disappear overnight while the winners of a very new game spend more and more time in Barbados or on the Costa del Sol.

In New Milton, Bob Gates, who played cricket on the Recreation Ground from 1927 to 1948, and Doreen Fernie, an attractive secretary, have taken on the invaders.

They have nothing to win but the status quo and I believe

that is how the glorious dead of my small town would have wanted it.

My father, for whom life was a bonus after the Somme, should have written this story. He would have been much amused by a sentence on page eight of Gateway Foodmarkets Ltd's elaborately printed proposal to enhance New Milton's future way of life.

'The company,' it says, 'is a major sponsor of English Heritage and also contributes to needy local children through its Help the Child campaign.'

My dad would have pointed out that New Milton already has all the heritage it needs and that its children, by and large, are healthy and happy. I suspect the rest of his views could never be printed.

FOUR weeks ago the *Daily Mail* took up the cause of a small Hampshire town whose War Memorial Recreation Ground was threatened by commercial desecration.

Those 3.6 acres of oak-fringed grass – once the home of New Milton's Cricket Club, still the headquarters of its football team and for 57 years a living tribute to local men killed in two world wars – are now safe.

The London-based property development company Trencherwood confirmed yesterday that it has abandoned expensive and advanced plans to transform it into a car park for a Gateway supermarket.

Chapter Two

1961–1972

AUSCHWITZ – THE MOST MONSTROUS MUSEUM

Just recently appointed as Sports Correspondent to the Daily Mail, *one of IW's early pieces was, surprisingly perhaps, this moving account of a visit quite outside his expected remit.*

Dateline: **Poland 1961**

Y OU drive up in the semi-darkness of a pine wood, jolt down into the dip of a level-crossing, and then swing right along a narrow road of shining cobblestones.

There is no road sign to tell you where you are, no milestone to measure how far you have come from the complacent warmth of your own little world.

There is merely a wrought-iron gate surmounted by the most treacherous three-word proclamation in the history of mankind. *Arbeit macht frei*, it says ('Work brings freedom').

I walked today among the ghosts of 4,000,000 people for whom this promise never held good. For these are the gates of Auschwitz.

Every bloodstained brick, every barb of wire, every machine-gun post, every gruesome relic, every gas-chamber and oven still stands.

For while the British have wiped Belsen off the face of the earth and the Germans divert you from Dachau, the Poles have turned Auschwitz into the world's most monstrous museum.

It stands, a huddle of grey buildings on a bleak plain that stretches out to a desolate horizon.

Admittance, as always, is free.

Four million people half the population of London, met degredation and death here in an area smaller than Regent's Park. Yet until you have walked these acres of agony, with sickness rising in your throat and turmoil deranging your mind, you cannot comprehend such a clinically stated statistic.

Around 80,000 people, among them not more than a handful of observers from the Western world, visit Auschwitz each year.

For many it is an appalling pilgrimage to lay wreaths somewhere within the squalid square mile where relatives died. Few, my guide told me, ever continue conducted tours past Block 11.

This is a two-storeyed brick building no larger than an English village hall. In its cramped cellar in the morning of 3 September 1941 600 Soviet soldiers were gassed. It was the first time that Zyclon B had ever been used.

At the far end of that dark dank corridor, guests are invited to crawl through a grille no larger than the entrance to a dog kennel.

I did so, and emerged into a claustrophobic brick box, so small that I could touch all four walls by sweeping one extended arm in an arc. Here relays of four naked men were incarcerated until they died of starvation.

From Block 11's upper windows you stare down into an execution yard untouched since the Russian Army smashed its way into Auschwitz on 27 January 1945.

Grass now grows at the feet of four gallows. And a simple bunch of chrysanthemums lies beneath the towering blank wall, where men were even refused the privilege of defiantly facing a firing squad.

They were lined up and shot in the back of the neck.

There are rooms of pictures, human hair, gold teeth, torture instruments. The tawdry rags of striped prison garments, a child's broken doll.

You will know it all if you have read Lord Russell or the evidence against Adolf Eichmann. You will know it all and you will know nothing.

For, until you have seen the single-line rail track that led from all over Europe to end in a blank concrete wall in this terrible field in the south-west corner of Poland, you cannot begin to calculate the price that was paid for our freedom.

I write these words for my own generation to whom Auschwitz is already a horror as improbably remote as the inquisition of Spain or Christian persecution in Rome.

I write them because today I was free to turn and walk back through the hellish gates which just 16 years ago had closed for ever on 4,000,000 of my fellow men.

BILL ALLEY – CRICKETER OF THE YEAR

BILL ALLEY, 43-year-old Australian-born Somerset all-rounder, was last night elected Cricketer of the Year. He polled 70 of the 162 votes cast – more than three times as many as England captain Ted Dexter.

Alley, whose 112 wickets and 1,915 runs this summer swept Somerset to fifth place in the county table, was chosen by rival county cricketers.

For the first time since the Brylcreem awards were inaugurated the title was decided by the voice of all capped county players in the country. Dexter, Yorkshire's Phil Sharpe and Hampshire's Derek Shackleton were Alley's nearest rivals. They polled 25 per cent of the votes between them.

ELOQUENT words and noble sentiments are entirely unnecessary to record the cricketing philosophy of William E. Alley.

'Listen, mate,' he said, 'I've only ever believed one thing. Don't even give your grandmother a full toss on her birthday.'

Bill Alley, the Cricketer of the Year who is old enough to have fathered at least four of our own current Test team, is inevitably Australian.

He never intends to go back there, but the creed of the outback, like his accent, will never leave him.

'Honest,' he said, 'if my best mucker came in with six ducks in a row behind him I'd bloody well bowl him first ball if I could. Mind you, I'd applaud him if he hit me for four.'

Bill Alley has played it that way across 38 years and half the world: for Hornsby School, for New South Wales, in the Lancashire League and lately for the benefit of his own kind of straight-talking cobbers in Somerset.

'I'm going to settle down there when I've finished,' he said. 'I've just built a bungalow outside Taunton. It's got a couple of acres. I'll get a few chickens, a couple of pigs and maybe a cow. But it won't be for a few years yet.'

The nomadic feet of Bill Alley, 44 next February, are still itching.

He finished an exhausting seven-day-a-week English season on Tuesday evening.

Flies out early on Wednesday morning for a tour of southern Africa, Rhodesia and a dozen games in the east.

Comes home for Christmas.

Leaves immediately afterwards for a seven-week long cricket campaign in the West Indies.

Reports fresh, and brimful with ambition, at the end of April, to try to boost Somerset to better than fifth place in next year's championship.

He had only four cricketless days this summer for he played in benefit matches on Sundays and representative games when his Somerset colleagues were resting.

Apart from his boots – which he appears to have worn since he was a blacksmith's striker, a boilermaker's mate, a professional welterweight and a dance-hall chucker-out in Sydney – he shows no signs of wear.

He says that any 40-year-old should feel the same way if he follows the rules.

'First, keep your enthusiasm. I get the same kick out of a cricket match now as I did when they let us out of school to play in the yard.

'Second, pick the right girl. I married a Lancashire lass and she's the greatest. She stays at home while I go off in the sun but she knows that's the way we make our living.

'Third, keep yourself fit and don't be scared to have a couple of beers in the evening.'

Bill Alley folded his £500 cheque and raced to catch the 6.30 to Taunton. Dusk was falling over another cricket season, and there was packing to be done before dark.

GOOD ON YOU, DOOK

Widespread astonishment greeted the appointment of the Duke of Norfolk as manager of the MCC team in Australia in 1962/63. IW was among those who recognized his success.

Dateline: **Melbourne 1962**

WE WERE having a few beers in a no-star saloon the other night when an Aussie mate of mine said: 'Don't look now, but there's a guy behind you who could save Australia from the Americans.'

In due course I turned to take in a scene that would have caused apoplexy in the protocol department at the Court of St James's.

His Grace the Duke of Norfolk was laughing like an old sea captain at a story that had just been told by a small man with a crocodile-skin face and thumbs through the armholes of his waistcoat.

The Duke was harbouring a schooner of Paddy Hannan's best brew between his Savile-suited elbows on the table.

Two other men, with the dust of the outback on their boots, were also in the school. For all I know one may have been Killer Webb who, according to a chalked proclamation at the end of the bar, was in the process of murdering all his mates at knock-out darts.

The Duke bade them goodnight at 10.50 p.m. to retire to a bed that not only sagged in the middle but also tilted alarmingly forward.

He was up soon after dawn to talk to farm kids over the Flying Doctor radio link, conduct his daily Press conference with English and Australian reporters and get to the cricket ground where he willingly appended his one-word autograph to anything from elegant albums to the backs of used envelopes.

This cameo from the daily life of a duke was enacted in the Klondyke-style township of Kalgoorlie. But it might have been Perth, Adelaide or even here in metropolitan Melbourne.

The Duke of Norfolk tossed the rule-book off the top deck of the Canberra the moment we sighted Australia.

He's played it by ear ever since and, if he will forgive an opinion that's not meant to be filppant, he's taken ten years off his age in the process.

The profound pace of his walk, which somehow seemed to turn an ordinary pavement into the aisle of Westminster Abbey, has accelerated into a zestful, swinging stride.

The right hand, which at first flapped distractingly up and down as he addressed an audience, is now thrust firmly into his jacket pocket as he faces a microphone with the ease of a Dimbleby.

He is here as manager of an MCC cricket team and if they had hired a high-pressure publicity tycoon at £5,000 for the tour they couldn't have got the job better done.

It was well illustrated a few days ago when, in an historic mix-up in Perth, both Ted Dexter and his rival Australian captain led their teams on to the field in the belief that the other side was batting.

Evening newspapermen, cabling and phoning urgent stories from the Press-box 80 yards distant, hardly had time to wind fresh paper into their typewriters before a complete explanation of the confusion was in their possession.

The Duke, slightly breathless from having hastened up 46 stairs, had interviewed both captains, sorted out and confirmed the full facts and was relaying them in short sentences to 30 reporters.

It is this appreciation of a newspaperman's problems that has guaranteed him glittering advance publicity across Australia. It may also account for the greatest gaffe of the tour to date.

On a television programme last week he was referred to throughout as the Duke of Bedford. But though the Duke may be only an also-ran in the stately homes league in England, he is a champion here in the eyes of both players and public. He has abolished the last remnants of apartheid between amateur and professional cricketers.

Round a massive circular table at an Adelaide golf club we were sorting out partners in a company that included the amateur Colin Cowdrey, the distinguished Sir Donald Bradman, the affable Tom Graveney, and an English journalist, so constantly close to the Duke's elbow that he has become known as Black Rod.

Yet the Duke chose for his partner one Frederick Trueman whose renowned vocabulary, when trapped in the rough, is sufficiently Saxon as to require an interpreter.

Throughout it all the Norfolk dignity has remained unimpaired. Those of us who deal with him daily have been informed that 'your Grace' is unnecessary and that 'Sir' is a quite acceptable substitute. No one, mercifully, has yet called him Dookie, though there was one narrow miss in Perth when it was averted by only a single syllable.

There a jazz-loving taxi driver of Greek ancestry was instructed by radio to pick up the Duke of Norfolk from a local broadcasting station.

'You Dook Norfolk?' inquired the swarthy young driver as he swung his showy Chevrolet up to the steps. His Grace affirmed that this indeed was almost the case, climbed in and was immediately asked: 'You just made a jazz record or something?'

The Duke is probably puzzled to this day about it. But the cabby later explained: 'Listen, any guy could have made a mistake like that. You never heard of Dook Ellington?'

The Earl Marshal of England, however, continues to shake hands, appear on television, talk on sound radio, suffer the advances of socialite boarding parties, talk to the Press, manage his team and shake still more hands as though he enjoys every moment of it.

Goodness knows how he will settle down under the old grey battlements at Arundel when it's all over.

WHEN COWDREY WALKED OUT WITH A BROKEN ARM

The England v. West Indies series of 1963 produced much memorable cricket, not least the occasion at Lord's when Colin Cowdrey, his arm broken by a bouncer from Wes Hall in the first innings, came out to bat to save the game for England.

Dateline: London 1963

STOP pounding, pulse, while I tell you the story of cricket's most legendary last over. It began at Lord's last night at 5.55. It ended at 6.

In those few minutes blue-bloods cavorted like children on the Pavilion balconies, newspapermen stood and roared.

So ended the second Test between England and the West Indies.

After 29 hours and 55 minutes England needed eight runs to win.

Wesley Hall, the world's fastest bowler, was turning at the end of his 22-yard run. Derek Shackleton, greying 38-year-old veteran from Hampshire, had to face him.

He was last man but one in. For England's last hope, Colin

Cowdrey was still in the dressing room with his fractured arm in plaster.

BALL ONE: Hall unleashed it like a bullet. At 90 mph it swung viciously away. Shackleton lashed out and missed.

BALL TWO: It was just as fast, but straighter. Shackleton dropped his bat on it and ran. Hall flung himself down the wicket to try to run out David Allen, racing from the other end. Hall stumbled and fell. England seven to win.

BALL THREE: Allen, calm as a Sunday afternoon cricketer, turned it away down the leg side for a single. Six to win.

BALL FOUR: Shackleton lashed out, missed and stumbled. He looked up to find Allen racing at him. He ran. But Murray, West Indies' 19-year-old wicket-keeper, cooly tossed the ball to his captain Frank Worrell. Worrell could not trust himself to throw. He had a two-yard start on Shackleton and ran like an Olympic sprinter to the other end. He won the race. Shackleton was run out by a yard.

England six to win, two balls to go. And in came Colin Cowdrey, left arm stiff at his side. For 30 minutes he had been practising batting one-handed in the dressing room for this moment and hoping it would not come.

Cowdrey, said many, was showing fool's courage to bat at all. It will already be eight weeks before he can return to cricket. Another blow could finish his career. But mercifully it was Allen facing the bowling.

BALL FIVE: Allen pushed it back.

BALL SIX: Hall, in utter silence, tossed it from hand to hand and looked imploringly at the sky. He began to run, gold crucifix flying out behind him. England could win with a six. West Indies could win with a wicket.

It was probably the fastest ball of Hall's life. It seared straight for Allen's middle stump. But Allen, a Pinocchio-like figure with quiff and up-turned nose, leant forward like a master and met it with a bold British bat.

Cricket's great last over was done.

TED DEXTER'S GLORIOUS INNINGS

To the end of his life IW continued to describe Dexter's innings v. West Indies at Lord's in 1963 as the greatest he had ever seen.

To CLEAR the decks for Dexter it must be explained that England have rarely come closer to totally and disastrously disappearing from a series than they did in the remaining 25 minutes of that morning. Edrich was out to the first ball he received, Stewart to the last ball before lunch. Griffith and Hall, like two huge hired assassins, seemed set for a bloodbath.

This was the background, then, against which Dexter's innings must be measured in years to come if we are some day to assess whether it was the greatest he ever played. All I can say is that not for a moment could I drag my eyes from that splendid Olympian figure. He came in at 1.12 p.m. with the England score at 2 for 1, withdrew for lunch, returned at 2.10 and left for good at 3.12 with the score at 102 for 3. He struck 70 runs off 74 deliveries but even those startling statistics tell next to nothing. It was the manner of their making that transformed

his deeds into the dream of all schoolboys and the fireside romance of old men. For me the Second Test and the earth itself seemingly stood still as he played one of the truly great innings of our time.

He simply stood and smashed anything that Hall and Griffith could hurl at him. The faster they bowled the more savagely he cut and drove and pulled them. Some around me in the Press-box recalled Macartney and Bradman similarly dismembering an attack. To my regret I never saw Macartney and watched Bradman only twice. But comparisons were pointless. This was Dexter, the enigma of even his own generation, rising head and shoulders above all his contemporaries.

Only once he smiled and that was when he thrashed Griffith through the covers to reach his 50. His bat flashed through like a scimitar and the crack was like a British rifle sending death down into some deep, echoing gorge along the North West Frontier. He held his bat at the highest point of that follow-through and waved it to acknowledge the ovation. There was no time, it seemed, to lower it and raise it again in the conventional salute.

Even that was not his greatest shot. There was another, hit from a later ball that Griffith flung out of the sea of faces from the unsightscreened Pavilion End, that almost defeated description. Dexter picked it up late in its flight. There was hardly time for any backlift so he simply jabbed it. Quite how he could generate such power with only wrists and forearms to strike it so hard in front of the wicket no one will ever know. But Butcher, at deep extra-cover, literally could not move more than a foot before it was past him and scorching into the boundary boards. It was perhaps as well for I suspect that it would have broken his ankle or splintered every bone in his hand. The ball never rose off the turf.

Griffith, at times, was hurling the ball into the wicket to get it to rear chest-high. Even that could not slow the cascade of runs. Dexter dragged one down so fast on the leg side that McMorris never saw it. It struck him on the leg and he fell poleaxed. Dexter spared only a cursory glance at the first-aid administrations. He prowled round and round his stumps with the tense stiff-legged walk that hints at monstrous impatience. He never rests on his bat at these times: he holds it either deep down the handle at the trail or across his chest, cradling it in the crook of his left arm. Dexter was once an infantry subaltern and it seems that these attitudes might well have been learned from the Small Arms Manual. He treats his bat like a tommy-gun.

McMorris, recovered, retreated to cover for the next over from Sobers. But there was no hiding place. Dexter smashed his next shot straight at his toecaps and McMorris, understandably, wanted to have no dealings with it. He stooped tardily and gingerly but the ball was through him and away to the boundary again before he had to commit himself to more pain. From the first ball of the next over Dexter swept Griffith for four.

Dexter had still been in single figures when he survived a vicious ball from Griffith that cut in and missed his off stump by a fraction. He also slashed at one late cut that again grazed his off stump on its improbable passage down to fine leg. But even his blemishes were brutal.

Hall and Griffith, the most volatile fast-bowling attack in the world, simply had no idea where next to bowl at him. Hall was hit for 23 off 2 overs after lunch, Griffith was no-balled seven times in his first 9 overs. England, from the threshold of disaster, were back in the game with 82 runs off the first 14 overs of the afternoon. Dexter had hit his first 50 off 51 balls and Barrington, like the perfect sergeant-major that he is, was intent only on giving his captain the strike. The crowd roared with approval every time he took a single, for Dexter's innings was now no matter for petty partisanship. Black spectators, I suspect, wanted him gone no more than white ones. Edward Ralph Dexter was out there in a domain where no critic could touch him. This was his thundering answer.

But shortly after three o'clock there was a fatal stay in proceedings. Griffith had been hammered out of the firing line and Sobers came down to the Pavilion End to bowl his seamers. His first over was an impeccable maiden to Barrington and its effect on Dexter was profound. The rhythm of England's crashing counter offensive had been lost. In Sobers' next over Dexter shuffled forward, bat slightly askew. It was his first indecisive movement in 80 minutes at the wicket and it was his last. He missed the ball as it swung in on him and struck his pad. There was to be no reprieve for the guerilla leader. Umpire Buller's finger went up and an innings that thousands will treasure in their memories for the rest of their days was over.

Dexter walked away briskly, like a man with other urgent business to attend to. But there was to be just one more memorable scene before he disappeared through the tall doors of the Long Room. All along the Nursery balconies, down the length of the ground, and across the three tiers of the pavilion there was a sudden upward movement as though Lord's itself had risen two feet off its foundations. It was an illusionary effect for it was nothing more than every man, woman and child, coloured and white, standing to applaud him each yard of the way back to the pavilion. Anyone who did not feel some tiny tingle down the spine must have been soulless or very, very cynical.

GEORGE BEST – AN IDOL WITH NO ILLUSIONS

IW's interview with 20-year-old George Best was prescient in terms of that wayward genius's later career, albeit his penchant for alcohol had yet to surface.

FOR SOMEONE under 21 with £160 weekly, a white 3.4 Jag, 70 shirts, a 600-strong fan club, a full-time secretary and half-shares in a booming fashion boutique, Master George Best is under no illusions about man's inhumanity to fallen idols.

'I'd be back in Belfast on ten quid and seven o'clock breakfasts and in two months nobody'd want to know me,' he said.

It could happen swiftly, he knows, in one of two ways. He could be destroyed by a broken leg while playing on the wing for Manchester United. Or he could destroy himself while still searching for something to replace the stern Presbyterian discipline which once packed him off to church thrice every Sunday. It is the second thought that disturbs him daily.

He doesn't smoke, drinks only rarely. He has cut back on his gambling to a cautious card-session on Saturday nights, and has conquered his compulsive spending. 'I once bought and wore twenty-two shirts in a week. I must have been stupid. Sometimes now I make myself get through a week on a fiver. But there are still girls. It's OK for you to write about it, because the Boss knows all about them. It worries him I think. It worries me too.'

Best's head, of course, has been over-exposed by Press photographers seeking to crown him prince of what their

39

caption writers call Manchester's swinging in-set. It is a handsome head, the head of a Nuryev or a Cordobes rather than the Brylcreemed bullet of the footballers of the '50s. It is not, however, a swollen head.

Best condones the publicity because it brings the teenagers panting out six miles from the centre of Manchester to his boutique, wedged between a print shop and a betting shop in the two-storey suburb of Sale. The music of Radio Caroline and the chat-up by the proprietor smooth the sale, it seems, of trousers that look as if they've been fashioned from tartan car rugs and ear-clips the size of sardine tins.

Malcolm Mooney, his business partner, is pleased. So is Best. In lieu of any other philosophy at 20 he plans to become the first British footballer to make £1 million. To this end, besides his partner, he has a business agent and a literary agent.

'No accountant?' I asked. 'No,' he said, 'but I'm getting one of those next week.'

Quite what he intends to do with his million, beyond buying a house in the Bahamas for his parents, he's none too certain. It's *now* that concerns him most.

'Maybe I should get married,' he said. 'I've always pretended there's no chance, but really I'd like it a lot. Right now I can't sit down for five minutes on end. I've got to be on the move all the time. Wednesday till Saturday it's murder. I know I've got to stay off the town and get to bed by eleven. But it drives me nuts. I don't read. Well, only the sports pages. The only thing that keeps me sane is remembering that there will be a party on Sunday and Monday and Tuesday.'

In contrast he suffers neither nerves nor self-doubt about his soccer. Critics rate him, age for age, the outstanding player in Europe. The Boss, Matt Busby, prices him beyond purchase. Best doesn't discuss it beyond maintaining it's as well he wasn't born English. 'I don't think I could ever have fitted into

England's plan,' he said. 'Here, I'm just told to go out and play football. If Ramsey had wanted me to change my style, I wouldn't have wanted to be picked.'

His views on life, such as he knows it at 20, are as unequivocal. Despite a wardrobe that is the despair of his landlady, he owns no dinner jacket. 'I dress how I want, or I don't bother to go.' And about reading: 'I don't care if people do reckon I'm an idiot so long as they think I'm a fairly nice person.'

'These attitudes,' I asked, 'aren't they like your hair-style . . . something you've cultivated?'

'Yes,' he said, 'they are. At least, that's how it started. But don't you see, I'm caught up in it now aren't I?

'I'll just have to watch my step,' he said, revving the Jag away in a racing start.

It was only Tuesday and there was a party to go to.

ASSASSINATION AT THE MUNICH OLYMPICS

The massacre of 11 Israeli athletes and one German policeman overshadowed the Munich Olympics of 1972.

Dateline: **Munich 1972**

THE XXth Olympic Games broke stride in Munich yesterday just long enough to pay tribute to the massacred Israelis. By teatime they'd carried out the dead and the show was on the road again.

Mr Avery Brundage's unilateral declaration that the Games must continue was not the only piece of showbiz fortitude to offend many thousands of people who took their grief to the Olympic Stadium.

In fierce mid-morning heat, they witnessed a memorial service so precisely staged for world television that it was more like a Hollywood Bowl spectacular. You found yourself looking for the drum majorettes.

What started as a solemn act of remembrance turned into a political rally and ended as a symphony concert.

When it was over the bewildered survivors of Israel's Olympic team straggled out of the stadium to search for a bus to carry them on the first leg of their sorrowful journey home. They had to watch out they didn't get knocked over by attendants officiously marshalling limousines for the VIP mourners.

They must have found the seating plan at the service ironic. They were placed centre-front of a mass block of chairs, symbolically protected from the world's chill winds by athletes from other nations.

The West German Olympic team, fetchingly attired in pale blue blazers which must have shown up well on colour television, stood round three sides of the square like guards in a lavish Wagnerian production.

One tenth of that protection 30 hours earlier might have been more appropriate.

All most people wanted to do in the Olympic Stadium yesterday was to howl their eyes out in private at the horrors of the night. Instead, they found themselves cast as extras in a world telly-cast of stage-directed sympathy.

All the right, trite things were said. Until, that is, Mr Avery Brundage rose to speak.

He is in his last week of office as president of the International Olympic Committee, and thank God for that, for his insensitivity to the occasion was beyond credulity.

He hurled himself at the microphone and used the bodies of 11 dead Jews to beat the drum of his ideology.

It was his cue to attack the commercialism which has increasingly infected the Olympic Games . . . then he could not resist the opportunity to go further: 'We lost the Rhodesians to naked political blackmail,' he rasped.

It was no spur-of-the-moment remark because he was reading his speech.

Mr Brundage may well be right. But it is unlikely that the Israelis, with 11 of their closest friends in a Munich morgue, found it an academic point.

Their dignity under stress was noble. The most emotional remark of Mr Samuel Lalkin, *chef de mission* of their team, was that 11 of his charges had died 'in the bloom of their lives'.

There was no criticism, direct or implied, of the circumstances which had permitted it to happen.

The real anger here comes from the sideline nations who witnessed the day-long cops and robbers show between German police and the desperate men of Black September only to wake up stunned by the news that every hostage had been murdered.

There is equally justifiable anger at the colossal bureaucratic blunder which permitted the unfortunate German Minister of the Interior to announce in public that the men's lives had been saved. Newspapers round the world published the escape story in good faith.

Opinion is divided in Munich, as everywhere, about the decision to allow the Olympics to continue. My own view is they should have been abandoned.

If you question that, I would only ask what your reaction would have been if gunmen had burst into the British headquarters in the Olympic Village and murdered Mary Peters, David Jenkins, Harvey Smith, David Hemery, Alan Pascoe, Ron

Hill, Lynn Davies, Precious McKenzie, Andy Carter and Anne Moore?

It may be unforgiveably cynical to suggest that it would have caused considerable office work to handle the ticket refunds, but the way the Israeli team left Munich yesterday to an almost audible sigh of relief from those passionate for the Games to continue was not an ennobling moment.

Israel's anguish, and indeed Germany's as the hosts who failed where they most wanted to succeed, should be shared by the world.

The competing Arab nations, as expected, did not turn up for the memorial service. They remained in the Olympic Village where they will continue to live. Nor did Tunisia carry it on television.

They are due to show themselves on the track today, and I can only wonder about the reception they will receive in such an atmosphere.

Montreal and Moscow, the next hosts for the Olympics in 1976 and 1980, must be watching it all with apprehension.

They may even be wondering whether the Munich Olympics, where the crowd will now think twice about raising its voice, are the last in the line.

PUT OUT TO GRASS

One of the emancipations of column-writing is the freedom it affords to watch the trivial, the absurd, the also-rans and the no-hopers. You have the chance to learn what it feels like to be the first man knocked out of a tournament or the last man riding in the Tour de France. You can hang around the unlike-liest places.

Dateline: **Wimbledon 1972**

COURT 14 at Wimbledon is so far from the Centre Court that it's damned nearly in the Old Bailey. It is the end of the line, the last stop before outer space.

People have been coming to Wimbledon since the days of Tilden and Cochet and never even noticed Court 14. This is understandable. It lies in the same latitudes as the lavatories, tucked away between two neatly clipped hedgerows.

You don't get assigned to Court 14. You get excommunicated there.

On the way down there this week I passed Hombergen playing N'Godrella on Court 7 and Bleckinger and Holecek fighting it out on Court 11. None the wiser I pressed on but Court 14 failed to yield any sudden flash of enlightenment.

A Mr Jiri Hrebec, from Teplice, was playing a Mr Szabolis Baranyi, from Nagyvarad, under the intense scrutiny of an Indian umpire and an English line judge who kept shrieking 'out' when the ball overshot the baseline by as much as five yards.

Hrebec and Baranyi took it pretty well. They swore only softly in what sounded like Serbo-Croat out of deference to their audience. This comprised me, a giggle of schoolgirls in candy-striped uniforms and a couple of smart middle-aged ladies with

45

wedding rings and roving eyes. Hrebec and Baranyi are very good looking in a sort of Central European way.

There were no commentators, no cameras, no reporters, no electronic figures flashing on scoreboards and when we all applauded a particularly good shot it sounded like a couple of dice rattling around in a bucket.

Just occasionally, to heighten our isolation, the tailend of a vast human roar would float down from the ivy-clad temple up on the hill: Billie-Jean must have missed an overhead smash on the Centre Court.

The roar testifies to the fact that more people than ever are watching Wimbledon this year but, for all that, Court 14, where no one knows anyone, is the symbolic site of the 1972 championships. Take Smith, Nastase, Goolagong, King and Evert out of the catalogue and what you have is a country fair tournament.

I do not speak, of course, on behalf of the cognoscenti who can rattle off Goolagong's career record like the creed. I speak with the tongue of 50 million others who are missing Newcombe and Laver and Rosewall and even Roger Taylor's annual sensation, and find this a non-vintage year.

What it has gone a long way to proving is something I've suspected for years. This is that you could dress up a couple of chimpanzees in sneakers and tennis shorts and still pack the Centre Court to the rafters.

Wimbledon, with its well-pressed suits, picture hats, modulated voices, exemplary manners, courteous officials, machine-turned efficiency and inescapable strawberries-and-cream, could almost function without any tennis at all. It is the last of the great middle-class festivals and nearly 30,000 people a day are clinging on to it as though it is their last stand against anarchy.

They will look you straight in the eye and tell you that, if anything, this year's Wimbledon is even better than the last.

It isn't of course. The politics of tennis have for one year reduced Wimbledon to below the credibility rating as a world championship, and to believe anything else is self-delusion.

The spirit of this year's Wimbledon is out on Court 14 where, incidentally, Mr Hrebec dusted down Mr Baranyi in three straight sets. It was a very nice tennis match.

Chapter Three

1973–1976

ROYAL SPORTSWOMAN
OF THE YEAR

IW recognized the peculiar pressures on Princess Anne and frequently saluted her for both her character and her qualities as an international sportswoman. The following piece, which combines several articles, reflects his admiration.

You could easily run away with the idea that pressure in sport is a cross to be borne almost exclusively by such as Frank McLintock, Tony Jacklin and John Snow. Indeed only the other day Don Revie was talking about 'the pressures that tear your guts out', and he's not a man given to hysterical complaint.

My submission, after a day amid the hacking macks and hip flasks of the horse world, is that no sportsman or woman on the face of the earth is currently under such intolerable pressure as Princess Anne.

Her dilemma is obvious. The world, literally, waits to see if she's just good enough to make the Olympics. If she does, there will be millions who'll nod knowingly and mutter darkly about Republicanism. If she doesn't, a thousand old ladies in Cheltenham will reach for the poisoned ink and fire off terrible Letters to the Editor and Willie Hamilton.

If in these last tense days leading up to next week's final selection at Badminton Anne shows the strain by so much as a frown, she'll be described as the petulant Princess. If she stares straight ahead she'll be written off, by others, as a haughty piece.

The dear girl can't win. I watched it all with ghoulish fascination at the Rushall Horse Trials in Wiltshire, and I wouldn't be in her riding boots for all the sparklers in the Crown Imperial. Little Raymond Bellisario, who keeps leaping out of the bushes to take candid camera shots of British royalty and then flogging them to foreign magazines, had set up his cameras at a point on the River Avon known locally as The Cattle Drinker, with one unmistakable intention in mind.

Namely, to snap Her Royal Highness Princess Anne Elizabeth Alice Louise, fourth in succession to the British throne, as she was flung headlong from one of her mum's horses into the freezing water.

It wasn't only trial by Bellisario. It was persecution by Box Brownie, Instamatic, binoculars, hand-held television cameras appearing out of hedgerows, rifle-microphones which can pick up intimate conversations over huge distances, officials dry-throated with protocol and, worst of all, hundreds of people just like you and me who pressed as close to her as they could and simply stared.

' 'Ere, look,' shrieked a woman who could have reached out and touched the Princess's shoulder, 'she's got 'er ears pierced.' It's all very well, I suppose, when Princess Anne is opening some Unmarried Mothers' Wing in Lanarkshire. I can tell you that in darkest Wiltshire on Saturday it was sheer bloody murder.

Well, most of them got drenched with nothing to show for it. HRH Princess Anne, as wilful as her strong handsome horse, came to grief at the undermanned 19th fence precisely where the equestrian cognoscenti least expected it.

It was almost like tripping over a mole hill after coming down from the Eiger north wall. For a zigzag fence that any respectable hunter should take in its stride would have presented few problems had the rain not started down on the Olympic eventing cross-country course just before dawn and had the 13 horses that preceded Princess Anne's Goodwill not churned the take-off area into a swamp. And when Goodwill got his hind leg tangled in the spars she crashed, collecting 60 penalty points, a critical mass of time faults, several bruises and mild concussion.

Mrs Phillips, the £2,916-a-month Camberley housewife, had been copping it all week from that bulwark of public propriety, the *Daily Mirror*. Its tut-tutting executives decided to publish an earwitness report concerning Mrs Phillips's colourful vocabulary.

Presumably the evidence was obtained by the traditional method of disguising a reporter as a Dutch Elm and planting him in the paddock. What he heard may have been naughty but it was never obscene. Just two bastards and a bugger off.

These were apparently provoked by (a) the sight of Captain Phillips coming off his mount like a stricken Apache, (b) the intrusion of a TV cameraman and (c) some child careering out of parental control and treading on one of Mrs Phillips's feet.

Anyway it was all published as a matter of public concern, thus provoking puritanical outrage among those readers with outside lavatories and republican leanings.

What intrigues me about these outbreaks of Lutheranism is that if it had been Harvey Smith or Freddie Trueman sounding off, they would have been congratulated in the public prints for their restraint in the face of intense provocation.

Not so, it seems, if Mrs Phillips blows her top in what she assumes to be a private place at a sport renowned for the vigour of its invective. She is portrayed as a haughty witch with her hand in the public till who ought to have more respect for her mother's subjects.

Well, as one of her mother's subjects I find it odd that there should be one law for the poor and an altogether harsher one for the rich and that's quite apart from the fact that I reckon Mrs Phillips has actually earned dispensation from the very boring business of being born royal.

This view comes entirely from having watched her ride for Britain round those murderous cross-country courses where one minute you're clawing up the side of Fort Knox and the next standing almost vertically in the irons as your horse plunges headlong into a river. In between there are up to 36 fences where, from time to time, riders break their necks.

Apart from Grand Prix driving, fighting Miura bulls and ski-jumping, it is the most vertiginous little caper I have ever watched and Princess Anne, who smashed her head on the ground and then rode on for another 17 fences at Bromont the other day, is pretty good at it.

And if, from time to time, her renowned spirit gets the better of her mother's English, it is probably because paragons don't often distinguish themselves in international sport. You will hear much, much worse at Lord's, the Wimbledon Centre Court and in any of the Fleet Street watering holes where the literati assemble to decide how the rest of the world should conduct itself.

While not wishing to advocate that the language of sport from now on should be pure Anglo-Saxon, I do reckon that Mrs Phillips has been harshly handled.

She's all woman, that one, and that's nine out of ten for a start.

THE GREATEST ALL-ROUNDER

The brief column that follows is an unashamed eulogy. There have been a handful of modern sportsmen as dominant in their own games – Nicklaus, Pelé, Viren, Ali – but the art of Gary Sobers was cricket and at its many complex facets he was the master. Recklessly generous and not always a paragon off the field, he nonetheless played cricket throughout his career according to a code of honour now almost forgotten in the desperate determination to win.

I T IS HARDLY classified information that a dismayingly large whack of Gary Sobers's cricket earnings down the years has come to rest with the bookmakers.

We all have our peccadilloes and Gary's has been for playing the horses. He could make Ascot in 55 minutes flat any day rain washed out play at Lord's and a million trembling rabbits can testify to his anxiety to catch the last two races at some night meeting at Nottingham.

Literature for Gary Sobers was *The Sporting Life*; mathematics the art of calculating the yield from a ten-bob each-way yankee; philosophy a matter of keeping your woes to yourself when you're taking a beating.

I use the past tense because Gary slowed down his gambling the day he got married.

It was just as well. Gary's talent for picking fast horses never quite matched his genius for destroying fast bowlers. He caught a few costly colds.

There's no moral tut-tutting about all this because no man has ever earned his money with such honest toil and few have ever given such enormous pleasure to others in the process.

When some sportsmen complain of fatigue you could almost laugh in their faces. When Gary Sobers talks of exhaustion your heart misses a beat. When he speaks of retirement, as he did for the first time yesterday, the sun goes in.

We must now actually contemplate the unthinkable prospect of a summer's cricket without Sobers and when we do that we can begin to think how fast and loose we have played with his incomparable talent. We have worn the man out with our insatiable demands.

As a matter of interest he had, as of midnight yesterday, played in 332 first-class cricket matches, played 527 innings, made 78 centuries, taken 942 wickets and held 360 catches. Add to that Cup matches, knockout matches, exhibition matches, festival matches, the ferocious pressures of modern Test captaincy, the constant pursuit by the Press and the savage strain of unending travel, and you can understand why, at 35, he is talking like a man at the end of his tether.

What saddens me, apart from the selfish dismay at witnessing the beginning of the end of a man who has given me more hours of delight than any other single performer, is what Sobers has made out of it all.

These things are relative. He will not retire into penury. For a lad born in a three-roomed stilted house and reared by a widowed mother after his father was drowned off Bermuda, he has done uncommonly well. But he's not been paid the going-rates for a genius.

Gary Sobers's weakness was not really horses. It was being born to cricket instead of golf, baseball or, maybe, American football.

In the past few weeks I have met his equals in these sports – Jack Nicklaus, Joe Dimaggio and Joe Namath. They are, or were, the best of their age and it goes without saying that they are millionaires to a man.

You will hear it said in certain circles in cricket that Garfield

St Aubrun Sobers has been a fool with his money. It is no way to speak of a man who has still lost less on the racetracks of the world than Jack Nicklaus slips in tips to his caddie.

BOYS AMONG MEN

Another nation whose soccer team less than distinguished itself during the final stages of the 1974 World Cup in Germany was Zaire. It was some years since I had had to write 'running copy' at a night football game, a process involving dictating one's report to London during the match in a series of brief 'takes' which are immediately set in type, leaving the reporter with only the result and the opening paragraph to dictate at the final whistle. The report, therefore, is virtually written backwards so that it can be included in a first edition which it would have otherwise missed Soccer correspondents and boxing writers are the masters of this technique which Paul Gallico, the greatest exponent of all in his days as a sports-writer, mockingly called 'literature under fire'. No literature follows and, in any case, Zaire at least had the grace to make the result a foregone conclusion as soon as they kicked off.

Dateline: **Gelsenkirchen 1974**
–**Zaire 0 Yugoslavia 9**–

THE LEOPARDS of Zaire made a memorable last-but-one appearance in the World Cup in a pitifully populated stadium amid the chimneys of the Ruhr.

If they sound like an ice-hockey team that's fairly appropriate. They run like lightning, occasionally with the ball. Their attitude to defence is curiously like that of the late Lord Cardigan of

Light Brigade fame. They charge straight at the guns regardless of casualties.

It just wasn't their night. They substituted goalkeeper Kazadi after three Yugoslav goals in 15 minutes. The poor chap was still dejectedly dragging his way along the touchline when the fourth goal went screaming past his replacement. He brightened perceptibly.

This goal brought renewed anguish to a Zaire team who appeared to be experimenting with a 1–1–8 formation. Mulamba N'Daye, a household name in Kinshasa, was so overcome with emotion that he kicked the Colombian referee on the fleshy part of the right thigh.

Whatever sympathy Mr Omar Delgado may have felt for his assailant he had no option but to remove him from the contest.

In truth, the Leopards could not afford to lose one of their colleagues at this juncture despite the fact that Yugoslavia had reduced their game to training pace and were concentrating primarily on avoiding too many multiple fractures.

After six goals in half an hour the seventh didn't come for what seemed ages.

Then it was only by courtesy of Dimbi Tubilandu, the unhappy substitute goalkeeper, who completely lost his sense of direction and palmed the ball with curious deliberation into his own net.

He was still adjusting his gloves when Petkovic fired the eighth goal.

How was it, the intellectuals of the Press-box began to ask, that Scotland could only beat the Leopards 2–0 in the opening match?

It also raised the question of whether the presence of a team as clueless as this provides the World Cup with light relief it could well do without. As long as the zonal system of qualification is maintained it will continue, occasionally, to happen.

But when you remember that nations like Portugal and

Hungary and Spain and – dare I say it – England aren't here it does lend some weight to the argument that the encouragement of emergent nations at soccer need not necessarily amount to inclusion in the World Cup final rounds.

The only question the match itself continued to raise was whether Yugoslavia could achieve double figures. They couldn't. They settled for nine goals, equalling the record for the final rounds.

The comedy was compounded afterwards when Zaire's manager, Mr Blagoje Vidinic, conceded that the referee was perfectly correct in sending off a Zaire player for kicking him. 'Unfortunately,' Mr Vidinic added, 'it was the wrong man. It should have been Ilunga Mwepu, not Mulamba N'Daye.'

PAUL GALLICO

Paul Gallico died in the south of France about 18 months after this piece was written. During that time he wrote me several notes of criticism and encouragement. I was astonished and grateful that a man who apportioned his time so ruthlessly should take the trouble. He was quite amused, I think, to know that a book he had written nearly 40 years earlier had actually fired another human being with the ambition to try sportswriting for a living.

MR PAUL GALLICO first came into my life when I was maybe 15 and bought a book of his in one of those oblong American Forces editions which had two columns of type on each page.

It was so grubby and dog-eared that it would have been dear at a shilling had the contents not amounted to the most magical prose ever written about sport in the rich English language.

Dempsey and Walter Hagen and Babe Ruth and Sarazen and Helen Wills Moody came tumbling out of its pages, reeking of liniment and after-shave or whisky or Worth, so that you were simply sitting there drowned in the golden age of American sport.

Gallico wrote them, warts, tantrums, grunts, vanities and all, chronicling their shortcomings, acclaiming their ability but, above all, stripping them of the glossy images that had been built up by years and columns of mindless obsequities.

He called the book *Farewell to Sport* and then, after 14 years of reporting boxing, baseball and tennis, went away to write about snow geese and cats.

He is now, of course, a distinguished novelist with a house in Antibes and a pied-a-terre mews cottage behind Eaton Square where two nights ago he poured himself a cut-glass of Irish whiskey and said: 'Paul Gallico and Mr Bushmills are now entirely at your disposal.'

Gossip came first, because for 25 years I had been curious why, in *Farewell to Sport*, he had concentrated his enormous powers of invective to knife Helen Wills Moody, the imperious Wimbledon queen of her day, out of the public's affection.

Gallico smiled: 'I was in love with her. I just liked to sit and look at her because she had that lovely Grecian nose. I remember taking her to the El Morocco where they had two bands, playing in relay, and when we'd been on the floor for what seemed about 35 hours she looked into my eyes and said: "You know, Paul, your dancing is very good for my footwork."'

It was not the oblique criticism of Gallico's fox-trotting that sealed the lady's fate. They later fell out over a business deal. 'That and the way she walked off the court against Helen Jacobs, pleading sick, were the reasons I beat up on her,' said Gallico. 'I never forgave her for either.'

But scurrilous locker-room secrets aside, what I really wanted to hear from Gallico was whether he believed any reasonably intelligent person could justify spending a lifetime getting passionate about anything so basically unimportant as two football teams or two boxers trying to win the same thing.

Reassuringly, coming from a man who has acquired much wisdom on his graceful passage to 75, his answer was yes.

'My disenchantment was not with sport,' he said. 'My disenchantment was with me. After 14 years of writing about sport seven days a week I had nothing left to say. I was beginning to repeat myself.

'But sport hadn't changed then and it hasn't changed now. It preserves adolescence, which is not a bad thing. It is a meeting ground for minds which might otherwise be completely empty of anything. Above all, it has a perpetual drama which even the theatre can't rival.

'Sport is all about some poor bastard of a golf pro who suddenly gets hot and comes away with $25,000. One day he's poor and the next day he's rich and nobody's written the plot.

'You talk of the golden age I was writing about. It's a golden age now. Cassius Clay is every bit as colourful as Dempsey, Lee Trevino could up-stage Walter Hagen. It's one of the tragedies that the golden age we so rarely recognize is the one that we're actually living through.'

Gallico still fences and in London this summer has sat mesmerized in front of the television watching cricket, which he rates an immeasurably superior game to baseball because of the additional dimension of the ball's movement off the pitch.

Tragically, for a generation who have never read the arenaside dispatches which he pounded out with speed and perception and glorious style, Paul Gallico will never write about sport again.

He is constantly under pressure to do so, to the point where he could make more money for one article in *Reader's Digest* than Dostoyevsky coined out of *Crime and Punishment*. He resolutely resists.

'My family will perhaps not enjoy me saying this,' he said, 'but my time is so short and my ambition remains so great to write something that will really satisfy me.'

It was Paul Gallico speaking. Not Mr Bushmills.

ROCK BOTTOM

Although he reported on top soccer games, IW, character-istically, did not forget the human story of teams struggling at the bottom of the divisions.

THERE was only a very small riot when Darlington were obliterated 7–0 for the second match running last Saturday. Maybe 20 men, some of them gnarled enough to have voted for Ramsay MacDonald, rose up in the stand and shouted, 'Tait must go.'

Tait is George A. Tait, who bought the chairmanship of Darlington Football Club 21 years ago by promising to under-write their expenses up to £75,000 over three years. He is widely disliked in Darlington because he is a foreigner. He comes from Newcastle, 33 miles to the north.

George Tait is an archetypal English football club chairman: self-made, thick-skinned, friendly, very rich, deferred to by his employees, envied by his contemporaries. In 1930 he launched out in the carpet business with £10 capital. He is now a millionaire.

He brought the only splash of colour to Saturday's freezing, fog-shrouded match: powder-blue 4.2 Jag, brown suit in bookmaker-check, ochre nylon shirt and one of those narrow ready-made bowties much favoured by 1959 band leaders.

What the demonstrators failed to realize, or blindly ignored, was that without George Tait there would have been no match to abuse. The economics of Darlington Football Club are so absurd that only philanthropy keeps them alive.

Take Saturday, when 1,088 of Darlington's population of 84,830 paid £232.55 at the turnstiles.

They had to give Southport, the visiting team, the statutory minimum of £250. Their wage bill for the week was £650. Printing 1,000 programmes cost them £28.75. They had to pay 15 gatemen and the nominal bill for police protection is still to come in.

But the financial strain is nothing compared to the nervous stress of being manager of the 92nd of the 92 League clubs with only three wins in 24 games. At Darlington they share it about a bit. They're now on their fifth manager in 15 months.

This may explain why Ralph Brand, who took over three matches and 17-goals-against ago, was stopped at the entrance and asked to pay 40p for the privilege of doing his job on Saturday.

Brand, at 35, is a one-time Scottish international who became so bored after two years as an Edinburgh newsagent that he took up the Darlington challenge in the one-to-50 gamble that it would launch him as the next Clough or Shankly in soccer management.

His style owes much to both of them. Short, with fanatical blue eyes, a busted nose, fearful articulacy, a drill-sergeant's vocabulary and about as much compassion as a Gestapo thumbscrew exponent, he last week flayed and cursed Darlington's 16-man staff through a practice match until they trembled in their boots.

'Get up, get up,' he screamed as a man fell from exhaustion.

'You'll die three times before I bring you off.' Then, back in the dressing room: 'Just get it into your heads that this time next season you'll be on the dole or driving a bus if you don't start fighting.'

On Friday afternoon a forward phoned Brand complaining of back pains. 'It must've been something I've eaten,' he said. 'Eaten?' scorned Brand. 'Jesus Christ, you must have swallowed a whale bone to get pains in the back. Listen son, get to bed and send your wife off to another bedroom. I don't want you waking up and finding your wife all nice and warm there beside you. Remember that you belong to me till five o'clock tomorrow. After that you can make up for lost time.'

Saturday dawned auspiciously for Darlington. They had their first full-strength side of the season. Then, at midday, goalkeeper Ernie Adams arrived. He was shuddering with flu.

Adams was sent home and Phil Owers, a quiet, shy lad who'd been cleaning the players' boots the previous afternoon, was sent for. Owers is a 17-year-old amateur who is still studying for his geography A-levels at Tech. It was to be his first League match. Ever.

After two minutes Owers went flat for a marvellous save. Of the seven goals that went past him one may just have been his fault. The other six left him helpless behind a defence that looked like a Toc H team appealing to Rommel's better nature.

As the seventh goal went in someone started singing 'We Shall Not be Moved'. A lot of people laughed. The alternative was to weep for Darlington's joyless fate and seemingly hopeless future after 99 years existence and 52 years in the Football League.

There is no moral to the story. Only, just a week before the League chairmen meet to debate whether the Darlingtons have anything to contribute to the future structure of English professional football, observation.

The local arguments – that 40p is downright robbery to get

in, that George Tait has failed them by spending none of his £75,000 on new players – are petty, pointless and parochial.

All Tait wants to do now is see the club steer clear of re-election and hand it back to the town.

All Ralph Brand hopes to do is to achieve that miracle, for it will be no less, and move on and upwards in the cut-throat business of football management.

In the end it comes down to a town visibly caring whether or not it has a football team and on that score, last Saturday, Darlington's apathy was even denser than its fog.

BODYLINE REVENGE

The Australia v. England series in Australia in 1974/75 featured the pairing of Lillee and Thomson, that most intimidating of Australian fast-bowling attacks.

Dateline: Sydney 1975

COMING fresh to this Test series is like walking into a pitched battle between the Mafia and the IRA. You knew they'd been at each others' throats but you couldn't believe it was this uncompromising, this violent or this uncouth. Practically none of the traditional courtesies of cricket survived the second day of this fourth Test.

Bats were thrown, oaths exchanged, umpires abused, obscene gestures made and, for much of the time, batsmen were subjected to some of the most viciously intimidatory bowling witnessed since the dark ages of bodyline.

All of it was enacted before a packed crowd, one-eyed in its allegiance, one-voiced in its prejudice and motivated less by the normal patriotisms aroused by international sport than the blood-lust you feel in the bullrings of Spain. The hostility came off The Hill like a heat haze.

Three points are worth making.

It was a thrilling and unforgettable spectacle, as war often is. Sydney cricket ground, with its Baroque architecture and domed pavilions, is the Grand Opera House of the game and the cast in this Test are almost all prima donnas.

There is no innocent party. England, released from the restraining influence of Mike Denness's diplomatic leadership, exchanged bouncer for bouncer, curse for curse and dissent for dissent.

There is, I believe, no lasting enmity off the field between the two teams. It is merely in public and before huge television audiences that they are indulging in a game which now has all the makings of a martial art. They appear, most of the time, to enjoy it.

This will make sad reading to those born to the literature of Blunden and de Selincourt and reared to believe that cricket is a synonym for words like honour, etiquette and nobility.

They will probably ascribe it to the age of long hair – half the Australian team, it must be admitted, wear Mexican desperado moustaches – and see it as another sign of moral decay. This would be coming it a bit strong.

In a somewhat embarrassed appearance before the Press, England's manager, Alec Bedser, conceded it had been an ill-tempered day but added that he'd seen a few of those in his playing era. Of course, he is right.

On this same ground, 43 years ago, diplomatic relations were almost broken off between our two countries because of the violence of the cricket exchanges and in those days England had an amateur, a gentleman and Wykehamist as captain.

This is not to condone the loutishness we have seen in this Test but to remind the new middle-class militants that good manners have never been exclusive to any one generation.

The new element now, I suspect, is a crowd, unfettered from an Empire and disenchanted with a Commonwealth, exhorting its young tigers to tear the old lion's tail out by the roots.

They bayed for blood yesterday and both teams did their damndest to spill it.

Thomson's mere emergence through the swing gate to start bowling was greeted by a roar barcly gentler than the one which accompanied Foreman to the canvas in Kinshasa.

Lillee, with The Hill at his back, was swept in to bowl on soundwaves of soccer-style chanting.

It could have been any old Sunday afternoon in the Rome Colosseum, and England, tired of the taunts and the humiliations and an Australian Press patronising them as overweight geriatrics, retaliated. Only the 12 Apostles or the late Albert Schweitzer wouldn't have done so.

These remarks, I fear, apply only to England's bowlers. When we batted we did so with something less than conviction.

It reminded you of a remark by Mr E. Hemingway, who thrived on blood and thunder. 'They fought,' he wrote of contestants in another sport altogether, 'as though they were condemned to it rather than if they had chosen it.'

They could have been England's batsmen at the end of a remarkable day.

RUMBLE IN THE JUNGLE

This is an edited version of IW's vivid and individual experiences
of reporting on the now legendary Ali-Foreman fight in the Congo.

Dateline: **Zaire 1974**

WHEN a reporter called Stanley passed this way in search of a doctor called Livingstone he was wise enough to be carrying smoke signalling equipment, cleft sticks and towing along a relay of foot-runners. We should have learned.

Up the Congo without any visible means of communications is no place for 600 journalists to be. This, of course, is why the Ali-Foreman fight has been receiving such filthy publicity from Sacramento to Surbiton.

It must be galling to a Zaire Government whose president, Joseph Mobutu, moved heaven and ten million tons of earthworks to get the fi . . .

London
As I was saying when a furious Zaire Government censor ripped last Friday's dispatch from my telex machine in Kinshasa: '. . . ght here and thus put his country on the map. For all our personal aggravations as journalists we should not be too critical. Now for the good news.

'There are few modern cities where you can walk about the streets in greater safety than Kinshasa. You could not meet people with greater warmth or anxiety to please. You could hardly stay in quarters more comfortable than those in which we have been encamped near the fighters.'

Unlike my earlier words, which were intentionally highly critical of Zaire's woefully inadequate communications system, this near eulogy of President Mobutu's capital and people never saw the light of publication.

Instead, they were borne away ahead of me to a darkened fifth-floor office where a Mr N'Godu, government official, gave me 25 minutes of his mind.

Invoking Bills of Human Rights was pointless. Explaining that censoring material mostly concerning a boxing match was to invite ridicule was useless.

Newspaper communications, I am the first to appreciate, are not the be-all of our existence. But one principle, even beyond the question of censorship, is involved.

It is whether a country which applies to stage a major spectacle, be it a heavyweight championship or the Olympic Games, is immune from criticism because it is young, emergent and black.

This is dangerous ground. There are those who will read into it attitudes of Colonialism and Kiplingism and racism, or, at the very best, insufferable paternalism.

I can only hope that regular readers of this space will recall that a succession of white South African Ministers of Sport have rarely received the time of day here and that George Best, Brian Clough, David Bedford *et al* may well think they have as much cause for bitter recrimination as President Mobutu Seso Seko of Zaire.

It is all a question of whether we are prepared to apply double standards. I, for one, am not.

In due course, if the contest is still on, I intend to return to President Mobutu Seso Seko's ring and report the action.

Kinshasa
The sun had the audacity to rise over Central Africa yesterday while Mr Muhammad Ali was still speaking.

His message was really quite trivial. He will require 10 million dollars, he informed the universe, to perform his next miracle in the boxing ring.

This works out at something slightly over £4 million an hour, or, alternatively, precisely twice as much as he received for exposing George Foreman as not quite the immovable object we thought.

Naturally, we shall pay it. We shall rob banks, surrender life policies, short-change widows and sell the new dishwasher to raise it. His recapture of the world heavyweight title here, on a morning the memory of which I shall take to the grave, entitles him to name his own price.

By the eighth and providently last round he had, according to a communal round-up of statistics, hit Foreman 65 times flush on the face.

It was then, from an entrenched and contemplative position, that he saw an opening which lasted as long as it takes to fire a hair-trigger pistol.

Foreman is a man of ingenuous honesty. 'A boxer,' he said when his mind was functioning again, 'never sees the big one that hits him.'

What hit him, in fact, was a Bren-gun burst of quick blows, a left hook that spun him round into the real line of fire and a right that put him on the floor for the first time in his professional career.

He sprawled there, blinking and subconsciously mouthing the count to himself. He had not one chance in 50 of getting up again. It was like watching a tank going over the edge of a bridge in slow motion.

He became so confused by Ali's tactics that he finished the fourth round hurling wild swings into the air, and later missed so badly with the punch that was meant to finish it all that he almost went through the ropes.

Ali slapped him on the bottom. Throughout the fight he talked to Foreman in all the clinches and carried on a running conversation with a black American reporter in between rounds.

In the fifth round he indulged in a piece of exhibitionism so dangerous that it would not be tried by the resident professional fighting farmhands in a fairground boxing booth.

He sagged back so far on the ropes that he was almost in the laps of the TV commentators. And there he stayed for well over a minute, defending himself from Foreman's frantic hitting only with his forearms and cupped gloves.

Ali took the wildest liberties and still rode back to the world title he regards as personal property with a performance of total genius allied to immense physical courage.

The fight that was reckoned to be his five million dollar retirement pay-off went precisely as he raved and bragged it would. 'I shall be the matador and Foreman the bull,' he told his Zairois brothers last week. The metaphor was exact.

Ali went down, too. Ten seconds after Foreman was counted out, he was knocked down as his faithful leaped into the ring. From then, long into the dawn, he was besieged.

'I'm going to haunt boxing for the next six months,' he shouted. 'I'll talk to the man who first offers me ten million dollars.'

You may say a man requires supernatural powers to command such a sum. But maybe Ali has.

At breakfast the sun went in and the rainy season started.

TERROR TOMKINS

There was a period during the quite recent history of Australian culture when it was possible to buy the most explicit pornography in King's Cross, Sydney, but quite impossible to lay your hands on a copy of *Portnoy's Complaint*. It had been banned, presumably on the assumption that any tacit acknowledgement of onanism could encourage the criminal waste of the gross national product. This ambivalent attitude should have warned me that *The Tomkins Papers* were likely to test Australian tolerance to the extreme.

They did precisely that. While completely fictional and written for fun, they provoked much acrid correspondence from Australia, where a couple of them were reprinted, and even inspired the management of a visiting Australian cricket team to contemplate legal redress. This they wisely decided against before it involved them in quite unnecessary expense.

In fact you could only parody Australia and Australians if you love the place to distraction, which I do. Brash, vigorous, generous, proud, chauvinistic and incurably insular, its sheer capacity for living far outweights its more hilarious foibles.

The only way to survive there, a fact not always assimilated by English immigrants until they are on the disillusioned trip home again, is to give as good as you get. If you can't beat them, join them. If you can't join them, beat them.

Hence *The Tomkins Papers*, the mildest of retributions for the calumny which the Australian sporting Press has cheerfully poured over successive generations of visiting Pom cricket teams. Long may this institutional harangue survive since there is nothing in sport to compare with an England–Australia Test match when the gates are closed and the heat is on.

Dear Mum,

Well it's just wot Dad said it would be like, freezing bloody cold and all the Poms which aren't on strike are saying the old country's knackered.

Incidentally is there any news about Dad's parole?

You can't move for birds here. They've got this thing called the Permissible Society. You don't have to join or anything. They're queueing up for a meaningful experience every time you come down in the lift.

I'm real sorry that you and Dad won't be able to watch the Test matches on TV. The reason is that the BBC are broke, cricket is broke and they won't do anything to help one another. They don't give a damn about the public so everybody suffers.

Give my love to Gloreen and tell her not to believe anything she reads about me and other birds in the papers. I'll definitely be fit in time for the Tests.

Did Sis get away with probation? They're much more lenient about things like that here. Some English blokes smashed up a football ground last week in Paris and then broke a lot of windows, and they've got the bloody cheek to call us wild colonial boyos.

By the way, please let me know whether it was only a rumour or not about Sharon. I know she's my sister but 14 is definitely too young to become a mum and I can do without that sort of thing damaging my image.

Thank Shirl for the picture postcard from Alice Springs. I know it's a long way from Sydney, but it's only right she disappeared in the circumstances. There are still some people who are very sensitive about that sort of thing and it might have affected the sales of my autobiography.

I still haven't met the bloke whose writing it, but he's

calling it *Rain of Terror*. I don't know what that means but the publishers say it's brilliant.

We were 1–5 with Ladbrokes for the Lord's Test and there doesn't seem much point winning if that's all you can make out of it. Obviously, we'd never bet on the Poms in case it got into the papers.

Well that's about all I can think of for now. Anyway, it's hard to concentrate here in the dressing room because everybody's banging their bats about over an lbw decision.

I didn't see it myself because I was looking up how to spell parole in the dictionary. This Test series has been a real education.

Your loving son,
Sgd. Terror Tomkins
87b, Whitlam's View,
Cronulla, N.S.W.

Dear Son,

I am writing this in Mr Robinson's because they came and took our telly away after Dad failed the identification parade. The Robinsons are real dinkum neighbours and they're only 73 miles up the road.

Also they've got a colour telly so we was able to sit up all night watching you stuffing the Poms at The Oval by saterlight. Mr Robinson got very wobbly and kept on shouting 'Goodonyer, Terror' and 'That'll teach the bastards to dissolute the Empire.'

When those Poms had to follow-up, Mr Robinson got out the champagne but this time I was sensible and stuck to wine. Gloreen had to go outside a few times and I've told her she'll have to mend her ways if she's going to marry you and meet all them Indian Rajers and the Queen and things.

Denis Compton was IW's first and greatest hero, and also became a good friend.

The young Wooldridge (*back row, far right*) was a promising left-handed batsman with the New Milton Cricket Club.

Wootton Post Office, in New Milton, Hampshire – where, some years later, IW was born.

IW goes back to the *New Milton Advertiser* to meet his first editor, Charles Curry.

IW revisits his birthplace.

Opposite page:
Above: IW wrote a brilliant piece about his flight with the breathtaking Red Arrows team, describing it as combining 'the horrific and the euphoric'.

Below: After supersonic acrobatics, IW reported on a rather more tranquil form of flight.

Left: The Cresta Run fully satisfied Wooldridge's continuing quest for an adrenalin rush.

Below: IW turned musher to report on 'the unimaginable hardship' of the Alaska dog-sled race.

IW remained fascinated by the continuing resonance of the Bodyline Tour of 1932/3, when Harold Larwood was instructed by his captain, Douglas Jardine, to bowl *at* the Australian batsmen.

British triple-winner at Wimbledon Fred Perry deserved to be cast in bronze – IW had no doubt about that.

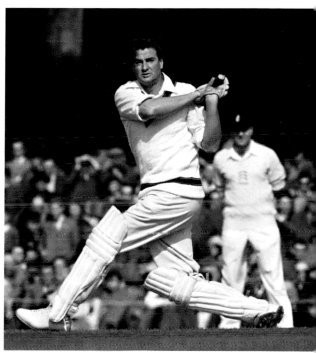

Jardine – pictured here in 1931 – remained unapologetic about his Bodyline tactics when IW interviewed him years later.

IW loved Miller's dynamism and carefree spirit, and treasured his friendship.

Members of the 1948 Australian touring side receive a guided tour of Balmoral. *Left to right*: Ron Saggers, Keith Miller, HRH Princess Margaret and Sam Loxton.

Enjoying one of the perks of the 'best job in the world', IW takes part in a promotion for Havana cigars.

For once, IW seems just a little 'tired and emotional' at a Brazilian Carnival Ball.

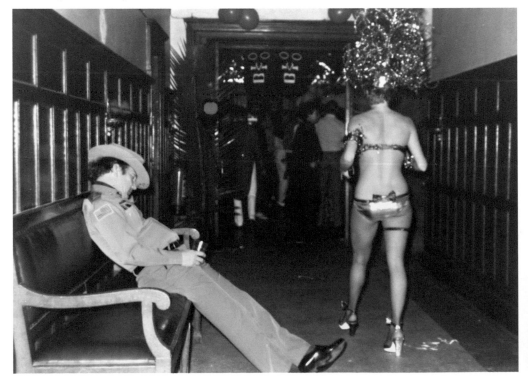

Funny thing was how all the Australian reporters seemed to be on holiday when we wasn't doing so well at Lord's. But this Oval Test is all over the front pages under headlines like *Tomkins Roasts Puny Poms*.

You'll be glad to know that our Shirl has been allowed back in skool after her little naughty. No harm done, touch wood, but of course she'll never be quite the same again. They grow up so quickly nowadays.

Gloreen's been working very hard at the slimming and is now nearly down to 16 stone. She's asked me to remind you about not stopping over in Bangkok on the way home, but I don't know what that means.

Your loving mother,
Signed Mrs Tomkins.

IDI AMIN – STILL THE HEAVYWEIGHT CHAMPION OF UGANDA

Four months before the Raid on Entebbe a somewhat less imposing commando, similarly uninvited, arrived in Uganda at dawn. My companion, uniformly crumpled after an overnight flight from Rome, was Monty Fresco, a Cockney Jewish photographer with the resilience and resource of all three of those races. It was a period in Ugandan history when foreign journalists were particularly unwelcome, a reality proved by my *Daily Mail* colleague Leslie Watkins the previous year when he was transported directly from Entebbe Airport to jail without passing go. While our real motive was to see how a nation was faring under the patronage of a bloodstained maniac we at least had the spurious excuse of arriving to cover a major boxing match which, predictably, never took place.

At the immigration barrier we were immediately invited to leave. 'S'orright, dawling,' said Fresco, waving a glossy photograph of President Amin under the eyes of a bemused man in uniform, 'yer guvnor's a personal mate of mine.' He started walking and thus we entered that satanic dictatorship.

For five days we were required to report each morning to the Ministry of Information. For five days Fresco was forbidden to take pictures. For five days he bewildered Ministers and Permanent Secretaries with a galaxy of outrageous lies, Kosher jokes, inquiries about their pension schemes, cackling laughs, dismissive waves, solicitous concern for their children and repeated reminders that to offend us would be to imprecate the wrath of our close friend, the President. On the sixth morning we flew 200 miles west by private plane to Semliki where we were granted an interview.

President Amin was childishly flattered to be questioned about his boxing career. He was more reluctant to demonstrate his sparring style. Even this failed to defeat Fresco's ingenuity. 'My friend 'ere,' he said, referring to an apprehensive reporter whose pugilistic career was as brief as it was abysmal, 'is a very fine boxah. Go'orn, sir, whack 'im.' Fresco got his pictures. Next morning we courageously caught the first plane out of Entebbe to Kenya.

There is a distressing postscript. The Minister of Culture and Sport referred to in this column was Major-General Francis Nyangweso. Eleven months later he was posted missing, presumed assassinated.

Dateline: Semliki, Uganda 1976

As BEFITS any humanitarian who only that morning had stepped straight from the breakfast table to save seven men from the firing squad, His Excellency Field-Marshal

Doctor Idi Amin Dada, VC, DSO, MC, was in benevolent mood.

The blades of his armour-plated helicopter had barely stopped spraying dust in our faces before he lumbered forward, hand extended, and said: 'My aides tell me you have come from London to discuss my boxing career.'

This was not necessarily the whole truth but one does not readily contradict a 19-stone statesman with a gun at his hip, even though he has recently been cleared of an allegation of murdering not fewer than 25,000 of his brother Ugandans.

'That is correct, sir,' I said.

Respectfully, his large entourage of Ministers, Permanent Secretaries and some unspecified gentlemen whose perspiration-flow appeared to be impeded by shoulder-holsters fell silent as President Amin began to recall his days as a pugilist.

In some respects they were more remarkable than Muhammad Ali's.

'I first won the heavyweight championship of Uganda in 1951,' he said. 'Then in 1952 I became champion of all East Africa. I used to train with heavyweights, middleweights and lightweights so that I was always ready to fight short or long men.'

His aides murmured approval at their leader's sagacity.

The President then added that he held both titles until 1962, which seemed a fairly safe cue to ask the name of the man who had the presumption to beat him.

'Nobody beat me,' the Field-Marshal replied.

'You retired, then?'

'No, I did not retire. I am still heavyweight champion of Uganda. Nobody is willing to fight me.'

At this the 48-year-old reigning champ shoved both thumbs behind a belt threaded with 36 bullets, and the ribbons of the VC, DSO, MC and 12 other decorations heaved on his massive chest as he bellowed with laughter.

His entourage were silent for perhaps half a second before breaking up. They slapped their thighs, as well as each other, and shrieked their appreciation of the President's wit so purposefully that two vile-looking birds rose almost vertically from a distant tree and fled towards the Sudan.

Understandably for a man who is now spokesman for about nine-tenths of Africa as well as heavyweight champion of Uganda, Doctor Amin – he conferred the academic title upon himself quite some while after awarding himself the VC – does not like squandering his *bon mots* in private discussion.

That morning, for example, he had invited a film crew from the government-owned Ugandan Television Service to accompany him into the yard of Kampala's Luzira Upper Prison, where seven convicted black-marketeers shivered in the sweltering heat.

They had been sentenced to death by an Economic Crimes Tribunal and were waiting to be shot.

President Amin, legs astride, planted himself in front of both them and the cameras and proceeded, with much finger-wagging, to denounce their wickedness in over-charging, hoarding and smuggling.

Then, first in English and then Swahili, he not only commuted their death sentences but set them free. One man collapsed. Another slid to his knees in gratitude.

All this was introduced on that evening's TV by a girl who, if anything, looked even less emotionally affected by news of any sort than Miss Angela Rippon.

At the time the President was performing his good deed for the day, we were flying 6,000 feet above Lake Idi Amin Dada (formerly Lake Edward) to a point 200 miles west of Kampala, famous for the ferocity of its Pigmies and its breathtaking views of the Mountains of the Moon.

It was here, during the afternoon, that the President was due to take a break from urging Mozambique into full-scale war with Rhodesia by opening the new Idi Amin Wing of the Semliki Safari Lodge. In view of our interest in Uganda's forthcoming world-title boxing promotion he might, we were informed, be prepared to discuss aspects of his distinguished sporting life.

In fact, due to an administrative hitch, the President had been informed only the previous evening that he was hosting a light-heavyweight world boxing championship planned for next Sunday week.

Heads, metaphorically speaking of course, will probably roll when he discovers that his Minister for Culture and Sport has pledged £250,000 to overseas white boxing promoters at a time when Uganda's sugar industry is dying because its refinery is broken, most of Kampala's buses are off the road for want of spare parts, and that among the commodities you could not get all on the same day in Kampala's ritziest hotel last week were: bread, water, salt, eggs or beer.

In short, for a man who'd never heard of either John Conteh or Alvaro Lopez and clearly had not the remotest idea of what weights they boxed, President Amin demonstrated his undoubted powers of magnetism by convincing the 300-strong audience who listened in to our interview that he's the Third World's Nat Fleischer.

'The fight will bring more world attention to Uganda,' he said. 'Already we are preparing 30,000 hotel beds for visitors from Britain.'

The fact that Kampala doesn't have 30,000 hotel beds and that getting into Uganda requires more persistence than getting out of Dartmoor should not be misinterpreted. The Field-Marshal was having one of his love Britain days.

'Next year,' he declared, sidetracking from sport for a moment, 'is the silver jubilee of her Majesty the Queen and I intend to come to London to take part in the celebrations. I respect her as my former Commander-in-Chief. Please pass that message to Her Majesty.'

Expanding on his own sporting achievements, President Amin briefly recalled his early days as a champion soccer and rugger player, marvelled at the way in which he had become a champion swimmer since he had had to train in a river, modestly conceded that he had driven in an East African Safari car rally and revealed to the world for the first time that he has recently taken up squash.

'According to affairs of state, I play either one or four times a week,' he said. 'It makes you sweat in five minutes.'

He also revealed, to his stunned Cabinet, that he intended to stage the Commonwealth Games in Uganda as soon as he had built the largest sports stadium in Africa.

His main sporting intention this year is to attend the Olympics in Montreal. When I pointed out that, like Uganda, Canada's Olympic stadium was not yet complete, the President thundered, 'Why?'

'Union troubles,' I said.

It was a foolish remark. It triggered, right there in the green hills of Africa, a political harangue which embraced the iniquity of all unions, the flaccid weakness of all non-socialist states and ended with the bellowed words: 'Everybody must obey the system.'

The President's aides nodded vigorous agreement.

Unfortunately, the Minister of Culture and Sport was not present. He was back in Kampala learning how to bounce a live televised picture of a boxing match off a piece of metal in the sky so that it comes down in London and New York simultaneously.

You may well wish to join me in wishing him luck.

'DO YOU SELL ANYTHING IN PACKETS OF THREE?'

Three months after our flight from Uganda I was watching a cricket match at The Oval in London. There was an intriguing advertisement along the boundary fence to the left of the Vauxhall End sightscreen. In large letters it bore the words MikroPul Ducon. In smaller letters it said Environmental Protection. By the end of the day I had once again learned the lesson that preconceived outrage has no place in investigative journalism.

Dateline: London 1976

THE ONLY problem about MikroPul Ducon, as advertised at The Oval cricket ground and therefore on BBC television, is whether you purchase it by the quart, the yard, the kilo or in packets of three.

'No doubt about it,' said my informant. 'It's the most brilliant coup of the year. It's a Greek firm, you know. Trust the Greeks to think up that "environmental protection" line.'

The implications, of course, were huge. If the BBC have banned Grand-Prix motor racing from their screens because some of the cars roar around with Durex written all over them, how could they conceivably televise the fifth Test from The Oval with MikroPul Ducon staring you in the face every time the ball ran down to the Vauxhall Stand boundary?

Well, millions of bewildered televiewers *did* see it on Wednesday when BBC screened the one-day Surrey-Essex match. So, bristling with puritanical outrage, one felt it only right to telephone the Surrey County Cricket Club and castigate them for the offensive tastelessness of their boundary advertising.

'Oh my God,' said a Surrey spokesman. 'Is *that* what they

are? It never occurred to us. I say, you're not going to print this, are you? You realise that the fifth Test will be blacked out on television?'

'It is the duty of a free Press to protect young children and elderly ladies from being affronted by this kind of nauseating advertising,' we boomed. 'Motor racing? Cricket? What's the difference?'

A low moan from The Oval indicated they knew all was lost.

To conclude our inquiries we called at a chemist's in London, EC4, waited until two lady typists had bought some shampoo, gestured a male assistant to the end of the counter and whispered: 'Three MikroPul Ducons, please.'

'I'm afraid I've never heard of the products, sir,' said the assistant.

'Really,' we replied nastily, 'of course, they *are* the very latest and presumably only very *up-to-date* stores stock them for really *discerning* clients.'

'Possibly, sir,' said the assistant.

So the search widened.

'Awfully sorry,' said a worthy-sounding man at the Family Planning Association, 'we don't seem to have them on our recommended list.'

'What on earth,' demanded a businesslike lady at the Association of the British Pharmaceutical Industry, 'are you talking about?'

'Very sorry old boy,' said a jolly chap at the Ann Summers Establishment up near Marble Arch, 'can't help you out at all.'

'If they're rivals of ours,' said a big wheel at the London Rubber Company somewhat brusquely, 'we've never heard of them.'

'I've just searched through all our reference books,' said an infinitely helpful secretary on the *Chemist and Druggist*

Directory, 'and they don't appear to be here. A Greek firm, you say?'

'Yes, a Greek firm,' we replied testily and promptly rang our correspondent in Athens to track down, once and for all, these Hellenic environmental protectionists whose cunning advertising was about to wipe cricket off the English television screens.

He drew a blank.

It was fast approaching teatime on the cricket grounds of England when we received a telephone call from a man in Shoeburyness, Essex.

'I understand from Surrey County Cricket Club,' he said pleasantly, 'that you wish to buy an air-conditioning unit?'

'Are you some kind of nutcase?' we demanded. 'Get off the line.'

'No,' he replied, 'I am the managing director of MikroPul Ducon, manufacturers of filters for cleaning dirty industrial and domestic air.'

'Do you sell *anything* in packets of three which have to be sent out under plain cover?' we asked weakly.

'Certainly not,' he retorted, 'air filters is our business and we are cricket fans to a man.'

'Thank you for calling,' we said. 'Forgive us our trespassing.'

'Not at all,' said Mr MikroPul Ducon. 'I'll send you a price list.'

JOHN CURRY'S GOLD MEDAL

John Curry won the Olympic gold medal for figure skating at the 1976 Winter Olympics, and also triumphed at both the World and European Championships in the same year. Sadly, he contracted Aids and died in 1994.

Dateline: Innsbruck 1976

THE PRICE of gold was written clearly across John Curry's face at lunchtime yesterday. He was deathly pale and the lines induced by remorseless training were almost vertical ravines.

Uncharacteristically, for he is by nature a courteous person, he was nervy, snappy and abrupt.

'Do come on,' he instructed his mother, 'I'm *extremely* hungry.' It was 12.42 p.m.

Mrs Rita Curry, a nice, small lady with the slightly harassed expression of a widow who has continued to run the family's light-engineering firm during the nine years since her husband's death, jumped a little and said: 'Sorry, I've got to go.'

She lunches rarely with John. The last time was in London in December. She does not know when the next time will be. It could be in America. 'I would so like to go and see what he's doing over there.'

They were a small isolated party in the dining room, high up in the Alps above Innsbruck. Mrs Curry had been staying there for 11 days without seeing her son.

'We spoke twice on the telephone,' she said, 'but he concentrates so completely I did not want to interrupt him. I shall not see him again after today. I'm going home on Sunday.'

They had all got to bed at 4 a.m. 'It was lovely,' said Mrs

Curry. 'We went back to the Olympic village and drank champagne.'

She is a kindly woman. She would remember to ring her factory back in Birmingham and give everyone the day off.

John Curry, at 26, is her baby, the third of three sons, who renounced soccer and rugger at prep and public school and then renounced Birmingham as well.

He was the one who left home at 18 and went to London to take courses in advanced skating and elementary sophistication. He became a £13-a-week receptionist at the National Cash Register offices near Madame Tussaud's.

He was the one who turned to America for the training that brought Britain its only Winter Olympics gold medal for 12 years before an entranced audience in the great ice stadium in Innsbruck on Wednesday evening.

He was the one who turned to his mother after his triumph and simply said: 'Oh Mum . . . !'

'That was all he said for a long, long time,' said Mrs Curry. She dashed in to lunch.

That was the private face of John Curry yesterday. The public face, squared frankly at a roomful of some of the world's toughest newsmen during an official Press conference seven hours later, was wholly different.

It was the face of the nerveless champion.

An agency report of an interview he had given earlier was already circulating the world. It said John Curry admitted to being a 'gay' champion.

'Gay' is a trendy synonym for a homosexual, and slowly the questioning got around to words like 'virility' and 'masculinity'.

Curry heard them coming and smiled at the room's discomfiture and said simply: 'I don't think I lack virility, and what other people think of me doesn't matter.'

When the official conference was over he was put under private questioning. He crossed spread hands like a referee counting out a boxer and said, 'Finish.'

His day of triumph had also been a day of tribulation. I am among 56 million Britons who care not whether John Curry is white, black, Moslem or Greek Orthodox.

All I know is that he skated the world out of the frame at the Olympics and the public face he showed yesterday revealed the qualities that had allowed him to do it.

'The two days before going into the arena,' he said, 'were the longest days of my life. It had suddenly hit me that there were a lot of people in England hoping that I'd skate well.

'A lot of people sent letters and telegrams. It weighed pretty heavily on me but I wasn't nervous.

'I'd had a sleep in the afternoon. Before I went to sleep, I concentrated on getting the mood I wanted to wake up in. That was the mood I did wake up in.

'When you start skating you see winning the Olympics as top. Now it's happened it all seems rather easy. There are some major skating competitions that make you feel as though you're pulling a coal wagon uphill. The Olympics weren't like that. They were on the flat.

'After I'd done my last triple I knew the hard part was over. I said, "Now just sit back and enjoy yourself." That's what I did.'

The American questioners, knowing well that without American sponsorship and Italian coaching John Curry would probably still be eating lunchtime sandwiches not far from Madame Tussaud's, asked him whether he considered he had really been skating for Britain.

'Of course I was,' smiled Curry. Then he said: 'But I love America. I love the energy of the place. I love the American attitude that before you start, all things are possible.'

There are writers who could sit down for an hour without

coming up with half such a perceptive accolade to the United States.

Curry calculated that 'very roughly' his final year's training for the Olympics had cost almost £10,000.

Didn't that come close to making him a professional? He smiled serenely at us all and said very carefully: 'I am an amateur as described by the rule books.'

Then, with a disarming frankness that caused the Olympic officials sitting close to him to drop their eyes to the floor, he confirmed that after next month's world championships in Sweden he will be on the open market.

'I will then know what options are open to me,' he said, 'and I shan't do anything until I've heard all the options.'

If the options are as good as most of the world's skating experts expect them to be, John Curry, of Birmingham, will join Franz Klammer, the Austrian skier, as the second young man to go on from the Olympics to become a millionaire.

What he plans to do is create a Theatre of Skating based in the United States, comprising half a dozen performers who believe, as he does, that skating can be raised from the plains of sport to the mountain peaks of the performing arts.

HYPE

Quite often those who complain about Press intrusion into privacy are accomplished publicity seekers, either merely gratified by seeing their names in print or anxious to remain in the public eye for commercial reasons. Surprisingly, Malcolm Allison, itinerant football manager, is not one of them. He is one of the most likeable men in the game. His life is generally in a muddle but to suggest this in print is to receive from him an invitation to listen to his philosophy, an enriching and entertaining experience if not a wholly logical one. An invitation to attend the launching party for his ghost-written memoirs was too good to refuse.

Dateline: London 1975

M R MALCOLM Allison arrived looking like death and announced he'd been up most of the night with Dorothy Squires, a statement which demands precise syntax at the best of times but even more so when you are crippled by a hangover.

A glass or three of Lanson Black Label brought the colour back to his interesting face and at the hour about six million factory workers were knocking off for lunch he borrowed a match and lit his first Havana of the day.

Then they wheeled in the obligatory blonde, a nice lady whose mum and dad apparently forgot to christen her because she's known as just Flanagan and comes from the East End and models things and has written three books, all of which, I gather, lean heavily on sexual intercourse for the plot. Flanagan must have had some sort of accident on the way because her lovely white ball gown had a big hole in the front which left her navel exposed to photographers, free-loaders, hangers-on and anyone else who felt disposed to press past in the crush.

After a while they rounded up Mr Allison, Flanagan and four other pretty girls and took them into the room next door where Flanagan hitched up her gown so that it wouldn't get crushed when she sat on Mr Allison. Coincidentally it revealed her knees and a disturbing acreage of thigh to the photographers, who'd also been invited.

About £300-worth of champagne later Mr Allison felt strong enough to answer probing questions about his autobiography, published Tuesday, at this Literary Event of the year.

In introducing Mr Allison, Mr Robin McGibbon, publisher, stated that Mr Allison was one of the most respected figures in the world of Association Football.

' 'Ere,' shrieked Flanagan, with that instant repartee for which the East End is renowned, 'Oi fought that was Georgie Best.'

Mr McGibbon, who had also been up most of the night with Dorothy Squires in connection with another literary project, showed pain at the interjection (Mr Best's autobiography having been brought out by the rival publishing concern of Stanley Paul Ltd) and invited the rest of us to put to Mr Allison questions concerning his philosophies about life, death, and the offside law, etc.

'Hey, Mal,' inquired a gentleman I presumed to be the literary editor of a distinguished British newspaper, ' 'ow much are yer goin' to bid for Rodney Marsh?'

Mr Allison cleverly parried this query and concentrated his full attention on the next which was: had he not, in a manner unbecoming to a gentleman and manager of Crystal Palace Football Club, knowingly subjected three ladies, to wit his wife Beth, Miss Serena Williams of the Playboy Club, and a Miss Christine Keeler, to considerable embarrassment by publicly revealing his emotional involvements with all of them in order to boost the sales of *Malcolm Allison: Colours of My Life*.

Mr Allison, whose shirt mysteriously had the words Mercedes and Fine Old Columbus Rum printed all over it, and was open down to the fourth button, replied: 'I have never tried to avoid anything. That's how it happened. It is now a controllable factor.'

In reply to my appeal for clarification, he said that when a man gets married he often tends to protect his wife so much that she doesn't know what the world is all about. In short, he implied that philandery is a fairly masculine trait but that, while some men tried to conceal it from their wives, he didn't.

By now Flanagan was displaying her boredom at the way the day was going by chatting up a handsome young reporter. Allison ignored her and announced his earnest intention to become a gentleman.

First he plans to spend seven years making Crystal Palace great again. Then he intends to set up as a freelance international soccer consultant, travelling to places like America and Australia and showing them how to manage and coach.

'I've seen them round the world and I laugh at them,' he said. 'They're crap.'

All this forward planning, I gathered, featured his wife as well as himself so now, maybe, we can all get some sleep.

Anyway, the need for further personal publicity hardly existed by the time the party reached its Hogarthian heights, which coincided with about six million factory workers heading for home. After only two days on sale the book has gone into a second reprint, as much a tribute to the perceptive way Mr James Lawton has written it as to Flanagan's much-photographed navel.

It just makes you wonder what heights Graham Greene could reach if he had the sense to stay up most of the night with Dorothy Squires.

HUNT VERSUS LAUDA

IW, slow to succumb to the excitement of Grand-Prix motor racing, was won over by James Hunt and his great rivalry with Niki Lauda, which culminated in Hunt's 1976 World Championship title.

Dateline: **Mount Fuji, Japan 1976**

I N THE long history of man's inhumanity to man there may have been more beautiful battlefields, but if so, I cannot imagine them.

Towering over you, 11,000 feet tall, pink and snow-capped in the setting rice-harvest sun, symmetrical as a lampshade and combining the mysteries of a semi-retired volcano and one of the Orient's holiest shrines, stands Mount Fuji.

Below you, shimmering with lakes and tinted by autumn, lie what could easily be the foothills of the Western Islands of Scotland.

The incongruous bit is at eye-level: a harsh, dark, snaking circuit of metalled road, almost three and three-quarter miles long, totally flat, and as clinically terrifying as an operating theatre.

It is here, where the souls of those who believe in the Shinto religion are said to come, that an English Anglican named Hunt and an Austrian Catholic called Lauda will fight for the Formula One racing drivers' championship of the world and, coincidentally, more money than you or I could ever earn in three lifetimes.

Niki Lauda, a millionaire already, does not need the cash. James Hunt, whose parental home in Surrey symbolizes exactly what they mean by the stockbroker belt, could take it or leave it.

But no. Separated by three points – Lauda's 68 in the red

Ferrari to Hunt's 65 in the orange Marlboro-McLaren – they intend to drive to the bitter end of a 10-month personal duel that has already seen Lauda come back from the priest's last rites and contributed in no small way to Hunt losing his extremely photogenic wife to an ex-rugby playing actor named Richard Burton.

You get nine points for winning, six for coming second. If Lauda wins here, he wins everything. If Hunt wins with Lauda second he takes the title by virtue of more outright Grand Prix victories. No other driver matters a damn unless he hoists Lauda off the track or zigzags in front of Hunt to stop him getting through.

There has never been a climax to a motor-racing season quite like it and there are chilling factors beyond wondering whether the two obsessed Europeans will be affronting other men's gods.

James Hunt has instructed his parents, both of whom wanted to come, to stay away. And Niki Lauda's wife, a lovely girl with swept up hair, looked 89 years old with concern when she came down in the lift yesterday.

It would be wholly libellous to call these men mad, but they are certainly not like the rest of us. It is a private war accentuated by the intense politeness each separately accorded the other yesterday.

Hunt, the eternal public schoolboy, said: 'We're perfectly good friends. At the American Grand Prix we had neighbouring rooms with a connecting door. This allowed us to annoy one another.'

Lauda, still horrendously scarred by his Nurburgring crash, which brought him to within 15 seconds of being burned to death, said: 'James and I don't see a great deal of one another, but don't forget it was the British who started cheating this year at the Spanish Grand Prix. There's no sport left in motor sport.'

On Sunday they will settle it, if their respective cars stand up to the strain at around 175 mph. 'It is not a dangerous course because it only has four real bends,' said Hunt, 'but only the Italian and Austrian courses are faster. You can even come out of the bend into the pit straight at around 130.'

Today they go into two days of qualifying drives to establish preferential, and possibly critical, positions on Sunday's starting grid. Yesterday, pottering around their pits 60 miles outside Tokyo they were merely watched by hundreds of bemused Japanese, who had not the remotest idea what to make of them.

This is Japan's first international Grand Prix and while Japan turns out cars like shirt buttons it has yet to produce a driver who can keep his foot to the floor when all around him are easing theirs.

They even missed the glorious irony of Lauda, Austrian star of the Italian Ferrari team, being driven to the track in a cobalt blue British Rolls-Royce.

Classically European, each gave the other the better chance. Hunt said: 'Niki has only got to race me while I've got to race the field.' Lauda said: 'My car was getting slower and slower in the last two races. I can't improve on a car if the engineers don't give me a chance.'

Lauda, upper face crenellated by stage-one plastic surgery and top half of the left ear charred out of existence, declared himself perfectly fit. 'If you are not perfectly fit you make mistakes and mistakes mean hospital,' said the man only recently back from an intensive-care unit.

Hunt, five years younger than Lauda, looked as Corinthian as C.B. Fry, but the tension showed in the myriad gestures he made to prove how relaxed he was.

One thing genuinely pleased him: that at least an edited version of the race is to be transmitted by BBC television, whose sudden aversion to motor racing allegedly had something to do with the advertisements scrawled all over racing cars just as they are now scrawled all over Lord's, The Oval and Twickenham.

Lauda, 50 yards down the pits, took pains to inform British readers that even in the darkest days of semi-consciousness it had never occurred to him to quit motor racing.

'I won the championship last year and I intend to win it next year,' he said. 'In fact I plan to make it three in a row.'

This implies that Niki Lauda intends to drive very, very fast on the world's third fastest race track on Sunday. Our own Mr Hunt is unlikely to be sluggardly.

The amazing thing is that neither of these modern matadors remarked on the breathtaking scenery. Mount Fuji could have been Fort Knox or the nearest Woolworths. Its tinted lowlands might have been Wormwood Scrubs or the Atlantic Ocean.

We can only hope that Mount Fuji's gods took no offence and accept that that's what separates the boys from world-champion drivers.

Chapter Four

1977–1980

FLYING WITH THE
RED ARROWS

In the vernacular of the 1970s the Red Arrows are something
else. Before you may fly with the RAF's aerobatic display team
you are 'invited' to take a medical which, far from being the
cursory check on heart and blood pressure I had imagined, is
a two-hour-plus physical and psychological examination of
one's capacity to withstand the rigours of high-performance
flying. Only afterwards does one understand the reason why.
To fly with them is a unique experience, encompassing the
horrific and the euphoric. I hope I shall be asked again, for I
have never enjoyed anything more in my life, but in the
meantime I would like to record my thanks to Mike Phillips,
who flew me in rehearsal and on the real thing; Frank Hoare,
who led his team with Celtic panache; and Mike Whitehouse,
player-manager of this incomparably disciplined bunch of
nerveless cowboys.

I T SIMPLY isn't true that your whole life flashes in front of
you, even when you fear that one-and-a-half seconds from
now you're going to finish up liquidized in the font of Ely Cathedral.

For one thing you don't really care, because of the raging
pain in both ears.

For another, the terror is so absolute that your brain has
hardly functioned at all since they explained what happens when
you fire an ejector-seat.

Around now, which is to say at the bottom of a near-vertical 400 mph dive straight at the roof of the finest example of Norman architecture in the whole of the Fens, a voice as calm as a cruising Concorde pilot's crackles inside your helmet.

'The next bit may be a bit uncomfortable,' says Mike Phillips, aged 33, a native of Horsham, a graduate of the University of London and an RAF flight-lieutenant at this moment piloting his plane in alarmingly close proximity to eight others in his 287th and final performance with the Red Arrows.

He does not exaggerate.

Suddenly, with a roller-coaster lurch that leaves your stomach in Ely High Street, you have somehow avoided the cathedral roof and begin to streak upwards.

It is then that a medium blow from a rubber cosh hits you across the nape of the neck, and some invisible stream-press begins forcing your head into your chest. You are incapable of lifting your arms and, momentarily, darkness surges in from all sides as you cling on to a keyhole of brilliant light somewhere in the middle distance.

This is what aerobatic pilots call 'pulling g', which is technical shorthand for their constant defiance of the earth's gravitational forces.

In that particular evolution over Ely, Mike Phillips, flying 12 feet from the wing-tip of Flt-Lieut Mel Cornwell to his left and 18 feet and fractionally below the tail of Flt-Lieut Dudley Carvell's scarlet plane immediately ahead, pulled 5½g. The effect, during the few seconds it lasts, is to make a 12-stone man weigh 66 stone.

At the zenith of that climb, as you collect your stomach and your wits and begin to enjoy it, there is one further small surprise.

You glance upwards through the perspex cockpit canopy to

offer thanks to heaven and there, 4,000 feet above you, are the green and ochre fields and small neat villages of Cambridgeshire in early autumn.

You are flying upside down without the slightest discomfort until a quick command from Frank Hoare, the Welsh squadron leader who runs the Red Arrows with autocratic democracy, pitches you into a violent right-hand roll and sends you splaying out into an empty sky.

This year, the RAF's Red Arrows have performed to live audiences totalling more than three million, including one crowd of 600,000 over an airfield in Germany. Their 102nd and final show over the Fens was to commemorate the granting of the Freedom of the City of Ely to the local RAF hospital.

Their display lasted 17½ minutes and, certainly to one layman privileged to fly with them, amounted to the next-but-ultimate thrill.

In their final act, mundanely called Piccadilly Circus, all nine planes streak in from nine different points of the compass at closing speeds of 800 mph and miss one another by narrow yet rigidly predetermined margins of air-space over a carfax about the size of Wembley Stadium.

I would like to be able to describe this denoucment in greater detail, but am unable to do so.

From 500 yards out my eyes were closed by an irresistible force called cowardice, and they didn't open again until Mike Phillips said: 'Okay, that's it. We go home now.'

On landing, he slapped his tiny turbojet on its nose in a small show of sentiment and walked out of his three-year career with the Red Arrows. He rode home from the airfield on a 90 c.c. Honda motorbike.

Three years is the most an RAF pilot can serve with the Arrows unless, like Frank Hoare, he is brought back as leader. During their tour with the most lionized aerobatic team in the world, they receive precisely the same pay as every other officer, deskbound or otherwise, of their rank. A flight-lieutenant gets £5,716 a year, and the leader £6,100.

These are the air aces of our day. They have comfortable middle-class Christian names like Mike and Richard and Martin and Nigel and Tim, and they fly, brilliantly and modestly, without attempting to perpetuate the laconic, wizard-prang, polka-dot neckscarf attitudes of their subsonic forerunners of the Battle of Britain.

'Élite?' questions Mike Phillips. 'No, we're not élite as individuals, but we're probably élite as a team.'

They are, in fact, so élite that an extraordinary chance came the way of the Red Arrows and their manager, Mike Whitehouse, earlier this year.

They were approached by an American entrepreneur, a kind of Kerry Packer of aviation, who wanted to buy them out of the RAF and promote them as the greatest flying circus ever seen, on salaries immensely greater than those they draw under the stringent restrictions of Britain's defence budget.

There weren't any takers.

There are those in Parliament who would deem it a political triumph to disband the Red Arrows, but to fly with them is to be reassured that there are still areas in British life where perfection, for perfection's sake, still exists.

Certainly to this layman, having retched and blacked out during rehearsal and been unashamedly petrified throughout 17½ minutes of actuality over Ely, quite how nine pilots fly in such perilously close formation under the enormous stresses of gravity remains a closed book.

To the newcomer there are many imaginative comparisons, but it cannot be altogether unlike being thrown over the edge of Niagara in a sealed barrel and then hurled back up to do it all over again.

It is a brutal assault on the brain and the nerves and the digestive system, but when, disoriented and upside down, you glance sideways and see the same wing-tip precisely the same distance from yours as it was 3,000ft lower a few seconds ago, you begin to relax and believe in the infallibility of the Sons of the Few.

DOG-SLED RACE

Covering the trans-Alaska dog-sled race in 1977 was one of IW's many extraordinary assignments. The following is an edited version of a number of on-the-spot reports filed during that epic race.

Dateline: Anchorage, Alaska 1977

I T WAS the great Jack London, mixing metaphors with another four fingers of whisky, who captured the God-forsaken wilderness in exactly two sentences.

'The Almighty,' he said, 'was pretty tired by the evening of the sixth day so he just tipped his barrow sideways and slung out what was left. Thus was born Alaska.'

He wrote that 70 years ago but nothing was different yesterday as Serge Amundson, bush pilot, revved his tiny Piper ski-plane across the frozen lake, banked steeply westwards and flew us low along the first 60 miles of the Iditarod Trail.

Ahead, the smashed molars of the Alaska Range. Behind lay jagged ice-floes. To the left and Canada, to the right and the Pole, there was only blinding whiteness. Outside it was petrifyingly cold.

Thirty miles out we caught the backmarkers. Twenty miles

on we were abreast with the leaders. The mushers waved, the dogs ignored us and pulled on demonically. There were just over 1,050 miles to go.

In Amundson's 31-year-old Piper PA14 we stage-hop the race and send back reports. In all there are 47 humans and 604 huskies down there engaged in the last great endurance race.

By daylight and darkness, across terrain of some danger and unrelieved desolation, in temperatures that have been known to plunge to 100° F below, sleeping rough and eating rougher and in the constant proximity of very wild animals, they are retracing the Gold Rush Trail of the 1890s.

They started in Anchorage, the bleak staging post of the big polar jets. They will finish at Nome, which is engagingly known as the Sodom of the North and stands out there on the Bering Strait staring at the blunt end of the Soviet Union.

It is a dog-sled race of unimaginable hardship and no one can remotely guess how long it will take. In the record year it was won in 14 days, 14 hours, 43 minutes, 45 seconds. Mostly the winning time is nearer three weeks. Back marker finishers have been known to take 29 days.

There is only one intractable rule. No fresh dogs may be harnessed en route. The same huskies must run every yard of the way and if they die in the effort, you must quit when you are down to five to save imposing intolerable strain on the survivors.

There were no flags or fanfares or mayoral send-offs. The mushers just slid away silently, faces set hard and eyes already concentrated on the western horizon. There were narrowed Asiatic eyes and flat expressionless features and cheeks creased as old boot leather, for slightly more than half the entrants come from long, proud lines of Eskimo and Indian hunters and trappers.

The rest are compulsive adventurers. Local businessmen who dog-sled for sport, all-American Hemingway fans up from Texas and Wyoming, one Norwegian who made his name ski-jumping, a US Army officer, a wealthy veterinary surgeon, and, unbelievably, two women.

Vicious winds combine with the cold to produce a chill factor equivalent to 70 or 80 below, a condition which frostbites any exposed flesh in around 30 seconds. In the 1974 race a chill factor of minus 120 was recorded. That year 15 dogs died.

The ultimate danger is a whiteout, when swirling snow blocks out the vision so completely that a hand stretched in front of the face is invisible. Then you stop and, if so inclined, pray.

Few of the competitors stay in any of the checkpoints. They drive on, guided at night only by the sixth sense of their lead dog, moonlight when available, or otherwise a thin torchbeam from a miner's-type helmet.

Rainy Pass, Alaska

The first 217 miles of the 1,110-mile Trail have been accomplished at a near-record sprint. The hard men like to storm through here before the weather closes in. All day the huskies have been toiling up the terrible gradient that gashes through the Alaska Range like a white-walled Khyber Pass. As you reach the ridge in Rainy Pass, the scenery changes from Christmas-card pretty to labour-camp grim.

Earlier yesterday, at the Finger Lake checkpoint, Gene and June Leonard invited us into a cabin barely visible above eight feet of snow to take tea. New-York-born Leonard, now a trapper, in last year's race was the man who found Colonel Norman Vaughan. At 21 Vaughan was in charge of all the huskies on Admiral Byrd's 1928 expedition to the Antarctic.

At 69 he was the oldest competitor in the 1976 Iditarod. Less than 200 miles from Anchorage he took a wrong turning and disappeared.

Three days of concentrated air search failed to locate him. On the afternoon of the fourth day Leonard found him. He was out of food and in the mid-stages of hypothermia. His starving dogs were eating their own harness.

'When I found him,' said Leonard, 'he was just wandering around. He had so little idea what he was doing that he didn't even care he'd been found. Sure as hell, he'd have been dead that night.'

Tom Mathias, a 38-year-old Michigan man up to compete in the last dog-sled race of his life: 'You want to listen to these guys. These are the real experts in Arctic survival. If you make a mistake around here, you can finish up dead.'

Nome, Alaska

Ten yards from the finish line, Rick Swenson made a lovely gesture. He halted his team, stumbled alongside them and almost hugged the remaining daylights out of his lead dogs, Old Buddy and Andy.

'Here', said the gesture, 'are the real heroes.' But no words came, for the Big Swede's lips were sealed by his own frozen breath. Icicles hung down like stalactites from his thin moustache and the upper reaches of his face were sand-papered scarlet by the awful winds.

He then re-mounted his sled, gently eased his huskies through the archway that dominates Nome's filmset Front Street, and thus won The Last Great Race on Earth. After 1,110 miles across mountain ranges, ocean, dangerous thin ice in canyon beds and passes where the cry of the wolf carries five miles, Swenson won by 800 yards from Jerry Riley, a musher of half-Indian, half European blood.

Swenson typifies the men taking part in this race. He won £5,400, which just covered his expenses of raising and entering a team. Every other entrant will suffer a loss and, as I write, 11 are into Nome, 20 are still out in the wilds up to 300 miles distant, and 16 have retired because of tired dogs, personal injury or illness.

Swenson has dimensions of hardness and endurance and a capacity for survival long lost to those of us now cradled from birth certificate to early retirement by government acts, central heating and union vigilantes.

It may not make these men better but it certainly makes them different.

'What,' I asked Joe Redington, aged 59, who arrived here in fifth position nine hours after Swenson, 'would you say to a European daily commuter whose world would end if he woke up one morning to find there was no hot water for shaving?'

'Well,' said Redington, whose sleep has averaged three hours in 24 over the past 17 days, 'I wouldn't say anything unless asked. But if I were asked, I would suggest that you only get one shot at this life and you might as well make the most of it.

'I don't think we're here to take things for granted. A race like this reminds you that the world doesn't necessarily owe you a living.'

HENRY LONGHURST – SIMPLY THE BEST

For many of his fellow journalists and broadcasters Henry Longhurst was the professionals' professional, and IW had a very warm regard for the qualities and the idiosyncrasies of the man.

Dateline: **London 1978**

Henry Longhurst would have deplored a solemn obituary. Incapable of writing a dull sentence in his life, he would have awarded nought out of ten, dear boy, to the reporter who reduced his death to a boring recital of facts.

'Dear boy', a phrase redolent of public school codes of honour, not necessarily very hard-working days at Cambridge, strict middle-class proprieties, a deep suspicion of all forms of Socialism, and huge rounds of large pink gins at a thousand golf clubs, was Henry's most frequent mode of address.

'Dear boy,' he said, recalling how two years ago, already ravaged by cancer, he determined to end his own life, 'what happened next was a remarkable tribute to the recuperative powers of Scottish whisky.

'I placed a quite adequate number of sleeping pills on the table. I placed a bottle of whisky alongside them and began drinking the whisky to alleviate the tiresomeness of what I was about to do. After half a bottle of whisky the world had infinitely pleasurable things to offer again. I woke up the next morning without even a hangover.'

Between then and his death at the weekend, Henry Longhurst gave a long interview to BBC television on what he chose always to call his life and soft times.

As the privileged interviewer, I drove down to see him the previous week in his house between the two famous windmills on the hill above Hassocks in Sussex.

'Dear boy,' he said, 'this will be the last lengthy piece of television I shall ever do. I would like it to be as good as possible.'

On the appointed day, he was desperately ill. He would not hear of a postponement. Between the ten-minute film-takes he retired to his room to recover his strength and breath. He emerged each time apologizing to the cameramen and sound recordists for the inconvenience to which he was putting them.

He then proceeded to speak the Queen's English with mastery and imagery and humour in a stunning valedictory performance that was the ultimate in professionalism.

One hour and half a bottle of gin later, Henry Longhurst and his adoring wife, Claudine, presided over one of the most uproarious lunches never to end with prodigious slander actions.

There is an even happier memory of Henry.

On the eve of the 1959 Ryder Cup golf match at the El Dorado Club, Palm Desert, California, there was an official dinner for the first 600 local millionaires to get tickets.

Henry Longhurst accepted an invitation to speak. When he picked up the toast list it was to discover that he came third behind a local dignitary and then a certain Mr Bob Hope. It was like being asked to bat immediately after Denis Compton.

Bob Hope, with a script honed by half a dozen Hollywood writers, was accorded a standing ovation.

And then, in the still buzzing aftermath, there arose this short, plump Englishman in the sort of dinner jacket that hadn't been modelled in *Esquire* magazine for quite 20 years.

Henry cleared his throat vigorously and began: 'My Lords ...' For ten, perhaps 12 minutes, he gave his audience pure Churchill, dazzling them with anecdote and philosophy in a style and accent and economy of perfectly chosen and permutated English words they had never previously heard.

For a moment, as he sat down and searched for the nearest drink, there was absolute silence. Then the audience rose again, and this time a standing ovation came from 600 people clapping with their hands high over their heads.

That is how I want to remember Henry Longhurst, whose death I do not regret. He suffered appallingly in recent years.

Other obituaries say he was 69 but that, of course, is nonsense. He crammed 120 years into his remarkable lifetime.

He had been an MP and raced motor cars and been a great amateur golfer himself, but ultimately his genius was in his use of the English language. He wrote golf for the *Sunday Times* and spoke of it on the BBC and the American networks with a command which has never been equalled.

There are those, even in death, who would depreciate his talents. They fail to understand that great writing is simple writing and that great commentating is the art of the very long silence.

Henry Longhurst could be a considerably difficult man. He would give you poetry when you wanted up-to-date facts. He would argue the case for Rhodesia as Nicklaus was driving off in the Open. He drank far too much too often.

It just so happens that, in our business, he was the best who has ever been.

DALEY THOMPSON –
BRITAIN'S NEW SUPERSTAR

When IW wrote this piece in 1978, Daley Thompson had just won his first gold medal in major competition, at the Common-wealth Games in Edmonton. During his remarkable career, Thompson won two more gold medals in the Commonwealth Games and no fewer than two Olympic gold medals plus a World Championship and two European titles. He has always remained very much his own man.

Dateline: **Edmonton 1978**

THE SUPREME irony was that the real pressures had only just started when Daley Thompson hauled his aching limbs on to the champion's rostrum and visibly allowed the acclaim of the crowd to massage the worst of his pains.

He is portrayed as a raving extrovert and some credence was lent to that misconception when he broke 48 years of Common-wealth Games protocol by insisting that the losers as well as the medallists take a curtain call. In his mood he almost certainly wouldn't have shown up otherwise.

But it was his day, no question of that, and they smiled their permission because you'd be lucky to witness anything better than Daley's performance twice in a lifetime.

Here, beyond informed expectation in the backwoods of Canada, he had just turned in the second greatest performance in the history of the decathlon. And that, since the decathlon is the ultimate test of any male athlete, made it considerably more than just watching a gold medal won.

By now you must almost know by heart the fine print of his deeds with vaulting pole and discus and his strength in the running and jumping disciplines that add up to the two-day, ten-event ultimate inquisition on the human body.

And doubtless, unless you are very odd, you will have shared our unashamed rejoicing here that this time it wasn't another American phenomenon or some Soviet automaton annexing the limelight.

It was a British boy, born exactly 20 years and 13 days ago of a Scottish mother and Nigerian father, now dead, in that part of London known as Notting Hill which is famous, or rather infamous, for reasons other than its profusion of restaurants.

It was a handsome, striking young man, with A-levels in geography and biology behind him, who now lives with a couple of mates in a flat in Turner's Hill, just outside Crawley in Sussex, where the neighbours are too well-mannered to question the colour of anyone's skin.

What, however, you may only partly know is what happened after our acclaimed young gold medallist stepped down from the rostrum.

Daley Thompson, exercising the ultimate human right and being an amateur within the loose interpretation of the definition now necessary to keep any athlete on any track anywhere, politely informed the entire world to go and get lost.

When the BBC television people arrived to herd him to the conventional after-triumph interview, Thompson said 'No' with a nerve that very few leading politicians possess.

Meanwhile the world's press, which is how someone will inevitably describe the 60 reporters drumming irritated fingers on unopened notebooks in a neighbouring interrogation room, vainly waited as well. Daley Thompson never showed up.

Some were outraged. A few, mostly Canadian, announced to one another that they would cut him to pieces. So began the real pressures for Daley Thompson, who now has to live with his astounding success.

In fact a very few minutes later, the affronted Canadians could easily have found their man sitting calmly under a maple tree not three miles away quietly counting the options now open to him. They are considerable.

First of all he has to accept the fact that, from now on, he has to be very good very nearly all of the time, and don't think that wasn't worrying him.

The reason he is driving himself is that, without a career or even a desire to do anything of significance outside an athletics track, he wants to be rich and famous and knows precisely how it can be done because there is the immediate precedent of the American decathlon star Bruce Jenner.

Bruce Jenner won the decathlon at the Montreal Olympics in 1976 and was rightly titled the world's greatest athlete. At that point Jenner, as he had a perfect right to do, decided to cash in his chips.

You can hardly switch on a TV set or open a newspaper in North America without seeing his face.

Advertising everything from after-shave to dog food, in a commercial in which he co-stars with his labrador pet, in demand for film roles that require overt masculinity rather than an ability to memorize anything more than five lines of banality, an old favourite on the TV superstars show, and prepared to drop anything to travel to Japan tomorrow to give highly paid blessing to any product, Jenner is guaranteed a minimum income of £5 million over the next five years.

Daley Thompson, being intelligent, has read all about it. 'What I would like,' he said on being asked his intentions for a future career, 'is to be another Bruce Jenner.'

I WAS A WALKOVER

This characteristic Wooldridge report from abroad is sketched
with colour, fun and a dash of adrenalin.

Dateline: **Surin, Thailand 1978**

A T THE weigh-in here the other morning, Boon Song tipped
the scales at a fraction over 8,550lb and then strolled away
to eat a hearty breakfast and rest up for the contest.

He had good reason, in the rising heat, to reflect sourly upon
the perfidy of man since his immediate opposition were coming
into the arena at a corporate 10,500lb. To any kind of champion
17½cwt is an awful lot to give away.

But Boon Song looked neither cross nor nervous. His character
reflects his name exactly. Translated from the Thai, it means
Get Lucky and he looked a monolith of affability and a cathedral
of self-confidence.

This was certainly more than could be said for the opposition:
72 crack troops of the Royal Thailand Commando who, despite
smart combat green and burnished toecaps, were edgy.

Smaller by much than Grenadier Guards but chunkier than
the archetypal Gurkha, they averaged 10½ stones apiece, which
isn't bad for a country which appears to live on bean shoots
and exotic massage.

But would it prove enough?

Every year for the past 18 years some 60,000 spectators have
come here in the third week in November to see the question
answered. The annual joust between the King's Elephant and the
King's Men is the highlight of Thailand's pachydermal year and,
coincidentally, the only possible reason for ever visiting Surin.

A stifling, clanking, jolting overnight trainmare out along

Thailand's eastern arm from Bangkok, Surin is half the size of Rochdale, eight times as dirty and uncomfortably wedged in to north and south by Laos and Cambodia. In short, no one in his senses would want to hang around here making home movies.

Except, that is, this week. Surin's Elephant Festival is to Billy Smart's Circus what Trooping the Colour is to a Boy Scout lope-past.

Not even the British, with their in-born outrage at the exploitation of animals, could take offence. Here the elephant, both tank and bulldozer to the Thai economy, enjoys the same status a thoroughbred racehorse does at home.

The allusion to Trooping the Colour is not all that absurd since it was at 11 a.m. precisely, the same hour at which our own Queen rides once a year on to Horse Guards, that the contestants in the King's Tug-of-War emerged from opposite ends of an arena six times the size of Wembley Stadium.

The National Anthem was played. Spectators stood in silence. The heat rebounded from the huge cantonment in dancing waves. No one moved until the swirling dust had cleared and there, exactly centre-field, stood Boon Song and the King's Commandos in knee-cap to eyeball confrontation.

The commandos were in twos, a thick rope between them. As they stiffened to attention their single opponent ambled to a halt, eyes half closed with indifference, and turned to submit to the rope being hooked to his harness. As an essay in absolute coolness, it reminded you of Denis Compton rolling out to bat.

Boon Song, at 30, is in the prime of a life which began with five years of schooling and will go on for another 40 years of shoving logs around until he is retired at 70 to live out the rest of his life in idleness.

But in no way was he gauche enough to admit that this was the highlight day of his existence.

He chose to look very bored as his mahoot, sitting barefoot

high up on his shoulders, thwacked him very hard a couple of times with a thick stick across the skull to manoeuvre him into precise position.

At a signal both teams took the strain, then heaved.

The sisal rope stretched audibly as the commandos jabbed their metal heel-plates into earth, laid back and pulled in unison to the shrill commands of a couple of officers wearing row upon row of plastic medal ribbons, apparently commemorating campaigns as yet unheard about in the West.

It wasn't remotely a contest. Boon Song waited until their elbows almost touched the earth with exertion and then casually walked forward to drag them over.

Eight reinforcements, adding around another 1,200lb to the commando end of the rope, rushed out from the shade.

Boon Song did not even turn his huge head to acknowledge their arrival. He waited patiently while they spat on their hands and kicked footholds into the ground. Then he walked forwards again and this time dragged 80 Thai commandos into disorderly rout.

Boon Song 2: Royal Thailand Commandos O was going to look so bad in the newspapers that the army proceeded to call up a further 20 men to raise their strength to 100.

They conferred. They spat and entrenched themselves again, and this time, as they took the strain, they bore the determined expressions of men who would sooner wear a truss for life than lose.

Boon Song courteously awaited their preparations and then he pulled. This time admittedly he was forced to acknowledge the military weight behind him by bending his knees to counter their initial onslaught. For a few seconds the rope did not move at all. But then, slowly and irrisistibly, Boon Song moved forward, gradually lengthening his stride until, for the third time in 16 minutes, he felt the resistance give.

It was then he knew, in sporting parlance, that he had white-washed the Royal Thailand Army.

Mr Seing Klang Pattana was ecstatic. He is Boon Song's trainer and had spent 14 of his 52 years preparing him for this moment. He has never left Surin Province in his life, but in a single morning, he had won Wimbledon, the FA Cup and the World heavyweight boxing title.

In his excitement he called upon the Governor of Surin to interpret, an act which in the strictly ordained Thai social structure is like asking Lord Mountbatten to fetch you a drink.

'He wants you to come with us,' laughed the Governor. 'He has something to show you. He insists on demonstrating that his elephants are not only strong but intellectual as well.'

We moved to the centre of the cantonment.

'Lay down,' commanded Seing Klang Pattana, and who, this day, could refuse him?

Waiting for five elephants to step over you, even when they've been trained by the King of Thailand's personal keeper, feels like playing last-across in front of the Flying Scotsman.

But they come forward, as gently as gorgeous ballerinas, delicately lifting their forefeet well clear of your body and just occasionally lightly scuffing your thigh with a back foot which instantly withdraws, as if controlled by some intensively sensitive radar.

'The elephant,' said Seing Klang Pattana, 'has only one problem. He is so ugly. But he has all the same senses as a human being, including a great sense of humour. When they are happy they make giggling noises.'

We went across to the winner's enclosure.

Boon Song was making noises that sounded like gurgling water. In fact, in a curious way, he reminded you of Muhammad Ali after most of his fights.

THE TEMPORARY DECLINE OF JIMMY GLEAVES

*This story has a very happy ending as Jimmy Greaves has not
had a drink for many years and is enjoying a splendid career
as one of the most popular of football pundits and after-dinner
speakers.*

Dateline: **Milan 1979**

I T WAS two o'clock in the Italian morning and to confess that
we'd had a drink or six would still be avoiding the truth, the
whole truth or anything like the truth.

Talking complete rubbish with utter conviction, I can recall
assailing Jimmy Greaves, then one of the supreme athletes of
our time, with the proposition that professional footballers were,
by nature, too indolent even to train properly.

It was the sort of slander one regrets the next dawn. In fact,
I was to regret it inside the next 15 minutes. 'Okay,' said Jimmy,
'we'll see about that.'

And so, as one does on these alcoholically inspired instant
Olympics, we lined up outside the Porto Dora nightclub to run
a foot-race of approximately 100 metres beneath the dimly lit
arcadian arches that grace one side of the piazza.

There were six competitors: Greaves and five of the British
reporters covering his brief and disastrous defection to Italian
football. He was lonely, dispirited, being carved to pieces by a
xenophobic Italian press, hated Italy for its preposterous charade
of masculinity and despised the miserable way Milan, his erstwhile
employers, played nine men on the fringe of their own penalty
area. In short, he welcomed our company.

At 70 metres it wasn't a contest. In his remarkable book,

published this week, Jimmy says he was two yards up on me, but that is symbolic of the man's generosity. It was more like seven and I was dying to make a public retraction.

It was then that Greaves pulled up as if hit by a bullet. Convinced that professional footballers, while faster, were prone to turn muscles under stress, we sprinted on towards our moment of triumph.

Unfortunately, unlike Greaves, I had failed in the half-light to see the spiked chain that blocked off the end of the arcade at a height almost guaranteed to emasculate any fool who ran into it at full tilt.

By sheer luck no irreparable damage was sustained. It only felt like a crowbar being laid across where it hurts most, followed by two somersaults, temporary blackness and, later, the suspicion that one nose, one elbow and one hand had all been methodically rubbed down with emery cloth.

That private incident occurred in the high summer of 1961. Last weekend, laying in bed in a small hotel in France, I read Jimmy Greaves's version of the episode in a review copy of his autobiography, entitled *This One's On Me*.

It is a terrifying book.

Its enormous strength is its simplicity: the unadulterated, scathingly honest, ego-stripping, no-bottle-barred account of the descent of a sports superstar into the labyrinths of such alcoholism that you suddenly wake up to a kindly policeman shaking your shoulder when you thought you were driving home safely or, worse still, come to in the alcoholics' ward of a mental hospital only a couple of miles from your home.

In a rage one night Irene, Jimmy's wife, poured every drink in the house down the sink. Jimmy, on his knees at the dustbin, went through every bottle praying for a few dregs.

It's a real man who will write that.

At the height of his sickness Jimmy Greaves was drinking half a bottle of vodka before he could get out of bed in the morning, between 12 and 14 pints of Guinness during the day and then a full bottle of vodka, sometimes more, in the evening.

Only a supremely fit athlete could have survived the assault.

Jimmy survived. The only point was that along the way he lost his super wife, a business grossing more than £1 million annually and, by the age of 31, a career which by then should have been mellowing from the sensationally precocious to the lucratively venerable.

Only those who saw Jimmy Greaves play can conceivably know what I mean. The rest will have to take our word for it. His genius was above statistics but if it's statistics you want, he kept doing things like scoring three goals against Scotland at Wembley and five goals in a single game against West Ham.

He was so good that if Trevor Francis is worth £1 million, the bidding for Jimmy Greaves would start today at around £4 million.

It is not without irony, therefore, that the proceeds of Jimmy Greaves's 152-page autobiography will not enhance his current lifestyle one jot. Such profit as it makes will merely go towards paying off the demands of the Inland Revenue during the years when he was dedicatedly drinking himself into oblivion.

Do not, I implore you, buy Jimmy Greaves's book out of sympathy. Buy it only if you wish to read a true, honest document about the pressures of pop-idolatry on a man who neither cuts his wrists nor takes off at a tangent when he realizes he can no longer cope.

Sid Vicious and George Best did it their way. Jimmy Greaves, son of a London tube-train driver, did it his gentle way, which was to turn, in a lonely room, to the bottle.

For years those who lived off his back never knew.

At his own expense Jimmy went into private clinics more than a dozen times in an attempt to dry out. Eventually the money was gone and the point was reached where they had to hold him down in an open ward in a public institution. It was here that he heard about Alcoholics Anonymous.

Today, at the age of 38, announcing himself merely as Jimmy Greaves professional footballer, he speaks about his traumas to others suffering a similar plight. He receives no fees. Nor docs he preach. He encourages.

For the past six months he has touched no drink stronger than Perrier water. He never looks back. He reckons that if he can get through the next 24 hours without alcohol he has won another League match. There will be 365 League matches this year.

The last time I saw him he looked a million dollars in a blue pinstripe suit. He was out of the immediate horrors and full of gratitude to Norman Giller, the young freelance journalist who had ghosted his devastating biography with perception and frankness. The two of them are now collaborating on a novel.

There are several reasons Greaves may have hit the bottle. He lost his first son, aged four months to pneumonia. He was cruelly rejected by England at the height of his genius. He began his career when professional footballers were paid like serfs. And, at the depths of his despair in Italy, he spent four months in the company of reporters who tend to drink rather a lot.

It is too late for expiation but not too late to report that *This One's On* Me will be published at £4.95 by Arthur Barker this Thursday.

WHY SEB COE IS THE GREATEST

In the year following the publication of this piece, Sebastian Coe won the first of his two Olympic gold medals in the 1500 metres and the first of two silvers in the 800 metres. Later, IW wrote about Coe's subsequent political career. Coe's more recent achievements, as the man principally responsible for bringing the 2012 Olympic Games to London, have been equally remarkable.

Eventually Sebastian Coe got to bed at 4.30 a.m., a pretty reasonable hour when you've just broken your third world middle distance running record in 41 days but a ghastly one when you have to get up exactly two hours later to face the first day of your life as a confirmed international celebrity.

It didn't bother Coe at all. At just after 7 a.m. he wandered into Zurich airport looking like a student about to discover America on 10 dollars a day.

He was in jeans, a creased windcheater and was cluttered with packages. The dark tinted glasses, so often the affectation of the anonymous craving attention, were strictly therapeutic. They shaded the strain lines beneath the brown, intense eyes.

At the finish of the big runs all the top men are within five seconds of oblivion. It plays havoc with the most finely tuned human body.

Coe didn't say 'good morning' to anybody. Everybody said 'good morning' to Coe. There were British businessmen, suddenly very proud to be British, and British reporters, who had spent half the night switching flights to come home with the new pride of Britain.

There were dozens of requests for autographs. Each time Coe smiled and said: 'Yes, of course.' The British reporters asked for an in-flight chat. Coe smiled and said: 'Yes, of course.' The Swissair captain sent down his prettiest stewardess to ask him to sign things for the entire crew. Coe smiled and said: 'Yes, of course.'

At London Airport the resident photographers asked him to drop his luggage and jog. Coe smiled and said: 'Yes, of course.'

It wasn't that he courted publicity. Coe is an increasingly rare phenomenon in British life, a person who would prefer to be pleasant than bloody-minded. He is certainly rare in sport. Many sports stars assume recalcitrance as a right.

Some 20,000ft over the English Channel I asked him what annoyed him. Coe was non-plussed. He'd answered about a million questions concerning lap-times and training schedules and, suddenly, he was speechless. He stared out of the window and then said: 'Honestly, not much. I'm pretty easy going. Well, there is losing, of course.'

This is not a eulogy. A little later, Coe said: 'I suppose we must be over Brighton by now.'

It was an angelically mischievous aside. Coe's only conceivable rival in British athletics is Steve Ovett, a tough and brilliant performer over the middle distances.

In the 41 days of Coe's world records over 800 metres, the mile and the 1500 metres in Zurich the night before last, Ovett had been upstaged out of sight. Ovett lives in Brighton.

Coe is 22, an economics graduate, has just finished reading a Saul Bellow novel and *The Best of Dorothy Parker*, has more than 250 jazz records, speaks tolerable French and is another rare phenomenon, a subtle Yorkshireman. He comes from Sheffield, although he was born in London, and is, I imagine, thoroughly enjoying something of a regional triumph. He never said so but I suspect that Ovett, more than any other motive, has inspired Coe to one of the most remarkable sequences of world records since the great American Negro sprinter, Jesse Owens, ended the era of white condescension on the track.

Obviously to run as Coe has run in recent weeks there has to be an inner hardness, for the physical demands are beyond the imagination of the average man. But all you see of him is the enduring charm and tolerance.

He is one of four children of an engineer.

At the astounding age of 13 Coe was offered a trial with Sheffield Wednesday which could have led to a career as a professional soccer player. He was a right winger of incredible speed. 'The only trouble,' he said, 'is that I kept being bundled into touch. There was no future in it, just as it took me only one game of rugby at school to realize there was no future in that either. What chance did a six and a half stone rugger player have?'

At 14, trying anything, he won the Yorkshire Schools cross-country title. That was it. Wednesday night's stupendous run in Zurich, confirming him beyond question as the greatest middle-distance runner ever seen, was a direct result.

Coe is utterly without conceit. It visibly did not even occur to him as he came through immigration at London Airport yesterday that the man who flicked through his passport recognized neither name nor photograph.

What did concern him was that the previous evening, for breaking the world record, he had been given a gold Longines watch. He hadn't asked for it and was suddenly confronted by an awkward situation.

He had neither the money to pay a large sum of duty nor the inclination to be caught smuggling. He declared it and to the eternal credit of HM Customs & Excise the uniformed gentleman said: 'After what you've just done for Britain, I reckon you're entitled to it.'

It was an admirable judgement. No £1 million-a-year public relations exercise could do as much for Britain as Coe has in recent weeks.

Altruism, however, has its limits. Coe said: 'No. I wouldn't swap my three world records for an Olympic gold medal in Moscow.'

It is a fascinating remark, for Coe is right on the inside of a sport which, under the pressures of commercialism, is changing before our eyes. Coe, as Olympian a figure as has been seen on a running track, believes the era of the modern Olympic Games to be over.

From London Airport we dropped him from a taxi on a street corner somewhere in West London. He chose that, not to burden his relatives and friends by bringing reporters and cameramen to the door.

Exactly 11 hours earlier millions of European eyes had been upon him as he ran, alone, to his historic triumph.

Suddenly, thankfully, briefly, the pressure was off. In the jeans and the windcheater and burdened by his parcels he walked down the street.

He drew not a second glance from the ladies of the district as they walked briskly to the supermarket.

THE MOSCOW GAMES

The Moscow Olympics were not due to start until July. But as early as January the controversy about whether Britain should attend them or not was already a bitter national issue.

Dateline: **London 1980**

MARGARET THATCHER's matriarchal concern for our country, you, me and the world, in roughly that order, is genuinely inspiring.

I fear, however, that her advisers have failed her badly over her stand on the Olympic Games.

No one would contest her public show of revulsion over the latest act of Soviet aggression. Most would applaud her courage in standing in the international arena to be counted.

Regrettably, her offer to house elements of the 1980 Olympic Games in Britain was based on spurious wishful thinking, impractical generosity and sheer ignorance.

No part of the 1980 Olympic Games will be staged in Britain. No part of the 1980 Olympic Games will be staged in any part of the world other than the Soviet Union, where they will open, absolutely on schedule, in the Lenin Stadium, Moscow, on 19 July.

Apart from the impracticality of the British venues, the simple fact is that Mrs Thatcher's aides, in common with some commentators and many bandwagon politicians, have not even bothered to swot up the history and rules of the Olympic movement.

Had they done so, they would realize that however much Mrs Thatcher and President Carter may wish Moscow to be deprived of the Games, it could be achieved only by a violent act of war.

That, in turn, would probably ensure that posterity, for us all, would be mushroom-shaped.

There will be Moscow Olympics. They will be grotesquely hypocritical Olympics. They will be grim, tense and unpleasant Olympics. They will be Olympics dismembered by boycott and disfigured by understandable protest. They will, in all probability, be untelevized Olympics.

But they will go on because no amount of muscle-flexing in the White House or shrill condemnation from Downing Street can alter it.

The reason is that Mr Carter's and Mrs Thatcher's advisers are unaware of the quaint idealism on which the Olympics were revived at the turn of the century.

One stipulation was that any city awarded the Games willingly conceded its authority to the Olympic movement during the period of the Games. In short that for 15 days or so it actually became Olympia.

Romantically schoolboyish though this notion may seem, it has already survived one test-case every iota as beastly as the Soviet assault on Afghanistan.

In 1936, when Adolf Hitler was already well advanced in his plans to incinerate Jews and set fire to the world, he decided to decorate the Berlin Olympics with eye-catching anti-semitic messages.

These could hardly escape the eye of Henri de Baillet-Latour, the then Olympic president, who summoned Hitler into his presence. An historic conversation ensued.

Baillet-Latour said: 'Mr Chancellor, your signs are not in conformity with Olympic principles.'

Hitler replied: 'Mr President, when you are invited to a friend's home you don't tell him how to run it.'

Baillet-Latour countered: 'When the five-circled flag is raised over the stadium it is no longer Germany. It is Olympia and we are the masters there.' The signs were removed.

It is unlikely that Lord Killanin will persuade the Soviet Union

125

to modify its militant foreign policy but it is quite certain he will reiterate that when the five-circled flag is raised over the Lenin Stadium it is no longer Moscow but Olympia.

Obviously there will be many athletes, spectators and officials who will not wish to go there but to imply that those who do are condoning Soviet military aggression is absurd.

If President Carter is really convinced the Soviet Union is on the march, why doesn't he drop a few professional parachutists into Kabul?

As alternatives go, pulling America's team out of the Olympics is as pathetic as shouting ya-boo through a keyhole and running away.

Mrs Thatcher's stand is no less bewildering. Only the other day she was defending the legal rights of British rugger players to tour South Africa. Now she wants to deny those same rights to British athletes bound for Moscow.

To write thus, of course, is to be branded a Trotskyite fellow-traveller and another bone-headed sportswriter who believes Afghanistan is a suburb of Sydney.

To write thus, in fact, is to know that there are dozens of mediocre politicians, from President Carter sideways, who are using the Olympics as a weapon because they are too scared to use anything else.

The Moscow Olympics will neither provoke war nor prevent it. They are now merely condemned to give us a hollow laugh of historic proportions when the Russians release the usual flurry of doves at the opening ceremony and sing us songs about eternal friendship and peace.

Far from staging a multi-million rouble propaganda exercise to the glory of Mother Russia, the Soviet Union has pledged to open its doors to the world at a time when its horrific ugliness has rarely been more exposed.

It is too good a chance to miss.

126

OLGA KORBUT – THE DANCING GYMNAST

The Olympics were played out in an atmosphere of suspicion and intrigue. They yielded many dramatic stories but, for me, it was an invitation to a late-night party that provided not only a nostalgic reunion with a legend but a sad insight into the pre-perestroika Soviet Union.

Dateline: **Moscow 1980**

WHEN she had exhausted the last of her flagging partners as dawn silhouetted the drab high-rises against the Moscow horizon, Mrs Leonid Bartkevich danced on alone.

She has always, of course, been a compulsive performer.

In the tiny seventh-floor apartment, before a small audience of three diplomats, two principals from the Bolshoi Ballet, a leading Soviet heart surgeon and a couple of reporters, she gave us the nightclub act that no roubles can buy.

To blaring music from the decadent West, there was first a slithering seductive send-up of Salome doing her thing and then a head-tossing, heel-kicking routine of sheer gypsy wildness.

She danced until the blue eye-shadow streaked her cheeks and was crestfallen only when the party was over.

The average Muscovite tends to be worthily dull. But Mrs Bartkevich, a visitor to the city, definitely doesn't hold with dawn bringing down the curtain on happiness.

It was that indefatigable vivacity that made her what she was in a more disciplined field altogether. Mrs Bartkevich is the former Miss Olga Korbut, the tiny bewitching elf who emerged, aged 14, at the 1972 Olympics and inspired a global gymnastics explosion.

There have certainly been greater women gymnasts in history: the austere Larissa Latynina, the serene Vera Caslavska, the ethereal Ludmilla Turischeva. But there has only ever been one Olga, who bounced on, beribboned and saucer-eyed, and simply turned the world's heart inside-out before bouncing out again.

If she infuriated the purists, which she did, they now concede that it was Olga who sold the gospel to an entire generation of sprites. Statistics confirm it. Before Olga there were 50,000 child gymnasts in Britain. There are now three million.

Multiply that by her impact on the world and it is probably quite reasonable to claim that no athlete in history has done more to propagate any sport.

Amazingly, it had never occurred to Olga herself.

Retired by two years, elevated to the title of Honoured Master of Soviet Sport but restricted now from travelling to the West, she said: 'I've never thought about it. If that is so, it makes me very happy.'

It was the guarded, party-line reply, but Olga – still only 22 but with the eyes of a woman of 40 – is well aware that had she been born in the West she could have turned her act into a travelling road show and now be a multi-millionairess.

What business entrepreneurs achieved for Sonja Henie and John Curry, after their skating successes at the Olympics, they could certainly have attained for Olga.

It was not to be.

Instead of a house with a swimming pool, two Cadillacs, an English butler and regular film contracts in California, Mrs Bartkevich has a three-roomed apartment in Minsk, a three-year-old car, which she is hoping to trade in fairly soon, one husband who is trying to change his job, a 15-month old son whom she adores to distraction and all the other problems familiar to 22-year-old housewives trying to make ends meet.

Rebellious to the end of her career, she married Leonid, a

member of Russia's nearest equivalent to a Western pop group. Leonid promptly quit and is now trying to set up on his own with Olga in the act – a courageous ambition in a country where private enterprise is not exactly encouraged.

In a brief respite from dancing, standing drink in hand in a corridor where she could almost hear herself speak, Olga loyally explained that by Soviet standards she is pretty well-off. 'The kitchen,' she kept repeating, 'is very, very big.'

She recalled our first meeting eight years ago, outside the Soviet Olympic team headquarters in Munich. She was famous then by only 24 hours, and I had attempted to interview her in execrable Russian, failing to understand a single word she said in reply.

'You gave me scent,' she said. And so I had, a tiny bottle which she almost snatched and popped down the front of her shirt before it could be spotted by the large lady chaperone hovering in close attendance.

No one hovers in attendance any more. Olga Bartkevich, née Korbut, has been summoned here to Moscow as a world-famous face at the Olympics. She undoubtedly enjoys certain privileges, but they do not extend to her husband accompanying her here by official invitation.

He is back home in Minsk minding their baby.

Olga has no particular ambition, she suddenly announced, to encourage her son to take up gymnastics.

It was an extraordinary remark from a woman whose example had launched millions of other people's children on to the beam. She said it with a look which I shall not forget.

It said more than all the words I have written here with considerable circumspection.

It may even have said that under the Soviet system you are as useful as your last gold medal. But, on the other hand, maybe she just wanted to dance again.

Chapter Five

1981–1988

BARRY SHEENE – THE AMAZING NUTS AND BOLTS MAN

In the 1960s a young man walked into the *Daily Mail* office, squatted on my desk and announced he intended to become the motor-cycling champion of the world. I asked him his name, just in case he made it. 'Barry Sheene,' he said. He survived it all and now, needing heat to ease the pain of his many shattered bones, lives in the Australian tropics.

Dateline: **Northampton 1983**

THE INITIAL impulse is to describe the man as mad. Charming, amusing, honest, slightly deaf, rich, sensual, patriotic, male chauvinistic but, above everything, mad.

It was a year ago this week, cresting the blind rise that leads to Silverstone's Woodcote Corner at 175 mph with his chin on the tank, that he hit an abandoned motorbike lying directly in his path.

Not unnaturally he has no recollection of what happened between then and waking up, feeling rather less than well, in Northampton's General Hospital. But the most credible witness says that he flew 30ft into the air, hit the ground 100 yards away and slithered for a further 200.

In itself this cannot be described as madness since no professional skill, no forked lightning reaction, could have avoided the collision.

Furthermore, if you reckon to gross something like £500,000 a year out of motor sport, you accept that the debit side can be sudden, violent death.

The madness argument is based on the evidence that seven years earlier the same man had come off at 180 mph at Daytona Beach and he has also fallen twice at Mallory Park, twice previously at Silverstone, at Brands Hatch, at Hengelo in Holland, at Quarter Bridge in the Isle of Man, at Anderstown, Sweden, at the Jarama track in Spain, at Imola, Italy, the Paul Ricard circuit in France and at Sugo, Japan, to name but a few painful mishaps.

He has pins, bolts and nuts holding his slender frame together and has suffered the grief of seeing three good friends die in motor-cycling accidents. Once, to get the grit out of his ravaged back, some nuns used a small scrubbing brush with an iodine chaser.

You would have thought that would have taught him a lesson but all he did was fit himself with a strong plastic back protector.

You would certainly reckon that last year's Silverstone pile-up, which almost smashed him to bits, might have warned him that the good Lord's patience was running out.

Not at all, Barry Sheene will be back at Silverstone again in Sunday's British Grand Prix and nothing said over a gastronomic masterpiece of a lunch this week could induce him to believe that it was anything other than the sanest possible way to relieve the boredom of another Sabbath.

No argument prevailed, not even the last-ditch reminder that his good friend James Hunt had the brains to get out of car racing the moment he made £1 million.

'Yes,' countered Sheene, 'but James had come to hate driving. I still love it. When I don't, I'll quit.'

In all else the man is logical. He is, paradoxically, a safety fanatic, refusing ever again to ride the lethal TT circuit in the

Isle of Man, detesting Germany's long Nurburgring track because of the time-lag in getting an ambulance or a rescue helicopter to an injured rider.

He is scathing about motor-cycling officials who have never ridden bikes at high speed but won't spend money on safety precautions. He has led riders' rebellions at circuits he regards as too dangerous. He is in fiery litigation with Silverstone over what he alleges to be the stewarding shortcomings that led to his horrific 1982 accident.

Materially, even emotionally at last, there is little more he could want.

He has a 33-roomed Elizabethan manor house standing in 22 acres in Sussex. He has his own helicopter and a Mercedes 500 SEL.

And after years of wild and indiscriminate wenching, highlighted by a summer mostly spent in bed with two Finnish sisters, he has found Stephanie, who divorced to be with him. They have a stunning relationship that comes only from mutual adoration and will marry when they propose to have children. Lovemaking and a large English breakfast, he suggests, knowing that Stephanie will only laugh, is the ideal morning preparation for a big race.

Not bad, you reckon, for a Cockney boy whose only known scholastic achievement was the highest truancy rate on record. Too bad, you argue, that with all that to live for the ultimate thrill remains driving motorbikes at very high speeds.

But he refuses to listen. He is literally partially deaf, anyway, from his years alongside engines, but the ultimate deafness is in his soul.

He is a stubborn man.

On the eve of a French Grand Prix, when a hotel manager ignored his entreaties to stop the booming dance band playing so that the riders could get some sleep, he carried a 26-inch colour television to a window and hurled it into the courtyard below.

In Finland, confronted by disgusting trackside lavatories for riders and their families, he poured ten gallons of 100 octane fuel into the loos, set light to it and blew the whole edifice sky high.

He refuses to go to restaurants that won't permit jeans or attend dinners where black ties are obligatory. The last time he wore a suit was in 1977 when he collected his MBE from the Queen at Buckingham Palace but even then, though both Tory and royalist, he would not wear tails and a top hat.

The Queen asked him then if he proposed to race on. He said he did. 'You be very careful then,' admonished the monarch.

There is no point at all in repeating the caution. Beneath the panache he is a careful rider. The madness is in not acknowledging that some day the surgeons might not be able to piece him together again.

MAGIC MATILDA WINS THE AMERICA'S CUP

The night of 26–27 September 1983 was mildly hectic in the *Daily Mail* office. Against a five-hour time difference I was attempting to report from America the greatest-ever yacht race. Edition after edition was sent out to the country carrying stories of an uncompleted and still unpredictable duel. Eventually America lost the oldest trophy in international sport after 132 years. What follows is an appalling piece of dictation, yelled down the telephone as *Australia II* crossed the line. But it was live history and for the first time a yacht race made the front-page splash in our final edition.

Dateline: Newport, Rhode Island 1983

IT HAPPENED and it happened in the manner of lurid fiction. *Australia II* sailed back from the Dead Sea here last night to beat *Liberty*, win the America's Cup and leave this nation speechless.

Two-thirds of the way through the accurately billed Race of the Century you would not have risked tenpence on *Australia*'s chances, at 100 to 1.

Outsteered by the brilliant Dennis Conner, outpaced by an American boat that had shed 1,000lb of ballast to defend 132 years of unthreatened high-seas supremacy, *Australia* looked irrevocably doomed as the unluckiest also-rans in sports and 'Waltzing Matilda' looked set to become a lament.

And then they won. They won a 4¼-hour race by precisely 41 seconds.

As America watched in helpless agony – and there is no greater frustration than urging a yacht to speed up in God's own good time – John Bertrand, *Australia*'s self-effacing skipper, sailed right out of nowhere, straight past *Liberty* and unerringly into the pages of sporting history.

So the seemingly impossible was accomplished. The trophy won by America off the Isle of Wight in the presence of Queen Victoria in 1851 and never endangered in 24 challenges, finally fell.

It is due to be handed over by the New York Yacht Club – in whose premises it has been symbolically fastened to a plinth by bolts – within the next 48 hours.

To its autocratic members and to millions of Americans, it will be akin to surrendering the Crown Jewels, for it was the symbol of American human and technological superiority. How they lost it on the fringe of the Atlantic on a warm Indian-summer afternoon just stirred by sufficient breeze to avoid another agonizing postponement will now become the plot for a dozen instant books.

The truth was that Conner, acknowledged by the yachting world as an unrivalled helmsman, gambled once too often.

The mild tragedy of the day was that the massive 2,000-vessel spectator fleet that had to turn back when Saturday's race was abandoned, did not reassemble to acclaim Bertrand's eventual triumph on behalf of the rest of the world. There were probably only 250 spectator boats in attendance when, after one aborted start and an anguishing 55-minute delay, a single cannon boom announced that Race Seven, the decider, was actually on.

Ironically Bertrand, whose starting technique had been the

Right: Paul Dacre, Editor in Chief of Associated Newspapers and Editor of the *Daily Mail* for IW's last fifteen years as a columnist.

Below: *Daily Mail* proprietor, Lord Rothermere (Vere Harmsworth), congratulates Drama critic, Jack Tinker, IW and, the then Editor of the *Mail*, David English, on their success at the 1982 British Press awards.

IW tried his Russian, learned during National Service, on the ever delightful Olga Korbut, as they danced at a party in her Moscow flat.

Another day at the office – IW reporting from the Olympics with friend and *Daily Mail* colleague Terry O'Connor.

Remarkably, IW was invited to join the four-man team from the Cayman Islands in the opening ceremony of the 1978 Commonwealth Games in Edmonton, for which he was later arrested.

Being chosen to carry the Olympic torch for a short stint, on its way to the Atlanta Games in 1996, was an honour IW was delighted to accept.

Ice-dancing was not often found on Wooldridge's beat but he admired, and reported on, the perfection of Torvill and Dean's gold-medal performance at the 1984 Winter Olympics in Sarajevo.

Carl Lewis won the 100m at the world championships in Tokyo in 1991 and set a new world record.

A face in the crowd
– this wonderful
image of Princess
Anne at the 1976
Montreal Olympics
won awards for
Wooldridge's
regular
collaborator,
photographer
Monty Fresco. It
was IW's favourite
image.

Above: The 'Dook' of Norfolk, as the Australian tabloids called him – pictured here (*left*) with Ted Dexter (*centre*) and Alec Bedser – was a surprise choice as manager of the MCC party on the 1962/3 tour down under.

Left: Basil D'Oliveira plays an innings that was to help free South Africa of apartheid.

IW revered John Arlott's gift for words – and his capacity for fine wines.

Former Test umpire Dickie Bird is another who is rarely short of a word.

Roy Jenkins presents IW with another of his many journalistic awards.

To get his shot, *Daily Mail* photographer Monty Fresco told Ugandan dictator and heavyweight Idi Amin that IW was a fine boxer. That caused IW to look rather worried but, fortunately, the dictator resisted Fresco's urgings to 'give 'im one, sah'.

one glaring weakness of the Australian campaign, scored his finest start of the series.

Unlike Conner, who had spent his Sunday rest day on a golf course with a laconic detachment first feigned on Plymouth Hoe, Bertrand had gone back to sea to rehearse start after start against two of his former rivals, Britain's Harold Cudmore and France's Bruno Trouble.

And with salutary effect. Although the official starting time placed America's *Liberty* eight seconds ahead, Bertrand went over on full acceleration and tactically dominated the first three miles of the 4½ mile first leg into the wind.

But such faint strains of 'Waltzing Matilda' as may have been sounding in Australian ears were soon drowned.

Gambling with one of those genius strokes that have built the Conner legend, the American skipper pulled *Liberty* over to the right of the course, collected a wind shift worthy of the term and hauled straight past *Australia II* to lead by 29 seconds at the first marker buoy.

A lead of that dimension, even at so early a stage, is generally a significant pointer. For *Australia* it pointed to defeat and there was worse to come.

She was 45 seconds behind at the second buoy, pulled back slightly to trail by 23 seconds at the third, but then slipped to a critical 57 seconds behind down the fourth leg. In yachting terms that is one foot in the grave.

The race defied all predictions. *Australia*, usually at her best beating into the wind, was floundering. Characteristically she is at her worst downwind yet yesterday it was on the fifth down-wind leg that she achieved her miracle, with some help from Conner.

She turned into it 57 seconds behind and emerged from it 21 seconds ahead in the great race for home. That 78-second improvement in a swift down-wind run changed the history of the America's Cup. It may not have been so had Conner not moved out again to find a windshift that was not there.

Liberty counter-attacked but left it too late.

She tried to lure Bertrand towards the spectator fleet. Bertrand wouldn't play. Victory and the America's Cup was firmly in his sights and his wisdom was rewarded. He crossed the line to a fraction of the reception he deserved.

The one reception he valued above all others was from the plump, beaming man aboard the launch at the finish line.

Perhaps it is quite inappropriate at this moment to recall that the man who has financed probably Australia's greatest sporting achievement was born in Ealing, West London. I will certainly not dwell on it.

Alan Bond made his vast fortune in Australia and spent £12 million of it on four challenges for the America's Cup. Last week at 3–1 down, with America in a seemingly invincible position, he never lost faith. Nor did he yesterday when *Australia II* looked out for the count.

He was the man who had the courage to believe that Bertrand would stay cool under the ultimate pressure, and the ultimate pressure was certainly applied in the final shoot-out.

TORVILL AND DEAN

There were few occasions in the 1980s when you could predict a British victory at the highest level with something approaching assurance. Miss Torvill and Mr Dean were the exceptions at the Winter Olympics. I am still equivocal about whether ice-dancing is sport or showbiz, but how often do you watch sheer perfection?

Dateline: **Sarajevo 1984**

T HE FIXED smiles could not mask the hopelessness. They came, two by two, condensed four years of training into four minutes on Mount Olympus and left.

Some hardly bothered to glance at the scoreboard for the sum total of their efforts was futility.

In ice-dancing the stars skate last and the very last couple on to the rink of the Zetra Stadium here last night were Jayne Torvill and Christopher Dean, the hallmark of whose genius is that they rendered all the 18 other couples impotent merely by turning up.

They won, of course. The sensation would have been if they hadn't.

But that was barely the half of it. You sat there, nervously at first, then with growing confidence, then simply spellbound, as they moved faultlessly to a victory that gave no other competitor the remotest chance.

You knew it was very, very good. But then came the moment that may well be the final acclamation of their amateur days – the row of nine sixes that declared that what they had just performed was, by the highest amd most Olympian standards, sheer perfection.

It had happened only once before in ice-dance history, and it was Torvill and Dean who had done it then, last year in Helsinki. They had no doubts themselves, skating down the rink to collect the flowers strewn on the ice by the 150 British spectators who had flown in for their performance and were flying straight out again.

But they were modest in their triumph, too, acknowledging with warm handshakes those who had come without a hope of beating them.

The audience, from across continents and ideologies, rose to acclaim them. On this night there was no argument, no controversy, only justice seen absolutely to be done.

That is the measure of the supremacy of the man and woman who for themselves, Nottingham and Britain, strictly in that order, took the solitary medal we shall celebrate at the XIV Winter Olympics.

I cannot prove that in those four minutes they became millionaires but I think it rather likely. When Miss Sonja Henie won the Olympic figure skating gold at Garmisch in 1936 she professionalized her talent so shrewdly that when she died of leukaemia, aged 57, she left £22 million.

Given inflation and the number of agents waving contracts in their faces last evening, I can hardly imagine Miss Torvill and Mr Dean underselling themselves.

Millions, not excluding the opposition, assumed they couldn't lose but, in fact, a fall or a bad blemish in style could have been very serious indeed because of the way ice-dancing is adjudicated by that stone-faced jury of nine, not-necessarily-just, persons who sit there with a gravity more appropriate to Nuremberg than the Olympic Games.

The ice-dance competition is fought out in three stages. The first, the compulsory dances in which Torvill and Dean visibly wiped the floor with the world, carries 30 per cent of the final marks. The second stage, in which they gave us their bullfighting routine, yields only 20 per cent of the the total.

But that left 50 per cent of the marks hanging on last night's free dance, a reward ratio cunningly devised to sustain the jitters and insomnia.

Those close to them say that Miss Torvill is the tough one during those awful waiting hours and this I quite believe. The *Daily Mail* gave a lunch a couple of years ago to Britain's reigning women world champions and, in the photo session afterwards, our cameraman asked Miss Torvill to sit, centre-group, on the floor.

The ice queen was outraged. 'I *never* sit on the floor,' she snapped, thus revealing a fraction of the character that made her unbeatable here last night.

Her partner, seemingly a perpetual study in blandness, proves at close range to be less cool than he looks. When he arrived here by train from Munich – they were taking no chances about being snowbound at some frozen airport – he was in a miserable tizzy about his baggage and the instant availability of ice to practise on.

The nerves were gone the moment he emerged with Jayne for the compulsory dances. It was here, so visibly a whole class superior to the rest of the world, that they demoralized the opposition.

European champions in 1981, 82 and 84; world champions in 1981, 82 and 83. What comes next for this transfixing couple?

I have not the remotest idea. Wait for the next book, for which the financial negotiations will undoubtedly be going on this morning.

FROM FEAR TO ETERNITY ON THE CRESTA RUN

In January the *Daily Mail* took 12 young readers to the Cresta Run to prove that guts are not exclusive to any one generation. After a dozen runs most were flying down like veterans. Our in-house competition was won by Nick Ovett, young brother of Steve, the Olympic athlete. In the circumstances one had to have a go. The following was written, champagne at elbow, after desecrating one of the supreme venues of sport.

Dateline: St Moritz 1985

YESTERDAY we rode the Cresta Run. To be more accurate we bounced down it like a pinball. After careful thought I declare it to be the second greatest thrill that life has to offer.

Heroics are as entirely out of order as false modesty. I am proud to have got down it in 79.55 seconds, which is half as fast again as Errol Flynn. I am not proud at all to confess I was so enduringly terrified that I doubt I shall ever do it again.

Morally there was no ducking it. When your newspaper brings 12 young Britons here to brave the Cresta, you have to grit your teeth, ring your insurance broker and shove off from the vivid blue start line across the ice.

Many claim that the waiting is the worst. I can now authoritatively dismiss that as utter nonsense.

The worst is roughly 18 seconds into it on the mildly banked bend named Battledore. It is here precisely that the novice is no longer boss.

It is here that the damned thing under you – a 60lb steel toboggan as aesthetically beautiful as a ripped-off oven door – takes over.

They kit you out with a pair of boots each with four metal teeth projecting from the toecaps. Till now you have been dragging these into the ice, just as they instructed you, arresting acceleration. You have done it so efficiently, despite one sledgehammer blow on the right hip when you hit the wall, that momentarily you enjoy it.

On Battledore that changes rapidly. Suddenly the Cresta falls away. It is not yet 9 a.m. It is minus 19°C. The Run is highly polished glass. And as its innocently beckoning camber hurls you violently to the right you are into a scenario roughly the equivalent of a thrashing nightmare.

Gravity grabs your 13 stone and your 60lb contraption with manic intensity. The toecap rakes are useless. You are out of control of your immediate health, let alone your destiny.

It is too late for discreet retirements, feigned muscle strains or the courageous withdrawals that are the privileges of the waiting minutes. Mayday calls will go unanswered. You are now heavily into this, brother, and the best thing you can do is keep your elbows tucked tight in and hang on. The dreaded Shuttlecock hairpin is down there somewhere and coming up to meet you very fast.

Somewhere to the right is a marker they told you to aim at to hit the line that gets you round Shuttlecock without flying off into the neighbouring forest.

Bloody hell, where is it? Gone. Missed it. Real trouble now. Blind panic. Jab a foot into the ice with a strength you never knew you had. Wrong foot. Slew madly to the right and smash the same hip against the wall again. Don't feel the pain. Swearing appallingly, out loud, far worse than can be reported here. Very frightened.

In his all-seeing glass eyrie high above the Cresta Run, Lt-Col Digby Willoughby, ex-Gurkha officer and now autocratic secretary of the St Moritz Tobogganing Club, broadcasts a commentary on what's happening to the poor initiates trying to negotiate his fiendish ice-chute over a relay system which echoes over much of south-east Switzerland.

Sometimes he is extremely generous. Mostly he is heavily sardonic. 'Lord X,' he is prone to say, 'has just negotiated Shuttlecock like a drunken crab.'

I am told he was kind to me. 'That,' he said, 'was an excellent execution of Shuttlecock for a beginner.'

I have news for Mr Digby Willoughby. I have virtually no recollection of getting round Shuttlecock let alone executing it. It comes up so fast that there is no time for academic reflection about how the brilliant young James Sunley glides round this terrible curve like a horizontal ballet dancer.

By luck, or maybe as a reward for a blameless life, the toboggan flew through there coincidentally with me upon it.

You glance up and exuberantly realize that you're past it. From here, they all say, it's plain sailing. They lie. In the very act of glancing up you wobble and smash the right hip into the wall again. This time it hurts a lot.

By now you are not thinking about wife, family, Queen, country or even Mr Digby Willoughby. You are thinking about getting off this thing as soon as possible. You are still alive, soldiering on in the name of journalism, and beginning to feel a bit of a hero.

It is then, having flashed through the infinitesimal shadow thrown by the road bridge that traverses a station of this sporting cross called Scylla, that you top the Cresta Leap.

I grope for a description of this latest horror: racing towards the brink of Beachy Head, perhaps, in a car with faulty brakes.

You have leather knee and elbow pads, helmet and goggles and metal plates strapped to the outside of your gloves to stop the Cresta ripping off your fingers. You've also got three layers of clothing but nothing helps as you crest the Leap, exit line completely wrong again, and once more the right hip pounds into the wall.

You know it is slowly turning into raw steak but you don't care any more. Your eyes are shut. You have given up the toecap rakes. You acknowledge the ice-chute known as the Cresta as your unrelenting master.

And then, sublimely, you feel the ground rising under your chest. With no effort on your part the thing is slowing down. It stops. You lie there for a few seconds, gasping. And then a nice man with a hook comes down and secures your toboggan. You could embrace him, even though he has three days of facial stubble. But, of course, he's seen it all before.

He drags the primitive machine away and you stand there, reflecting on 79.55 seconds of curious life.

The *Daily Mail* team gather for champagne. Photographer Graham Wood is the hero. He half slid off his toboggan round Shuttlecock, regained it somehow, and made it in 70.33 seconds. Alwyn Robinson, just the oldest among us, was down in 86.57. Promotions manager Desmond Nichols flew off at Shuttlecock the first time, waited for a nervy hour and then negotiated it with intense concentration in 101.51 seconds.

The great Cresta runners watched us with quiet amusement. By their standards, we had just run a six-minute mile. But they are kindly people. 'Well done,' they say.

The Cresta breeds a fraternity like that.

TEST OF BRAVERY AGAINST THE WEST INDIES QUICKS

The piece that follows reflects the apprehension of standing yet again in the firing line of a merciless West Indian pace attack. Supplication is not for the professional sportsman but occasionally a sportswriter is entitled to question the morality of playing games in a certain manner.

Dateline: **Trinidad 1986**

JUST OCCASIONALLY a sports event generates a tension that makes the waiting a physical agony. You only had to watch England's cricketers at the nets yesterday to know that this Trinidad Test is such a landmark in many young lives.

There was no skylarking. There was neither leg-pulling nor laughter. The intensity of it was epitomized by Ian Botham, normally a lax rehearser who just slogs a few sixes to loosen the muscles. Yesterday, heavily padded from right shoulder to knee, he batted as though his family's lives were at stake.

They are aware that England's eyes are upon them, ready to heap scorn upon ridicule, imply cowardice or leap on the band-wagon in the unlikely event that they beat the West Indies in a proper cricket match.

Their one-day victory here on Tuesday did more to set the Caribbean alight than restore their own confidence. Five-day cricket against the most relentlessly hostile attack in history, played before a crowd which in the past I have heard literally bay for blood, is a very different ball game.

If I were 20 years younger and an experienced Test batsman,

my heart would still miss a beat on the way to the ground. Indeed, I might even feel that a minor injury sustained in a small traffic accident before we got there would be no inconvenience.

It will not happen, and I shall be hooted down here even for suggesting it, but the batsman I would like to see in the England team is the highly paid commentator, Geoffrey Boycott.

He is such a raving egocentric, so battle-hardened in situations like this, that he is capable of throwing off the years and writing a new chapter to his own glory, coincidentally helping England along the way.

It is not only Boycott's accumulative obsession that England needs at the moment, it is his meanness of spirit. You simply cannot take what the West Indies are currently hurling at you and still play to the Queensberry Rules.

At the height of the bodyline fracas 54 years ago Bill Woodfull, the Australian captain, uttered one of the frequently quoted remarks in sport: 'There are two teams out there and only one of them is playing cricket.' The wheel has turned the full circle. The West Indies aren't playing cricket at all. They are waging war.

Under no circumstances must England squeal and to their immense credit no England player has attempted to do so. Four potentially lethal bouncers an over is no way to play the game, but while I can write that since I don't care about the repercussions, David Gower would be pilloried here even for hinting it.

This is an extremely volatile part of the world. The most innocent remark is analysed for racialist undertones.

Gower, happily an intelligent and perceptive man, is performing a superhuman job on the diplomatic front and deserves a few dazzling innings out there in the middle as a reward. However, the attack he will face here these next five days is from a different planet to the Australians he emasculated at The Oval last year.

That said, England should not be napalmed out of it in three days, as they were in the first Test in Jamaica.

Compared with the murderous ice-rink pitch at Sabina Park, the wicket here is a drawing-room carpet. Based on clay, as in tennis, it takes the venomous speed out of the half-volley and restricts the bounce. By the fourth day, and pray God there is a fourth day, we may actually see some intellect restored in the shape of spin bowling.

Inconceivable though it may seem, the two teams get on very well off the field. On it they can be quite remorseless.

I do not believe cricket should be played in this fashion but I am clearly out of date. Television appears to have decreed that vicarious audiences want the thrill of Grand-Prix motor racing and bullfighting introduced to cricket. It will, of course, destroy the game if the violence continues.

Men will make or break reputations here in the next few days. Unashamedly I take the unusual course of wishing England well.

They are up against it. The disparity between West Indies and any other team in the world is now such that you almost regard losing on the fifth day as a triumph. We sleep uneasily here to see how it will work out.

It must be hard to imagine that merely watching Test cricket can be nearly as nerve-racking as playing it, but that's how it was yesterday as England gave every indication of vanishing on another funeral pyre.

Their dressing-room balcony affords no privacy so the grief was cruelly evident. Graham Gooch was slumped deep in a chair, staring at a magazine whose pages never turned. Wilf Slack's eyes were fixed on something somewhere in the middle-distance. Peter Willey looked pale. He was entitled to. The 24th ball he received could have killed him.

All three were out. The Test was ten overs old. England were

30 for three. Even watching it, from the cowardly comfort of the Press-box, provoked nausea. The sight of England's remaining batsmen, padded up against protracted collapse, did nothing to suggest the day would improve. They looked like men on Death Row.

It was the ball from Patrick Patterson to Willey that did it. It rose like a deflected rifle bullet from only fractionally short of a conventional length and screamed straight for his face. He had no hope of avoiding or playing it. By the grace of God and self-protective reaction, he got part of his bat in its path. But, of course, he was out.

While cricket like that is in progress, you tend to forget what made you fall in love with the game in the first place: the skill, the unspoken code of honour, the beauty of the grounds.

David Gower's battle for form and Allan Lamb's courageous batting did provide an hour's respite in which to enjoy, in the dragging intervals between balls, the stunning setting of this Trinidad arena with its mountain backdrop.

We deserved that for the doom-laden mood was soon to descend again. A colleague bet me five dollars to ten that Ian Botham wouldn't survive it for half an hour. He won with a luxurious 18 minutes to spare. Inevitability had set in again.

For the retreating batsmen the agony of dismissal is compounded by the cacophony of hearing the manner of it vividly described over hundreds of transistor radios tuned to ghetto-blasting levels. Even the mellifluous Etonian tones of Henry Blofeld do nothing to alleviate the misery of the moment.

But, outgunned, out-firepowered and out-classed, England, by contract and fixture list, are stuck with this tour. It is hard not to feel sympathy for them.

SEVVY DRIVING ON THE BURMA ROAD

Severiano Ballesteros has the reputation of being extremely testy. But when he turns the charm on, playing against him is no worse than having a nervous breakdown.

Dateline: **Wentworth 1986**

IT WAS like tackling *The Times* crossword in front of Einstein. Or driving James Hunt to the airport. Or writing a letter to Graham Greene.

You know the true giants are invariably tolerant, yet lunch – in this column's case two stiff gins and a bowl of soup – rested in the stomach like suet pudding. One is old enough to recognize the symptoms of a bad attack of nerves.

At 2.42 p.m. precisely the starter at Wentworth's Burma Road calls this column's name with all the enthusiasm of an auctioneer selling off a job lot of back copies of *Farmers' Weekly*. One steps forward, waxen-smiled, armed with a four iron.

As anyone who knows anything about golf will tell you, a four iron is probably the most stupid club a man can carry on to what the critics have called the most intimidating first tee in Britain. Even if stupendously struck, it will hardly get you into competitive play on this switchback par four.

Why, then, take a four iron? Because it is the only club with which your correspondent, an occasional golfer, can make contact with the ball on a reasonably regular basis.

Shrewd thinking, though I say it myself. The usual purple mists cloud the brain at the top of the backswing but somehow the ball flies 170 yards straight as an arrow into a fearful lie in some transverse rough.

152

Like every amateur who has ever played in a pro-am we thank Our Maker for sparing us an air swing.

Proceeding down the fairway, an arm falls lightly round my shoulder.

'Why you hit four iron?' he say.

'Because,' I say, lapsing into the pidgin-speech we British use instead of foreign languages, 'I no good with any other club.'

'Rubbish,' says Severiano Ballesteros, the best golfer in the world.

'You just stand up there and hit the ball with any bloody club you please. We all friends here, unnerstand?'

This you are not going to believe. Our foursome, also involving Dennis Hart, a Scottish travel agent, and Ian Chubb, a Bell's Whisky man, all got down in five at the first hole. So did Sevvy, who may well deliberately have punched his second shot left of the green to make the rest of us feel better.

At the short fifth, we halve another in par. 'Estupendo,' he cry. We are feeling better now.

The knees have stopped quivering and mists are clearing. This was Sevvy's being-nice day to the public.

Ballesteros flew in to Wentworth by helicopter. Since he's staying in a not-distant hotel for this weekend's European event at Sunningdale, he could, possibly more swiftly and certainly at one-tenth of the price, have come by car.

But it was a day for style, not economy. When the rotor blades stopped he stepped out to devote an entire day to publicizing the La Manga Club, a sports resort in South East Spain, to whom he is attached as travelling professional.

True, La Manga rarely sees him. His brother, Manuel, runs the place. But Sevvy is the flagship. Eight days a year he dedicates himself to promoting its activities with all the intensity he gives to winning championships. It involves playing golf with the likes of me.

This he tolerated with a smile and no semblance of impatience. Understandably. It is not possible under the terms of his La Manga contract to state precisely how much he earned for his day among the golfing lower classes but had it been a one-off job the price would have been minimally £25,000.

He chats amiably along the fairway. 'No,' he says, 'I no learn a single word of English until I seventeen. Then I began to travel and picked up a few words.' He now speaks English engagingly. 'No problem' is his favourite phrase.

'No problem,' he laughs as you hook another tee shot into foliage. 'Funny game is golf. It's the only sport which the professionals practise all the time and the amateurs never practise at all. Do you practise?'

'Never,' I admit.

'Yes, I can see that,' he says. 'Me, I am like a pianist. When I am not playing in tournaments I still practise six, seven hours every day. It is the only way I know to stay where I am.'

The great man demonstrated the controlled draw and slice, issued a few tips, signed autographs and dispensed bonhomie all day, earning in the process slightly more than Max Faulkner won in prize money during his entire career.

SAIL OF A LIFETIME

We were to spend five months in Australia covering Dennis Conner's campaign to win back the America's Cup. It was an idyllic period blighted in only one respect. The apprehension in this column about jumping off a 12-metre yacht in heavy seas was justified. I slipped a spinal disc and take this opportunity of thanking Dr Ken Kennedy, the ex-Irish rugger international, for giving me hell but getting it back.

Dateline: Fremantle 1986

VIEWED from a helicopter yesterday the passage of KA8, the glorious royal blue, gold and scarlet-hulled South Australian 12-metre, must have given considerable cause for alarm.

So erratic was its progress into 15 knots of Indian Ocean headwind that it may well have been assumed that its helmsman was off his rocker, hopelessly drunk or simply working his ticket.

In fact, he was none of these things.

Firstly, since he can't even swim, he was petrified about falling off the bloody thing. Secondly, having got on it, he was constantly in a panic about how he was ever going to get off again out there in a high-pitching sea.

Well here we are back on dry land, probably for ever, to offer sincere thanks to the captain and crew of *South Australia* for permitting a landlubber Pom reporter to have 20 minutes at the helm of their 26 ton, 65 foot, £400,000 toy and thus get a closer glimpse at this America's Cup game.

Boy, that's some sport out there. The horizon spends all the time disappearing up its own axis, the deck is never there when you feel like putting your foot on it and driving it is like coming very fast down a motorway on a 300 horse-power eiderdown.

When all the canvas is up the noise is amazing. There are two distinct sounds, a constant groaning, which reminds you of about 2,000 mortally wounded men on a battlefield, and sharp cracks that sound like small-arms fire in films about the American Civil War.

'See that tall building,' commanded Phil Thompson, pointing out a Perth skyscraper that was swaying around on the distant shore like a metronome, 'try steering for that.'

Phil was in charge for the day while John Savage, *South Australia*'s resident skipper, was having a 10,000-mile service in a local clinic in preparation for the start of Australia's four-syndicate battle to find the one yacht that will defend the Cup.

Behind us, in what appeared to be a 2ft 6in. high broom cupboard, navigator Steven Kemp and tactician Gary Simmonds were hammering away at a computer which would probably win the World Chess Championship on its own. If I could have understood what they were saying I would have assuredly complied, but merely steering *South Australia* at that skyscraper was like wrestling with Geoff Capes.

'Keep her at 7.9,' yelled Phil.

The problem was 7.9 of what? There were three computer dials and nine switches immediately behind the wheel. One of the dials was registering 8.6. 'That's the one,' shouted Phil. 'Get the boat speed down to 7.9.'

But how? More significantly, why? What's the point of coming out here to make Dennis Conner look an idiot and then slow the boat down?

Phil had no time to explain. Instead of heading for the Perth skyscraper we now appeared to be en route for Durban, South Africa, with only a few sandwiches on board. Phil jerked the wheel with his left hand and there, dead ahead, as we slalomed down a wave, was the skyscraper again.

The answer, apparently, is that when you're beating to wind-ward – which is to say sailing directly into a headwind whose natural instinct is to blow you back to where you've just come from – you close-haul the yacht to 25 degrees to the wind at an optimum speed, which gets you to the turning buoy considerably quicker than going much faster at an angle of 35 degrees.

That achieved, the sense of power when you've got her going is like being Prime Minister or piloting Concorde.

While you are striving to retain the foregoing, there is one further thing to remember. Lurking at your shoulder is a metal branch which sticks out from the mast down to the back end of the boat and scythes across the deck every time you tack. This is called the boom. It weighs about 240lb and if it hits you in the head you'll probably get washed up in the Falkland Islands.

Meanwhile, there is the nagging terror about disembarking. *South Australia* will be out here all day, rehearsing hard. One has to leave them to it. This means jumping from the swaying 12-metre into a bobbing chase craft about the size of a Serpentine rowing boat.

It's only a five-foot drop but what concerns the layman, I can authoritatively report, is the gap of water that keeps yawning between the two hulls. You close your eyes and go for it. Back on shore John Savage, returned from the clinic, laughs.

These guys walk on water every day. 'It's just like ball games,' he said. 'If you're born with a ball sense you don't think about anything. You just do it. It's the same with the sea. If you don't have an affinity with it, you'll find it hard.'

I found it hard.

South Australia's 11-man crew never laughed once. They were as impeccably mannered as the wardroom of the QE2.

Meanwhile, a mile or two down the ocean, 12 of the challenging yachts were fighting it out to take on *Australia* at the end of next January.

The America's Cup is an extraordinary business. Yesterday our education into it was marginally widened.

FROM ETON TO LAS VEGAS

Stuart Wheeler had been drawn to the possibility of becoming a bookmaker, but never expected anything to come of it. Then in 1974, sacked from his merchant banker job for picking too many dud shares, he set up the spread-betting firm IG Index with £30,000 (including just £300 of his own money). In 2003 he sold his shares for £40 million.

WHEN THE 3rd Earl of Birkenhead died suddenly, aged 48, two years ago he left a bequest of £5,000 to his good friend Stuart Wheeler.

Mrs Wheeler said they should buy a picture with it as a permanent memorial but Mr Wheeler had a more radical idea. Thus next week he flies out to Binion's Horseshoe Club in downtown Las Vegas either to multiply or lose the lot on the green baize of the World Poker Championships.

Sitting alongside such cut-throat casino luminaries as the legendary Amarillo Slim, Tree Top Jack Strauss and Pug Pearson, Stuart Wheeler may appear an incongruous, even improbable, figure.

He dresses like an off-duty high church bishop, wears the sort of spectacles favoured by nuclear mathematicians and will call his bids in the cut-glass accent that only Eton, Christ Church, Oxford, the Welsh Guards and three years at the Bar can polish to perfection.

However, Amarillo Slim won't be deceived into fiscal indiscretion. He knows what a 'What's My Line?' panel wouldn't guess in several light years: that Wheeler is one of Britain's most brilliant and successful professional gamblers.

What started with a six-shilling winning bet at a West Country point-to-point when he was seven and progressed with a nerve-racking but profitable £140 on the Peter Cazalet-trained Flaming Star at 6–1 while he was at Oxford sees him now, at 52, the boss of a 20-employee company called IG Index whose offices look down on one of London's most fashionable squares.

In practice it's an upper-class betting shop. Its clients speculate on such weighty matters as tonight's closing prices on Wall Street or tomorrow's price of gold. 'All perfectly legal,' said Wheeler, 'the Inland Revenue know all about it. But it's gambling, pure and simple.'

Every year, though, Wheeler leaves for his spiritual home: Las Vegas. There, for an average 17 hours a day, he plays bridge and blackjack, mostly becoming what it is physically dangerous to become in that wild west town – a consistent winner.

In his first year in 1965 he proved conclusively that the punter *can* beat the house at blackjack by winning $3,500 at a session. 'If you are numerate and absorbed by gambling anyone can do it,' he said.

What he meant by numerate, of course, was the phenomenal ability to recollect the cards already played and calculate at immense speed the number of 'ten' and picture cards remaining in the shoe.

'I've had my bad moments,' he conceded. 'I was playing in Caesars Palace at six o'clock one Sunday morning when the pit-boss suddenly said: 'You're not losing. We don't like your type here. Cash in and go.' I went. You don't mess about in Las Vegas. Too many bodies have been found out in the desert.

Since then he has taken the precaution of playing a one-hour session in one casino and then moving on to another.

But this year it will be poker, played for keeps at the highest level in the world.

Some 150 gamblers will each stake $10,000. One man will scoop an enormous prize. Thirty-five others can get a small return on their investment. The rest will lose. There is no pulling out to save a fraction of your stake.

'To me,' explained Wheeler, 'it is a purely academic business. It's exciting, of course, but there is nothing reckless or compulsive about it. Basically it's all down to mathematics.'

One ventured to ask what the late 3rd Earl of Birkenhead would have felt about his legacy hanging on a running flush?

'Good heavens,' cried Wheeler, gently changing the tense, 'he will be tickled pink.'

THE EAGLE HAS BARELY LANDED

The Winter Olympics in Calgary were a disaster. Unseasonably mild weather, bad siting of the events and a schedule that dragged proceedings out over three weekends to scalp even more money from television rights, conspired to create a shambles. The media were mostly in a foul mood. Consigned to a Press Village of wooden huts, miles from a decent restaurant and served by a laundry that contrived to lose about 4,000 pairs of underpants, they conspired to make their own fun. I wasn't in a foul mood at all and joined wholeheartedly in the unspoken conspiracy to present The Eagle as the hero of the Games.

Dateline: Calgary 1988

EDDIE 'The Eagle' Edwards, the Cheltenham plasterer, completed his Olympic campaign in glory last night. He jumped – and lived – and broke his British record.

A crowd of 60,000 roared their approval as the Eagle soared

71 metres, three metres better than his previous best and ten metres further than any other Briton.

In brilliant sunshine, with the violent gales of the past week abated, Eddie launched himself off the rim of the terrifying 90-metre ski-jump, wobbled only fractionally and landed not quite on his backside to an ovation that will not be out-decibelled at these Winter Olympic Games.

That he thumped down at the 71-metre (237ft) mark, a point which the world's ski-jump stars soar past like long-range bombers on entirely different missions, mattered not one jot.

The triumph was that Eddie was down on two skis without troubling morticians, surgeons, or even the anxiously waiting stretcher bearers.

His position in the competition – 55th and last. But Britain's first and only Olympic ski-jumper was jubilant, delivering his famous arm-waving salute to the gallery.

In the second and final round, Eddie decided to play it conservatively. His style was more confident and his landing more decorous at 67 metres. For the great eccentric, the Olympic Games were over. Now Eddie can get on with living, though clearly his life can never be the same again.

The supreme irony of all the Eagle fever was that almost simultaneously another Briton, Wilfred O'Reilly, was winning a gold medal in the short-track skating event and smashing a world record in the process, while virtually ignored by the Press and TV cameras who preferred to crowd round the foot of the ski-jump.

Fears for Eddie's safety were such that despite his survival in coming an unchallenged last on the less intimidating 70-metre hill last week, concerted efforts were made yesterday to stop him jumping at all off the 90-metre Big Brother switchback.

'Eddie the Eagle has been wonderful world publicity for ski-jumping,' said Torjborn Yggeseth, Norwegian director of the event. 'But all the time we have been worried what that publicity would turn into if he crashed and broke his legs.

'Under Olympic rules we did not have the power to ban him from making the first of his two jumps. But yes, we did go to the British delegation and asked them to withdraw him. Evidently they decided he could manage.'

Eddie's best effort left him a mere 47 metres behind the winner, Finland's Matti Nykaenen whose longest jump was 118 metres.

Britain's low-flying Eagle was suitably modest in defeat. 'Perhaps I shall make a bit of money out of what has happened here,' he said. 'But to me jumping is the only important thing. I hope all the publicity will encourage a lot of British kids to take it up.'

He added that he was happy to have done his best for his new army of fans at home.

Aged 24 now, with years on his side, he confirmed he will definitely be jumping at the next Winter Olympics. 'By then,' he said, 'I think I have every chance of being the best in the world. Who knows?'

Eddie Edwards woke up yesterday to the reality that he is now a household name from Vladivostok to Virginia.

He spent the morning making arrangements to jet down to Los Angeles and grant an interview to Johnny Carson on the world's most famous TV chat show, as well as discussing business affairs with his two agents, one here in Calgary and the other in London.

To date his only firm contract is a $2,000 deal for marketing Eddie the Eagle T-shirts but there should be at least another £250,000 in the pipeline.

What bugged him – as it would perplex any young man of 24 whose status precisely two weeks ago was that of a jobbing Cheltenham plasterer – was what he's going to do with the rest of his life.

Eddie Edwards isn't a fraud. No man with the guts to switch-back off a 90-metre ski-jump, which is nearly the height of St Paul's, is a fraud. Nor is he a loser. No man who comes hopelessly last and yet wins more attention from the world's media than any sports star at the Olympics can conceivably be a loser.

What Eddie Edwards has become is the freak product of intense media hype. The serious Olympics were getting bogged down by the weather. Eddie, with his bottle-end glasses, wit, warm personality and absolutely no hope of winning anything was a godsent alternative.

The reporters, the cameras, the microphones moved in. Hype created more hype. More and more Press conferences were called. Star columnists were flown up from America merely to get a glimpse of him.

Eddie kept his nerve and sound, west-country common sense. He played up to the circus. But what, in the end, did he have to sell? Nothing. He remains without question, the worst ski-jumper ever to appear at the Olympics.

'Eddie doesn't jump, he drops like a stone,' said the Norwegian with an anagram for a name. Having earnestly tried to get Eddie excluded for his own safety, Torjborn Yggeseth maintained: 'In Norway, we have a thousand eleven-year-olds who can jump further and better than Eddie. I think he should stop now before there is a tragedy.'

Eddie is an enigma. His honesty is so patent that as you listen to him trot out anecdote after anecdote about his boyhood escapades with girls and bicycles you just wonder if he could possibly be inventing it straight off the top of his head. His ability to handle the awkward question is devastating.

An American reporter asked him: 'Eddie, if you have made a thousand ski-jumps, why is it that you're still so bad at it?'

'Have you ever tried it?' Eddie snapped back. End of discussion.

It is hard to see how he can settle back into plastering walls in Cheltenham and going to the cinema with his girlfriend, Hannah, whom he professes to love dearly despite the fact that he never once saw her when she was flown to Calgary by a British newspaper.

'I thought that was disgusting,' said Eddie. 'They were trying to exploit our love and I was having nothing to do with it.'

There have been oddballs in sport before. A Japanese runner once 'won' an Olympic marathon by leaping on to the course less than a mile from the end. A golfer named Maurice Flitcroft once conned his way into the British Open and hacked his way to an horrendous score.

Both were treated with unanimous derision as men who had desecrated great events.

Eddie is different. The sheer bravery demanded of any man hurtling headlong down a ski-jump insulates him from criticism. Eddie did what none of us writing about him would do for a million pounds.

It is just possible he is the oddest oddball ever to invade a sport. Was it a calculated quest for the international limelight or did it all happen by accident? I have been with him at length here and I honestly have to confess I do not know the true answer.

'Anything happen today, Eddie?' you ask.

'Yes,' he beams. 'I ran into Princess Anne when I was taking my dirty underpants to the laundry.'

Eddie the Eagle may just become the international celebrity with virtually nothing to celebrate. Before you decry the way the world is going, simply climb to the top of a 90-metre ski-jump and look down. It is the headlong route that has pitched Eddie Edwards into another world.

TOAST TO DENIS COMPTON, A CHILDHOOD HERO

My hero and friend Denis Compton reached 70 during 1988. Colleagues and opponents came from all over the world to honour him at an unforgettable dinner in London.

Dateline: London 1988

S TATISTICS kill any damned story so here is a handful to get them over and done with.

In Benoni, South Africa, he once scored 300 runs in 181 minutes. In the English summer of 1947 he scored 3,816 runs and hit 18 centuries. In the 1950 Cup final he played left-wing for Arsenal when they beat Liverpool 2–0. By his third marriage he has daughters named Charlotte and Victoria, aged ten and three. He was born in Hendon on 23 May 1918, which means that next Monday will be his 70th birthday.

The subject of that thumbnail biography is also averse to statistics, largely because he can't remember his own or anyone else's. Records were for Bradman, not the greatest all-round British sportsman of my lifetime.

Denis stamped the hallmark on his golden talent at an unusually early age. At 14, playing at Lord's for London Elementary Schoolboys, he scored a century memorable less for 100 runs than the sheerly luminous manner of their making. Tousled, athletic, impish, assured and happy, he radiated the persona that years later was to cause his disciples to start queueing at daybreak to watch him bat.

Image, a phoney modern word, is that which the moderate

would wish upon themselves. Style is the genuine article, a God-given grace to accomplish without apparent effort.

Compton had style. He had such style that an entire generation of schoolboys, of whom I was one, tried to walk, run and throw like him. We ladled on the Brylcreem because that's what Denis used and we neatly turned our shirtsleeves two folds back because that's what Denis did. No caning hurt when you'd played truant and cycled miles to watch him bat: it was a privilege, a mere percentage of the admission price.

He was immensely courteous to the kids who worshipped him. I have to this day the autograph he signed for me at Dean Park, Bournemouth, in 1946. Some 50 of us milled around him as he came off for lunch. He promised he would sign for all of us provided we formed an orderly line. We did and he kept his word and thus, without effort, he created not fanship but idolatry.

Denis scored 115 that day. I can remember two shots now, an off-balance sweep that only Vivian Richards could emulate, and a cover drive he fashioned by coming down the wicket to a slow left-arm spinner who had yet to release the ball. His hair, Brylcreem or not, was in a tangle and his shirt was open down to the fourth button and he was the nearest thing we'd ever seen to God.

It must have been hell going in to bat in front of him as Jack Robertson did for years. Robertson, a consummately elegant player capable of making 200 every time he batted, could hardly have been unaware that all but his close relatives wanted him to get out so that God would come in and start orchestrating lightning and thunder. Of course these are the recollections of an impressionable schoolboy but fanciful they are not.

In a contemporary essay called 'Genius Unrationed', Neville Cardus, the master of our game, wrote that in the immediate post-war years 'Compton's cricket symbolised the hopes and renewed life of a nation that had emerged from the dark abyss of war . . . They sat in the sun and the strain from those heavy years fell from all shoulders as Compton flicked the ball here, swooped it there, drove it right and left.'

It wasn't all roses. In the Old Trafford Test of 1948 he was two not out when he nicked a blinding no-ball bouncer from Lindwall into his face. He went off to be stitched, consumed a restorative brandy and returned to score 145 not out.

He also drank a large brandy at half-time in the 1950 Cup final. It was his last football match and he played a storming second half but wishes it to be known that this was not necessarily the stimulant upon which his career was fuelled.

In life he was, and still is, charming and scatter-brained. The legendary stories of him scoring centuries with borrowed bats and arriving for the start of play in last night's dinner jacket and advancing down the ground at the height of a Test match to discover the result of the 2.30 at Ascot are all true, and I am delighted that Peter West is at this moment occupying his retirement from television by assembling them into a long-due biography.

Inevitably there is the temptation to compare him with some of the present-day sportsmen but that could introduce an unwanted jarring note to his 70th birthday celebrations.

Denis Compton doesn't qualify as a paragon. He has about as much commercial acumen as the average Poet Laureate. He was simply a genius of a ball-games player who has lived comfortably with celebrity, laughed at life and endowed us with vivid memories that many will carry to our graves. It would be a serious oversight not to wish him a particularly happy day on Monday.

SEOUL – THE UNFORGETTABLE GAMES

Not even the Ben Johnson drugs scandal, which provoked the suspicion that you could no longer believe what you were seeing in sport, could diminish Seoul's triumph as stage managers of the Olympics.

Dateline: **Seoul 1988**

L AST EVENING, as the darkness came, Korea bade us farewell with the most staggering and emotional closing ceremony in the history of the Olympics.

A nation flattened by recent war, took as its theme global unity and peace. With immense dignity, with dance and song that reached back into a millennium of culture, with the greatest pyrotechnic display ever to transform a night sky into day, they told us how pleased they were to have played host to 160 nations united once again by sport.

It transcended the cynicism of drugs, the curse of commercialism, the strident nationalism some nations brought here. It invited us to hold this fragile Olympic movement together. There was hardly a dry eye in the house.

The most glittering gold medal of all at these Games goes to South Korea. I was one of thousands convinced they couldn't do it in the face of superhuman odds. They did. No Olympics have been more graciously staged. None, in these seething days of political discord, has been more secure.

Three weeks ago, South Korea was on the fringe of the Third World. Its elevation to the First World is confirmed by a simple question: which future Olympic city can follow that?

Their success was due more than anything to the pride and calmness of Seoul's people. In almost a month here I have not seen a scrap of litter in the streets or a smear of graffiti on any wall. Twice, searching for taxis in a hurry, private motorists have pulled up and driven miles out of their way to drop me at my destinations. Last night brought the ultimate test.

The closing ceremony, rehearsed for months, was choreographed as an exercise in perfect symmetry. It was severely disrupted when the athletes broke ranks and overran the stage. There was no bad behaviour – it was their Olympics anyway – but it was rather like a bunch of tourists squatting on Horse Guards during Trooping the Colour.

We watched with fascination as the plain-clothes security guards handled it. With gentle persuasion, never touching anyone, they controlled what could have degenerated into an almighty shambles.

If Ben Johnson deigned to watch it all on television back home in Canada, I hope he was ashamed. He and many other athletes dragged the Olympics to the brink of disaster here. It took the Koreans to remind us that the Games are greater than the cheats.

On that score, these were the finest Olympics I have ever attended. You could not move a yard, of course, without being searched. Security was as tight here as in Crossmaglen. The justification was that as the Olympic flame flickered and died last night not one person had been touched by international terrorism. A miracle.

South Korea, heroically, has done its part. It is now for the Olympic movement to purge itself of the poisons that endanger it. It must launch an all-out war on drugs. And it must realize that the vast sums offered by rival American television networks to become 'host broadcaster' of the Olympics with all the privileges that entails, must be resisted.

Much of the world takes the American TV feed. Much of the world, therefore, has been given to understand that these Games were a hick-town sports meet.

Why? Because the United States seen as head-to-head rivals with the Soviet Union, got their severe comeuppance there. They were run into the ground not only by the Soviet Union but by East Germany, population 19 million.

American television stumbled over any foreign name of more than two syllables, made it perfectly obvious that it had no idea where countries like Senegal and Surinam actually were, concentrated on American athletes running tenth, moved gear from screech to hysteria when America won anything, offered commentary of ignorance and near illiteracy and generally patronised the world.

There have been moments of disillusion here, no more so than when it was proved that a British performer had fallen into the drug trap. It is to be hoped that he will be banned for life, just as a British pole vaulter thankfully was a few weeks before he was due to come here.

The war against drugs must be ruthless and uncompromising. That is one message of these Seoul Olympics. The other is that, given a host nation with the will to move mountains, the Olympics are still alive. Only just, badly dented, an endangered species. But what other international movement in this world of turmoil could have got 160 nations together under one roof for a fortnight of deadly competition?

We leave Seoul on a note of delicate optimism, sincerely thanking our hosts on the way out.

Chapter Six

1989–1990

MIKE TYSON –
THE PRISONER

Interviewing Mike Tyson was no more difficult than talking to any other mixed-up man of 22. Getting access to him was the problem.

Dateline: Las Vegas 1989

WHEN YOU finally get him on his own, away from all the hoodlums and the hoods, Mike Tyson turns out to be the strongest puppy in the world.

He has this engaging habit of emphasizing exciting points about Duran or Ali or Joe Louis by stabbing you in the shoulder with his right forefinger.

Since this is made of teak and has the diameter of a broomhandle it not only endangers your collarbone but truly makes you wonder what it will feel like when he sticks his thumb and the other three into a boxing glove and lets Frank Bruno have it.

He is shy and wary, particularly of the British press whom he has clearly been given to understand are only interested in his sex life, his rocky marriage and such wild antics as breaking training to rush up to Canada to do something about one or the other or preferably both.

When we settled to talk about boxing he immediately relaxed. Boxing is the only world in which he is equal to its historians and superior to all contemporary exponents.

It transpired that he actually wanted someone fresh to talk to. He is bored. Bored most of all by being virtually a prisoner of his own handlers in a hotel suite in a ghastly town in the middle of the Nevada Desert.

They give him new toys to play with, like the 175,000 dollar Lamborghini he now uses to drive the two miles to the gym, but when you observe him struggling with the mysteries of a manual gear shift you wonder why handlers so disciplinarian in one respect can be so irresponsible in another.

'Bored, bored, bored, man, is what I am of this place. Stuck in here all the time drives me crazy and I've got another five weeks of it.'

Actually it's rather more than five weeks and it's not strictly true he never gets out. Now back in training he is leaving the hotel at 4 o'clock each morning to run in streets as yet unpolluted by traffic fumes and the human hassle world heavyweight champions invariably attract.

Later, around 1 p.m., he drives to the gym accompanied by a convoy of vehicles containing security guards, sparring partners and other men of dubious countenance and unspecified employment.

One appears to do nothing more than bring Tyson's ghetto-blaster, a three-feet long instrument of torture which is likely to inflict more damage on Tyson's eardrums than any opponent ever will.

Although his recent sparring sessions have been conducted behind the bolted and grilled doors of Johnny Tocco's windowless training establishment, the wild noise can be heard a block away.

I must explain that such direct quotations I use from Mike Tyson in this story are heavily expurgated. The reason for this is that on average every fifth word he utters would tend to cause offence in print. Frequently he splits a word into syllables and slips the other word in between.

It is utterly innocent because it is the argot of where he came from and also where he is. Boxing's brutality is not confined to the ring.

I asked him if he's afraid of anything: snakes, spiders, heights, cocktail parties full of Ivy League socialites, things like that.

'I ain't afraid of nothing,' he said instantly. 'I ain't afraid of getting hit or hurt but that don't mean I'm not nervous. I'm as nervous as hell before the start of any fight. Nervous that something might go wrong. Nervous I don't do as well as I should. It's adrenalin, ain't it. Pours through you like fire. You can't wait to get started and then all the nerves go and you're in there, hoping you'll do it right.'

He giggled slightly before amending this declaration. 'Yeah, I do get scared. I get scared at night when I get chased by monsters. Happens all the time. I dream a lot and I'm always getting chased by monsters.'

Is he ever scared that with his phenomenal strength and aggression he could kill a man in the ring? The casual question shocked him. He took some time to reply, as though the possibility had never occurred to him before.

'God forgive an accident, man,' he said, and this time he went a whole sentence without swearing.

Then he got annoyed. A legendary fighter called Joe Louis finished up in this very town of Las Vegas as a celebrity 'greeter' at a huge casino-hotel. Mr Louis's greetings were often less than convincing since he was in a wheelchair, frequently with his once-noble head lolling from side to side. And then there was Muhammad Ali, of magnificent physique and wit, now reduced to human wreckage by going many fights too far.

There was no time to ask the question. Tyson pounced. 'That's **** man, that's ******* ****. I hate hearing people speak that ****. You can tell people who speak like that to **** off, man. Boxing is a business that is totally different to any other business. Why it's **** is because people who talk like that don't come up with no solution. They just sit there and say how lousy it is that those boxers finish up bad. They don't realize a lot of us started bad so where's the ******* difference? When you go in there you're going to get hurt. Everybody gets hurt. You talk to me about Ali. Do you know that Ali really needs the money?'

Tyson angry is an awesome sight. The eyes, brown around the pupils, blaze. There was no question that he threatened violence but there was also no question of your correspondent provoking him still further by asking him what happened to the 40 million dollars Ali earned before descending into a living hell?

Tyson was much happier refuting a rumour I reported in last Friday's *Daily Mail*. It was to the effect that such is his passion in a fight that he has no recollection of knocking any opponent out, that he merely comes out of a trance to see them lying at his feet.

'Are you crazy, man? How could I fight like that? That story is rubbish. I know everything that goes on in a fight. I can tell you afterwards when everything happened and how it happened and I can tell you almost every punch. I know this game man, I really know this game.'

He knows its history, its legends, its unsung heroes, its cowards because he studies nothing else. The long hours of his lonely vigil in the Las Vegas Hilton are filled watching filmed fights of all of them back to the days of Carpentier.

'I don't read books. I don't watch much television. I sit there and I study boxers.'

So who were the greatest? Which ones would have given him the hardest fight? Was there one among them who would have beaten him?

Tyson was now intense, concentrating on getting the words right because this was the only question of vital importance.

His integrity was at stake because his opinion was genuinely sought.

'That's a great question, man. I'm telling you there ain't no answer. How the hell can there be one? How can you ever tell about Marciano versus Ali when you don't know how either man was feeling on the night or whether he made a mistake he wouldn't make in a million years. I'm in this game and I know about it and I'm telling you again there ain't no answer. No one will ever know.

'But if you ask me a different question, nothing involving heavyweights and who'd give me the hardest fight, I'll tell you and nobody can argue because Duran, as a lightweight, was the greatest fighter ever seen. I've watched him for hours and hours on film and I'm telling you he was so tremendous that nobody could live with him.'

Returning from the sublime to Frank Bruno, Mr Tyson declined to say anything derogatory or provocative about his next opponent, thus casting grave suspicion over the publicity handouts which quote him as saying he will crush Bruno like a British egg.

But are they friends?

'Stupid question, man. We're just about to fight. What do you expect me to say, that we're going to finish up hugging one another? I hardly know him. I ain't saying nothing one way or the other about Bruno. We'll just fight, that's all. It's stupid to think that boxers love one another just because they've fought. It's you writers who make up things like that. Some fighters hate other fighters for the rest of their lives after they've lost. I ain't going to get drawn into it.'

Of course he will get drawn into it. For two weeks before the fight, after Bruno has joined Tyson in Las Vegas, they will give frequent press conferences and, at the behest of publicity agents, mouth all the familiar banal rhetoric that gives boxing such a bad name.

Statements like 'I'm feeling great' will be accorded the most profound significance. Tyson is worth much more than that. He is a fascinating member of the human race, terribly unhappy here as a young man of 22 is entitled to be when he has already grossed in excess of 50 million dollars, knows where none of it is, is being sued by his estranged wife for 125,000 million dollars and comprehensively ripped off by businessmen who reassure him they're his friends.

I asked him what career he would have liked had he not been a boxer. 'Nothing, man,' he said. 'I'm just a fighter. It's the only job I have.'

I asked him what he most wanted in the world. 'Some peace man,' he replied, 'just some ******* peace.' The man who is scared of nothing looked furtively around to see if the hoods had overheard him.

Later, outside the gym, our photographer, Monty Fresco, asked him if he'd indulge in an utterly spurious picture allegedly involving an arm-wrestling match between the world heavyweight boxing champion and a *Daily Mail* sportswriter of indeterminate age. His handlers pointedly looked at their watches, but Mike insisted.

'Jeez, I can't stand the pain,' drawled the man who could have snapped my arm like a matchstick. 'You British guys, are you all like that?' This remark may not significantly shift the betting on the Tyson–Bruno fight. But it was an interesting insight into the mind of a lonely genius who has the world's admiration but is craving for simple love.

FRANK BRUNO – THE AMBASSADOR

Returning to Las Vegas for the Tyson–Bruno fight I could only marvel at Frank's composure in an atmosphere of unrelieved hysteria. He was to lose, of course, but surviving five rounds conferred him with heroic status.

Dateline: **Las Vegas 1989**

REPORTERS don't write for posterity. They write to daily deadlines, well knowing tomorrow's story will insulate the next day's take-away.

Yet somehow I hope that years hence someone may produce a fading dog-eared cutting of this column and show it to Frank Bruno's children.

Not, I swiftly add, to suggest it has the remotest literary merit but to let them know how their father comported himself when the time came to secure his, their mother's and their futures.

So, young ladies, here goes:

Your father did not have the most privileged of upbringings, as I am sure he won't have told you.

As far as you are concerned there have always been large cars to transport you to good schools and bring you home again to toys, books, your own bedrooms and the family swimming pool.

But these things have to be earned. They don't fall into your lap. And your father earned them just about the hardest way I know.

He went into professional boxing, acquitted himself with much distinction and then, to the astonishment of many and the horror of some, was negotiated into the position where he could fight an American named Mike Tyson for the world heavyweight championship.

Your father, probably with you and your futures in mind, accepted the challenge.

So I must tell you a little about this Tyson. Only 22, bull-necked, ghetto-hardened, street-educated, as at home in the fight ring as though he had been born in one, with a punch in either hand that could literally kill a man, he stalked the world looking for his next opponent.

Very few would fight him. And those who did, even those if you will forgive me saying so with credentials greater than your father's, regretted doing so.

This Tyson was incapable of losing fights. He won them with such frightening violence that their duration was no longer registered in rounds but seconds. Your father, Frank Bruno, volunteered to become the next contender. Either that or someone talked him into it. Whichever, your dad went off to train and get himself supremely fit in the wilds of Arizona. He should have stayed there until just hours before the fight but regrettably, under some contractual agreement, he was required to present himself in Las Vegas, a 20th century Gomorrah.

The idea was that your father's presence at a number of Press conferences would boost the sale of tickets which, for all the furore in Britain, were not selling all that well.

In fact, they were going so badly that if you had the nerve to sit it out at a roulette table, someone would have given you a free one, so keen were officials to show a global TV audience that the place was packed.

So, initially, your dad was dragged into a meeting with the Press to apologize for his utterly justified remarks about being kept hanging around like a hick punter when he arrived at the huge hotel where the fight was to take place.

Although your father conducted himself with dignity, I have

rarely witnessed anything more embarrassing. Until, that is, they stage-managed for a massive attendance of TV, radio and Press, a conference with both fighters.

The Tyson entourage, 14 in number, arranged themselves on the left-hand side of the podium. Some wore caps. Most wore tracksuits, chewed gum and looked extremely menacing. Heading the British delegation was a man from Savile Row. Superbly dressed in understated bespoke tailoring, with a subdued and beautifully knotted tie, he looked like an ambassador, which indeed he was.

This man was your father.

For an hour he was forced to listen to a banal harangue, embracing world politics, apartheid, Greek philosophy, Shakespeare, quotations from Winston Churchill and quite slanderous allegations about his business rivals in the world of boxing, by a man named Don King.

Had I been your father I would have walked out, I would particularly have walked out when this odious self-appointed windbag warned Mrs Thatcher gratuitously – though it was hard to understand quite where she came into it – that early next week 'Frank Bruno will be returned to Britain in an incapacitated state'. To compound this appalling remark he added: 'Funny things happen in boxing rings and we don't want to be responsible for them.' Even Mike Tyson, sitting four yards from your father, was stunned by the sinister implication of that statement. He shook his head slowly, dissociating himself from it.

In many years of writing about sport, I have never heard anything quite so evil. Well, your father took it, staring straight ahead. The sickening thing about boxing is that the men who do the fighting are discussed as though they are so many pounds of horseflesh.

When, finally, his turn came to answer questions, none remotely intelligent, your father handled them with admirable brevity. Being a fighting man he is no master of the English language, but even so his replies were gems of dignity.

Obviously he said he was here to win the world heavyweight title, to which Tyson obviously replied: 'I'm the best fighter in the world and he's going to be in a lot of trouble on Saturday.' Press conferences before big fights are arranged to provoke exchanges like that. They are designed to make headlines and capture the opening minutes of the television news, thus generating the interest which sells seats in the arena or closed-circuit TV venues across the world.

Your father went along with all that. His voice was firm, his composure under provocation quite superb. I wrote earlier that he looked like an ambassador. Well he is. He is probably the best sporting ambassador Britain has sent into foreign fields for many years.

The only problem is that beautifully mannered, elegantly dressed, self-controlled ambassadors are hardly expected to prevail in the murderous fire of a world heavyweight boxing ring. Especially when a man called Mike Tyson is advancing from the opposite corner.

I snatch this opportunity to write positively and affectionately about your father before the contest because, deep down, I believe his only motive for being here concerns his love for you.

Frank Bruno is a brave man and, as Mr Dave Allen used to say, may his God go with him.

AN UPSIDE-DOWN DAY

In the lazy days before Lord's and Wimbledon there was time to test out the ultimate hangover cure with the Toyota air acrobatic team.

Dateline: **Henley 1989**

HENLEY was a picture yesterday two weeks before the Royal Regatta.

Chimney pots clean on the inside. TV aerials burnished brightly. Hardly a loose slate anywhere. For this bizarre information you are indebted to Nigel Lamb, who insisted on showing me the place his way.

This involved two sorties along the Grand Challenge Cup course at a height of 500ft flying upside down in the open cockpit of a biplane at 145 mph. Not to be recommended after a farmhouse breakfast but an enriching experience when you finally force your eyes open.

The nervy bit for the newcomer is fixing the safety belts: two straps over the shoulders, two under the crotch, one round the waist, which all clunk-click into a central hasp.

Nigel tightens all these for you, comfortingly explaining that you should now feel like a trussed chicken. Then he suggests you might like to fasten another single red belt round your middle. 'What's that for?' you ask suspiciously. 'That's in case something goes wrong with the others,' he says, bumping down the grass runway of Booker airfield and banking away towards Henley.

He's already confiscated your loose change and cigarette lighter. 'Don't want these falling out and jamming up the works, do we?' he says reasonably. Nigel seems to spend half his life flying upside down. He and his wingman, Richard Manning, once flew the 22 miles from Calais to Dover completely upside down in close formation. Actually it is terrific fun when you get used to it. So were the rolls and the loops. What wasn't such fun was when Nigel stood the plane on its tail and threw us into a stall turn. It's then that you understand the brilliance of these stick-and-rudder aerobatic pilots.

He warns you that it's coming. 'Tense your leg and stomach muscles,' he advises. 'It'll stop the blood rushing to your head.' All the same the universe suddenly goes mad. Utterly disorientated, conscious only of an engine that sounds like a thousand sheets of ripping calico, a split second of total blackness and you've come through 7g, which momentarily transforms your body weight from 13 stone to 91 stone.

The tyro simply cannot comprehend how these men do it. Nigel and Richard Manning do it all the time in tight formation. In the loops they are just six feet wing-tip to wing-tip apart.

They will be doing it at 85 airshows and sporting events throughout Britain this summer in the scarlet and white livery of the new Toyota aerobatic team. You wouldn't dream of going up with them, of course, unless you knew their pedigree. In fact, you are as safe as houses. Nigel Lamb, 32, has flying in the blood.

He is the son of a World War Two Spitfire pilot and trained with the Rhodesian Air Force. Richard Manning, 41, is an ex-RAF fighter pilot and instructor to the Red Arrows display team. They can fly anything. For Toyota they fly immensely high-powered Pitts Specials with a 200 horse-power Lycoming engine.

The planes are so small you could park them in a domestic garage, so light they are only half the weight of a saloon car, so manoeuvrable they can roll through 360 degrees in one second. They fling them about all over the sky, utterly under control despite g-forces even greater than those felt by the Red Arrows pulling out of big dives.

'How can you think straight in circumstances when I think my skull is going to burst?' you ask. Nigel methodically explains the physiological workings of the inner ear, the speed at which messages can pass from eye to brain. I understand none of it, comprehending only that it's rather like ball-sense in other sports: either you have it or you haven't. 'Well, you don't pull five or six-g the first time you go up,' reasons Nigel. 'You step it up gradually. If you flew with us every other day for a month, you'd be used to it.' I rather doubted that.

They work immensely hard. Some days in this frenetic summer season they will zigzag across Britain to fly up to five displays in different locations in a single span of daylight. They are professionals, of course, but they are not businessmen. They are sportsmen of the highest calibre.

Both could have become staid civil airline pilots. But their affinity is with the great seat-of-the-pants barnstorming aviators of war and peace, from Baron Manfred von Richthofen above the trenches of the Somme to the mad Russian, Kharlov, who flew under three successive bridges of the Moscow River for a lark.

They will entertain millions of spectators this year not only to keep their overdrafts in check but for the sheer joy of flying. 'Luck,' says Nigel Lamb, 'is finding someone to pay you for what you love doing best.'

Both were trained as military pilots and Nigel says: 'For me the greatest pilots of all were the pioneers, the fantastic air aces of World War One who discovered all these things we do today with better planes.'

Back on land after 7g we had lunch on Booker Airfield where the restaurant is named the Red Baron, the *nom-de-guerre* of Baron von Richthofen. It rather made the point.

DESERT ORCHID – STRAIGHT FROM THE HORSE'S MOUTH

RED RUM was the people's playboy, Arkle the austere aristocrat. Now an entire nation has a love affair with Desert Orchid, the grey with the elegant stride and human brain. Last year he consented to be interviewed for these pages and won the Gold Cup. This year, for an entirely different reason, he again tells his story exclusively to *Sportsmail*.

Dateline: **Cheltenham 1990**

A H YES, *Daily Mail* isn't it? Woolgar or Wooldirge or something? Came down to interview me last year. Took rather a lot of liberties as I recall. Lots of smarmy remarks about my celebrity but you couldn't resist that crack about my sex life, could you? If I had my way they'd put the shears to a lot of you sportswriters, too.

I'm in two minds about getting you thrown out of the yard. But I'll tell you why I won't. It's out of respect for the readers of the *Daily Mail*. When your paper ran that poll about whether or not I should run in the Grand National NINE THOUSAND of them wrote in saying it was unthinkable. Phew, that was a relief I can tell you. Sweated up a bit that morning waiting for the *Mail* to arrive. It's the last tabloid we take, you know. Suits my politics and, anyway, I find the others disgusting.

It wasn't actually running in the Grand National I objected to, although I must say that Aintree isn't exactly my kind of place. That Red Rum forever parading up and down like some geriatric pop star and – God, I can still smell the after-shave – I was introduced to that Derek Hatton one year. Not too sure about him. Reminds me somewhat of you.

Actually, if you pace yourself and keep clear of about a dozen absolutely brainless nags, the National is no big deal. The big ordeal, pardon my little pun which you may use if you wish, is flogging up to Liverpool. All those road works on the M6. Forever jerking to a stop and then lurching off again.

It's all right for you. I suppose you ponce your way up there on the Orient Express, swilling champagne on expenses. Well, we have to *stand* all the way. Bet you didn't even think about that. Next time send that nice Lynda Lee-Potter. Look, don't bother me with your idiot questions. I've had quite a week of it, I can tell you. Quite a year of it, come to that.

Posed five times for my portrait – once with the Queen Mum which appeared on 25 million Christmas cards in aid of injured jockeys – and been subjected to three different television documentaries. I can't begin to tell you how dreadful those television crews are. They come down here in jeans and T-shirts, always bragging about that scandalous 'Death on the Rock' programme and shouting for bacon sandwiches.

Honestly, there are days when I'd like nothing better than just to stand outside Horse Guards in Whitehall and be photographed by tourists. No stress, no strain. Jingle off back to Knightsbridge Barracks and get the old head down. Can't do it, you see. Price of fame. Have to put up with the likes of you barging in here as if you own the place.

As I say, your feet wouldn't have touched the ground if it hadn't been for what your readers did for me. NINE THOUSAND against 200. Boy, that was some brilliant stunt. Well, I might be an arrogant horse and I'm definitely becoming an intolerant one. But I am not ungrateful so let me advise my *Daily Mail* friends to back me to retain the Gold Cup. I mean, going back yonks, that Golden Miller won it five years in a row. Golden Miller? Absolute poofter, I'm told.

My price – 5–4 on last time I heard – is of course lasting testimony to the philanthropy of the bookmaking fraternity. To be frank I rate bookmakers hardly higher than journalists or public relations consultants.

You're all parasites feeding off stars like myself and those England and Scotland rugger players who will be mincing one another to pulp at Murrayfield on Saturday and not getting a brass farthing for it.

Last year you cast doubts on my chances by saying I was inexperienced on left-hand tracks and may not handle a soggy track. Dear Lord, I nearly hit the roof when I read that. Well, it didn't become a right-handed track overnight, did it, and what about the weather? It simply hissed down all day. So don't start injecting any of your own fatuous opinions this year.

Do you know why I won? Because the horse that headed me over the last fence was called Yahoo. I'd thoroughly snubbed him in the paddock, I can tell you, but there he was under the sublime misapprehension that he had a chance. I mean, no one ever loses to a horse called Yahoo, does one?

This year, of course, my opponents include Cavvies Clown, my stablemate here at Whitsbury. We're not close. He has the occasional touch of halitosis and takes the *Independent*. Occasionally, when I'm doing a television interview or chatting with Lord Oaksey or Peter O'Sullevan, he gives me this sort of pathetic look. I'm sure if you go up there now he'll talk to you for hours. A bit like some football clubs I could mention. Doing all right, but hardly a friend in the world.

I see that Bonanza Boy is also mentioned as a conceivable rival. I simply choke on my lunch. I mean, I have nothing against Bonanza Boy personally. Probably has quite a future with the Field Artillery. Extrovert, friendly, amusing. Reminds me a bit of Ron Atkinson. He'd run with four pounds overweight of gold bracelet on his hocks if they'd let him but essentially, if I may say so, secondary modern.

You see, one has to be aware of one's status if you are to get anywhere in this life. I openly admit I have never been overburdened by modesty but then I'm Desert Orchid, a rare hybrid too precious to flail around in that squalid rough and tumble up at Aintree.

Cheltenham has class. Which reminds me, Gloria Hunniford will be arriving any minute. Heavens, she can talk, that one. Sometimes I can hardly get a word in edgeways in my own interviews but she's a kindly soul and I never object to speaking to her.

Now scarper. And remember, this year no cracks, no double entendres, no flowery notions of your own. And don't bother to look me up in the winner's enclosure. The conversation between the Queen Mother and myself will, as always, be entirely off the record.

HEARTBREAK PENALTY SHOOT-OUT IN THE WORLD CUP

As it turned out, this was merely the first exit by England from a World Cup in a penalty shoot-out. Two more were to follow in 1998 and 2006, and they also lost on penalties in the final of the European Championship in 1996.

Dateline: Italy 1990

T HEY TURNED away, inconsolable. But England's controversial World Cup journey was over, beaten in the dreaded penalty shoot-out.

First, Stuart Pearce smashed his shot straight at the splayed legs of Germany's goalkeeper Bodo Illgner. Then Chris Waddle struck his high and wide of the goal.

The irony was that last night in Turin, in quest of a Roman spectacular World Cup final against Argentina and a global audience of billions on Sunday night, England played the finest football of their month-long, often-criticized campaign.

The Germans, as we have noticed before this century, tend to bring out the best in Englishmen in a tight corner.

And so it proved yet again as England dominated the first half of the semi-final, fought back to level the score 1–1 in the second, shared with Germany a pile-driving shot against a goalpost in extra time and then formed up to decide the issue from the penalty spot.

Germany's first four marksmen hammered unstoppable shots past Peter Shilton – at 40, and with 124 internationals behind him, the oldest and most experienced goalkeeper in the Cup. England couldn't match it.

After the game, even as hooligans back home in England were taking to the streets, manager Bobby Robson said: 'We did our best, we gave our all.' And so they did, before two passionate sets of fans roaring with rampant nationalism.

It was a cruel way to go, but Robson's consolation, in his last significant match after a harassing reign as England's manager, was that his team rose out of frank mediocrity to match Germany, the clear favourites, thrust by thrust in 120 minutes of wonderful football.

The penalty shoot-out – and I would have written such had England won in those tense closing moments – remains an absurd way to settle a campaign which has been four years in the making. For one young man in his first World Cup, Paul Gascoigne – who broke down in tears at the end of extra time – the result made no personal difference. A yellow card, his second of the tournament, would have seen him denied an appearance in Rome anyway. He ran his legs off for his country and gave every sign that, with the onset of maturity, he can become one of the game's truly great figures. Robson raced on to the pitch to console him.

PETER USTINOV'S TIGRESSES OF THE CENTRE COURT

IW loved style and wit wherever he found it and Ustinov was his perfect interviewee.

Dateline: **Wimbledon 1990**

A s ONE would anticipate of so urbane an observer, Sir Peter Ustinov wouldn't dream of saying anything directly derogatory about the manners and morals of modern tennis. The darts landed feather-end first.

Thus of Miss Monica Seles:

'A wonderful new talent. I'm fascinated by that grunting every time she hits the ball. She seems to be shouting "Har-ee". I hope she doesn't marry a man of that name – her wedding night could be quite awful for the neighbours.'

Or thus of John McEnroe:

'A great entertainer of the modern idiom. Even if no one had told me I would have known he's the son of a lawyer. He's not just a complainer, he's positively litigious. I have this vision of him as an old man, rushing up and down the sidelines in a wheelchair like Raymond Burr, shouting, "I object."'

The simplest question provokes this wealth of imagery from Britain's newest theatrical knight, who has loved tennis for 60 of his 69 years.

He began playing it before he went to Westminster School and recalls that he reached the zenith of his career shortly thereafter.

'My parents, being foreign and somewhat artistic, did own tennis rackets but I don't think they discovered what they were

192

actually for. However, they encouraged me to learn at a place called the Anglo-Russian Sports Club, which was somewhere down near Barons Court. It was full of old Czarist emigrés and when I was 15 I won the gentlemen's singles, defeating an elderly Russian colonel.

'My prize was a stack of four ashtrays. It remains the only thing I have ever won at tennis in my life.'

Since then, one is given to understand, it has been an unremitting series of humiliating defeats, wrenched hamstrings and disastrous embarrassments at pro-celebrity tournaments, all culminating in a crashing fall on a Caribbean hard court last year which removed the skin from both knees and convinced him to hang up his racket.

'I do have another souvenir of which I'm rather proud,' he remembered. 'It's a photograph of me standing at the net while my doubles partner, John Newcombe, is serving. What it doesn't record is that exactly one second later the ball struck me with extreme force on the back of the head, so I speak with some authority on the speed of the modern serve.'

It is the bewildering pace of the 1990s game and the sheer noise and mayhem of the big arenas that strike him as the major changes in tennis in the Ustinov years. But again there is only implied nostalgia for the days of delicate artistry, exemplary manners and crowds that merely swivelled their heads in enthralled silence.

'Tennis is only reflecting life in general,' he reasoned. 'I was watching at Queen's Club last weekend and I found myself asking, "What's happening, what's gone wrong?" And then it struck me. Queen's, of course, can afford to be much more exclusive than Wimbledon and I suddenly realized that the tennis was being played in relative silence. You could even hear one of those car burglar alarms going off down the road. You would never notice a thing like that at Wimbledon.'

Impressed though he is by today's power play his choice of

his all-time favourites was another oblique reproach: Donald Budge, the American who won Wimbledon in 1937 and 1938, the Czech-born Jaroslav Drobny, who was champion in 1954, and, among the women, Althea Gibson, Kay Stammers and Evonne Goolagong.

Miss Gibson, the black American, won Wimbledon in 1957 and 1958. Miss Stammers never won Wimbledon at all, being flattened 6–2, 6–0 by a block of Alice Marble in her only final in 1939.

'I know, I know,' acknowledged Ustinov, 'but there was something so ethereal about her being so exquisitely frail and utterly, defencelessly English. Althea Gibson was quite different, but my admiration for her was the quite astonishing breakthrough she achieved for her race in the sport.

'Oh, there was another woman, too. A Polish girl just before the war – you'll have to check the spelling I'm afraid [understandably since her name turned out to Jadwiga Jedrzejowska] – who was quite bewitching. Slim as a wand, but hit the forehand with incredible force. As a matter of fact, she rather reminded me of myself.'

Had it been any other rather greying, rather expanding old gentleman of 69 rummaging through the lovely pin-ups of an incurably romantic youth, today's young tigresses of the Centre Court might justifiably be irritated that names like Navratilova, Evert and Graf never appeared to cross his mind. Indeed they might even question whether he still had a mind to cross.

But palpably Sir Peter Ustinov, a man of laser-beam wit, effortlessly beautiful English, apparent total recall, overwhelming charm and the astonishing stamina to bring them altogether in the three-hour, one-man show with which he has recently been rivetting London audiences to their seats, can hardly be accused of rampaging senility.

Indeed at his chateau outside Geneva last week he appeared simultaneously to be talking tennis, correcting the proofs of his latest book, writing a newspaper article, buffing up his variety of Australian accents – he takes his show down to Sydney next month – and impatiently waiting for first the afternoon, then the evening World Cup soccer matches to come up on television. He has watched practically all of them. His heroes are the referees for their highly dramatic sentencing by yellow card.

Audibly in parentheses he sighed: 'Italy has had so much to put up with that it would be almost offensive not to let them win.'

But he can and does talk seriously about the game he loves most. 'Tennis has been a joy to me throughout my life,' he said, and what clearly disappoints him is that some now engaged in it at the highest professional level appear to find no joy in it at all.

'The stress on those very young players is intense,' he said. 'I think they'll probably learn to cope with it but I compare them, almost, to some little girl of ten in the Third World who suddenly loses her parents in some tragedy and has to bring up the rest of the family.

'It's an unnaturally oldening process and when they're burned out they still have most of their lives to live. Look at Bjorn Borg. What happened to him was terrible. He won Wimbledon five years in succession, became disenchanted but didn't know what to do afterwards. Mostly they have ancilliary business interests, of course, but they don't understand them. They don't know what they're doing.'

He doesn't dispute, however, that the stars of today know what they're doing out there on court as never before. They have won his admiration if not quite all his affection.

'I was standing with Donald Budge and Fred Perry one day watching the young Rod Laver,' he recalled, 'and Donald said, "Fred, I don't think we could have stood up to him." Games progress like that but you can't see where they'll end. The speed of tennis now is blinding.'

But it was a final recollection of the gracious Budge that confirmed, I suspect where his heart lay.

'Six years ago I was in New York. I was alone it was my birthday and I was simply waiting to appear in the theatre when I received a call. "Peter," it said, "we want you down at the tennis club." I was due on stage in four hours, but I went. When I got there Donald Budge had fixed up for me to partner him in a doubles match against Gardnar Mulloy and Tony Trabert. Imagine that, three great champions and a rather plump actor who, at best, should have been there as a war correspondent. It was the most wonderful birthday present.'

The unspoken question, of course, was whether today's champions, with the passing years, will turn out to be comparable gentlemen?

Or will the savagery of modern combat have left its mark?

THE RETURN OF DEADPAN PIGGOTT

Lester Piggott retired from riding in 1985 and subsequently served a year of a three-year sentence for tax irregularities. In 1990, at the age of 55, he decided to resume racing and rode the last of his 4,493 career winners in 1994.

Dateline: Leicester 1990

THE LEGEND is now encased in the husk of a human body but, for all that, Lester Piggott came back as though he had never been away.

It wasn't the winners he never got. It wasn't even the inimitable style. It was simply the aura this man radiates merely by purring up to a race-track in a pale Mercedes, discarding three inches of Havana cigar and sliding back into the silks of the only world he has ever truly understood.

It was worth walking to Leicester's friendly, utterly unfashionable racecourse yesterday to witness that. And to see him crack the bleak smile of a man exorcising the demons of the past five years, one of them very solitary indeed.

What tickled him was that as he emerged to meet the clamouring Press, a rare concession by a sports star never in danger of winning the Great Communicator Award, it began to bucket down with rain.

Beneath the only available umbrella, well knowing that many of his inquisitors never knew Leicester even had a racecourse until despatched there at breakfast, he proceeded to give an interview of sufficient duration to know they would be comprehensively soaked. Lester likes reporters and excise men in equal measures.

The voice, ever seemingly parched, now matches the face: ghostly grey and deeply corrugated rather than merely etched by the years of wasting that delivered him to yesterday's startline, aged three weeks short of 55, at an incredible 8st 5lb.

Someone asked him how he could conceivably achieve it. 'I missed Sunday lunch,' he said.

Someone else asked him about his riding technique since his 4,349th and last winner at Nottingham almost exactly five years ago. 'Same as before,' he said. 'One leg either side.'

He delivers these one-liners without a flicker of a smile. You have to fathom Lester Piggott and it's about as easy as fathoming the Piltdown Man. Unless you've signed him exclusively – and even then you can't be sure – you'd never know the reason for his comeback yesterday.

Unlike Muhammad Ali, he doesn't need the money. Unlike Frank Sinatra, he can live without the adulation. It was, perhaps, the sheer pleasure of performing in an art at which he once was peerless.

It's a colossal risk, of course, for comebacks in sport so often tend to become memorial services for the living. This was not so in Lester's case.

His first ride yesterday had a crowd approaching 2,500 – normally there would be a quorum of spectators at Leicester on a Monday – roaring him home. Among them were his two daughters, Maureen and Tracey.

For Maureen, now wife of trainer Willie Haggas, it was a race of divided loyalty as her husband had saddled Punch The Air. Her father was riding the 5–1 novice Lupescu. Priorities were soon resolved. 'Come on, Dad. Come on, Dad,' yelled Maureen.

Dad did come on but not quite fast enough. He lost by a short head to the odds-on favourite Sumonda, piloted by Gary Carter, an experienced jockey who is only 30 years his junior.

Maureen relaxed in the box of Barbara Bassett, a charming lady whose husband, Michael, died after 32 years of marriage earlier this year. Mrs Bassett chose this day to reunite her family at a quiet race meeting at which her late husband's horse was having its first run. She found herself engulfed in the Piggott comeback and perhaps took comfort from its huge distraction.

Lester's wife, Susan, wasn't present. She will be at Chepstow today when he takes up the reins of one of her horses, still pursuing his 4,350th winner and the first of his second coming.

His second and third mounts yesterday yielded a seventh, then a 14th place, and brought no spiky criticism from the man who was 11 times champion jockey.

In the old days he would have worn the doleful, undertaker's glare of deprivation.

Yesterday Lester Piggott, genius horseman and enigma, simply looked a happy man. At long last he knew exactly what he was doing once again.

SEB COE STILL ON THE WINNING TRAIL

IW admired both the athletic talent and the character of Sebastian Coe from the earliest moments of a great career.

Dateline: London 1990

THERE IS no telling what the prospective Tory candidate for Falmouth will do here on the athletics track in the next few days, but whatever it is Sebastian Coe cannot lose.

He is every mother's son, every girl's dreamboat, every schoolboy's idol, every spinster's sigh, every reactionary's recollection of how young men used to be.

An American sports columnist, here to report the emotions of Coe's valedictory appearance after 13 years astride the international arena, has described him as a latter-day Lord Byron. This may be mildly unfortunate, in view of Byron's club foot, but you will get the drift.

This week, while his rivals for that Falmouth parliamentary seat are washing up in winter, Coe will be rarely off your screens, enjoying in brilliant sunshine the biggest free-hit campaigning in the history of politics.

Coe has invariably displayed a shrewdness beyond his years. Back in 1981 he announced he would be retiring in 1984. Then, in September last year, he invited us all to a Press conference in London to hear an unspecified announcement. TV crews, radio men and reporters who hadn't stirred out of bars for years cluttered the Connaught Rooms to hear Sebastian Coe, dropped from Britain's team for the last Olympics, confirm he was about to jog off into the sunset after an illustrious career.

It wasn't quite like that. Sebastian proclaimed instead that he would be competing in the Commonwealth Games in New Zealand for a last shot at a title he'd never won. He allowed it to be dragged out of him thereafter that, yes, he was contemplating a career in politics and no, his views were not aligned with the right wing of the Conservative party.

Anyway here he is, preparing for the final of the 800 metres, at which he still holds the world record, and one heat and the final of the 1500 metres at which he was never beaten in the world from the autumn of 1976 until the summer of 1983.

Some athlete. Some man. At 33 he still has the profile, if not the legs, of Byron. He is superbly fit and utterly relaxed. He is far more perceptive than many now clamouring to interview him because he knows he has nothing more to prove. If he loses – and there are runners here who can beat him at both distances – he will do so with the utmost grace. That, even in the turmoil of the zenith of his career, has always been his forte.

Unlike Steve Ovett, with his abrupt dismissals and occasional tearful emotionalism, unlike Daley Thompson, with his occasional yobbish obscenities, Coe has always kept his cool. He is the man who realized there is life out there after sport. Not merely life as the part-time expert in a TV commentary box or as an occasional celebrity panellist on 'Question of Sport' but as someone who recognizes that, essentially, sport is for the birds.

Sir Roger Bannister, the first man to run a sub-four minute mile, became one of the world's most prominent neuro-surgeons. Chris Chataway progressed from television journalist via Cabinet minister to merchant banker. Coe may have failed his 11-plus but he is of that mould and don't for a moment think he doesn't know precisely what he's doing here. He's going into politics.

The world he is leaving has become tawdry as well as tough and not to have been diminished by it is remarkable. I would be deeply disappointed to learn that Coe is not a millionaire, but he has never been seen scrabbling for money in the marketplace or selling snippets of information to the popular Press. Always he has employed high-powered agents to handle his business affairs.

His big advantage when he heads next Monday into public life is not only his fame as a legendary athlete but his utter classlessness. Born in west London, reared in Sheffield, is neither of North nor South. A state schoolboy who won his way to Loughborough, he was neither deprived nor privileged. One of four children of a repertory actress and an engineer, he had the good fortune of inheriting from both the ethics now known as work. He was once made to sit down on Christmas Day and do two hours' concentrated homework.

His emergence on the international athletics stage was, appropriately enough, at San Sebastian, Spain, in 1977 when he won the European indoor 800 metres in fractionally outside the world record time. If some dismissed it as a fluke, Coe's father, Peter, knew better. Father and son had been working for it for years in the hills of Derbyshire.

Peter Coe, now 70, is a slender, bespectacled, lugubrious man who ruled his family like some Victorian patriarch and, recognizing his son's potential, became his coach. Wrongly I saw him as one of those fathers who, second time round, live their lives through their children's achievements.

In the span of 41 days just before the Moscow Olympics Sebastian smashed three world records. He was the hottest Olympic property in Moscow since Jesse Owens and was to run, as here, in both the 800 and 1500 metres against not only the world but his close British rival, Steve Ovett.

Coe ran a simply terrible race in the 800 metres. He got boxed in and then, in desperation, tried the outside with a colossal surge. But he'd left it too late. Ovett, who had elbowed all opposition aside like a street fighter, deservedly won by three yards. Coe got the silver. It might as well have been brass. He was inconsolable.

On the steps of the Moscow stadium later that night I was present when Peter Coe berated his son for sheer idiocy and decided that no human being, blood-related or not, was allowed to address another human being like that. I wrote about it for the *Daily Mail* and, because of it, found myself embroiled in a terrible row with Coe's father. Two days later we'd both come to our senses.

More significantly Coe had to live with himself during the six days between then and his 1500 metres final. Pursued every yard of the way, every hour of each day, by reporters and photographers, he scarcely knew what sanity was. When sportsmen speak of pressure, that was pressure.

He won the 1500 metres, of course, with one of the great runs in history. He crossed the line looking maniacal and, glancing back only recently, I see that my front-page lead story, written fast after that night's events in Moscow, was only slightly less so. He has broken records and hearts but he can never savour that moment again.

He has had a fashionable catwalk of girlfriends and remains unmarried. He has a newspaper column which is not about sport. He has that gamin look which attracts the young and a persona which convinces the elderly that he really cares.

Sebastian Coe is on the move again and nothing that happens here will make much difference. The only thing is that, in crude sporting parlance, he has stuffed all his immediate political opponents sincerely out of sight.

POCKETS OF RESISTANCE IN THE DESERT

Since it lacks his favourite ingredients of athleticism and physical bravery, IW rarely chose to write about snooker, but the seemingly incongruous conjunction of billiard hall and desert tempted him on this occasion.

Dateline: **Dubai 1990**

MORNING prayers rang out from the minarets yesterday as we drove out from the oasis on the threshold of Armageddon.

Dug in to our left was an international task force capable of blowing the Middle East back into the Middle Ages. To our right, in the steaming Gulf, floated the most lethal concentration of naval and air fire-power since D-Day.

Up ahead, according to military intelligence, Saddam Hussein was nursing enough toxic retaliation to guarantee the ugliest of conflicts.

But none of the foregoing, you'll be relieved to learn, disturbed the green, rectangular worlds of Steve Davis and Stephen Hendry as we sped out through the desert sand. Indeed, if it weren't for the rising heat we might have been heading for a 15-frame exhibition match at the Conservative Club in Milton Keynes.

Steve Davis, six times world champion and far more amusing than you'd ever guess from television, talked books. He is a discriminating reader and has demolished the entire works of Tom Sharpe. Stephen Hendry, the new champion at 21, spoke engagingly of his trip to China last week.

'War?' cried Davis, scanning the horizon for any adversary more threatening than an audibly dyspeptic camel. 'What war?'

'Tension?' queried Hendry. 'I mean, you'd never know anything is happening, would you?'

It is not that global strategy to two of the greatest snooker players in the world is confined to jamming the white so tight up behind the pink that the last red is unassailable. It is simply that they do not renege on professional engagements even when, during an alarming wind-shift in history, they are contractually beckoned to the flashpoint of the world. This is more than can be said of some of their journalist compatriots.

Yesterday, after winning their late-night, first-round matches in the Dubai Duty Free Classic – so named because it is sponsored by what Dubai claims to be the poshest and least rip-off duty-free shops in the world – Davis and Hendry struggled back into their black-tie evening gear at dawn to do a favour for a pal.

It is true that one does not immediately address His Highness Sheikh Mana bin Khalifa Al Maktoum as 'mate' but he's a friendly soul, besotted by thoroughbred horse racing, whose current assignment – as a prominent scion of Dubai's ruling family – is to persuade the world that this tiny emirate, hemmed in by guns to the right of it, guns to the left of it and poison gas ahead, is not about to be blasted off the planet Earth.

'Of course,' he acknowledged, 'the situation is serious. My family' – there are some 40 Maktoums, 12 of them running any government department of importance – 'have all returned home to be prepared for what some may see as a crisis. But tell me, what crisis have you seen here?'

Good question. For all the doomsday headlines of the international Press, you can stroll around this Gulf state, play golf, watch polo, drink alcoholic cocktails and dress for a dinner party at which you'd never know the Iraq invasion of Kuwait had occurred. It is extremely British in all respects but three. There is not a scrap of litter in the streets here. There is no graffiti on the walls, and there is virtually no crime. Three days ago, two men who had fallen over drunk in the street each received ten lashes at a public flogging. A prominent restaurant in Dubai is called Thatcher's and it is mostly over-booked.

Yesterday Steve Davis, having just beaten the Canadian Jim Wych 5–2, and Stephen Hendry, 5–1 victor over England's Neal Faulds, willingly contributed to this air of peace on behalf of the Maktoum family and the Dubai government.

Both are considerably more than millionaires. Neither received a penny for venturing into the Arabian desert soon after dawn to engage in the most bizarre frame of snooker since some bored British Army officers invented the game. The camel and its bewildered handler were genuinely passing. The planting of a snooker table in sand dunes was what might be described as Dubai's most demonstrative contribution to peace in the Gulf. 'All remains normal here,' says a nation whose holiday bookings have suddenly been torpedoed by the Middle East crisis.

The Dubai Snooker Classic is actually being played in the air-conditioned luxury of the Al Nasr Sports Club and watched by white-robed men so intensely involved in the game that they burst into ecstatic applause last evening when Stephen Hendry inadvertently went in off the blue.

His Highness Sheikh Mana bin Khalifa Al Maktoum plays the game himself three times a week in his private sports complex and is eagerly anticipating his first break of 20.

Recognizing a comparable duffer, he suggested sending his personal helicopter to air-lift your correspondent over there for a match. Virtually anything, you will gather, is available to anyone here who will propagate the opinion that Dubai is sitting this one out.

'We are, you will understand,' said His Highness, 'essentially interested in business and commerce.' Actually, he was much more enthusiastic when talking racing.

His real interests are at Newmarket and Ascot. And as owner

of the Willie Carson horse that jumped the shadow – thus losing the race – in the Breeders' Classic at Belmont, he had to conceal his grief at one of the freak disasters of the turf lest it be compared with his sorrow at what is happening in the Middle East.

It is hard to say who has his priorities right down here. Apart, that is, from Messrs Davis and Hendry. They are simply playing snooker while the winds of war gather above their heads.

OLYMPIC LOGO

Controversy over the logo for the 2012 London Olympics gives this piece a surprising topicality.

A s you will readily appreciate, a newspaper becomes progressively more philistine the closer you get to its back pages.

Not for us the dancing wit of Jack Tinker's theatrical notices, the thunderous denunciations of Peter Paterson's TV reviews, the acute perceptions of the Keith Waterhouse and John Edwards columns, the blazing ridicule of Ann Leslie getting stuck in to another bunch of unspeakable foreigners.

No, it's blood and gore down here in the sports pages, mate, where three-syllable words cause consternation and Arsenal's deprivation of two League points is the biggest talking point since the Abdication.

Yet there comes a point when even muddied oafs must confront the world of the arts and question whether its contempt for sport is such that its rare contributions to it are dashed off in a drunken stupor between 3.00 and 3.05 a.m.?

Behold a drawing of such witless ineptitude that, if perpetrated by a teenaged Slade School of Fine Art student, the unfortunate child would be instantly conveyed to the nearest job employment bureau or passing ambulance.

This is Cobi. And Cobi, I have to tell you, was unveiled this week as the official mascot for the 1992 Barcelona Olympic Games.

Cobi is destined for maximum exposure, all of it indecent.

Cobi will appear on lapel badges, T-shirts and letter-heads. Cobi will see the light of day on tea towels, neck-ties and head-scarves. Cobi will desecrate not only postcards but a nation's postage stamps.

Cobi will decorate anything that sells because Cobi, poor chap, is the copyrighted property of the trading licensing contractors who now flood the temple of the Olympics with all manner of tawdry commercial junk.

It wouldn't be so bad – though on second thoughts even that's a lie – if Cobi hadn't been launched to an audience gaspingly more appreciative than that which saw the curtains drawn back on Leonardo da Vinci's Mona Lisa some years ago. I have literature in front of me which describes the artist, Javier Mariscal, born Valencia, 1950, as the master of schematic avant-garde design. Be that as it may, I am in no hurry to commission him to tamper with my window-box.

Anyway, that's what's going on these days in an Olympic movement that used to be about foot races and punching opponents on the nose.

In apologizing for this rare and unseemly incursion into arts appreciation, I should add that the Barcelona Olympic Committee are simultaneously producing a Games poster by one Enric Satue which is shortly to be distributed around the world.

Down here in the sports department we believe that it comes very close to illustrating what we think of the arts intruding on our tiny world.

JOHN ARLOTT – OVER AND OUT

As a wordsmith – and a lover of wine – IW admired the unique style of a great professional and was proud to be his friend.

Dateline: **London 1990**

FOR THOSE privileged to know him, the enduring memory of John Arlott is less of a man crouched over microphone or typewriter than of a slightly florid squire discoursing brilliantly from the head of his own refectory dining table.

As midnight turned to morning the tie came off, the shirt buttons came open one by one and the subjects ranged wider, ever wider. Cricket was the least of it. The spectrum spread from Gladstone via bullfighting. Thomas Hardy, drinkable clarets, the unconscious use of the iambic pentameter, Freddie Mills and feudal England to Dylan Thomas and beyond.

An early night was 2 a.m. and Arlott had a house rule that where you dined you slept. He never quite recovered from the death of a son in a horrific car crash and no guests of his were permitted to leave the premises after submitting to his legendary hospitality. Knowing the long history of his refectory table he calculated one night that at least half a million bottles of wine had been consumed at it.

These were magical evenings and they held the secret of his eminence and unique style as a broadcaster.

It was the immense breadth of his erudition that was the font of his incomparable imagery with the spoken word and it was the good fortune of cricket, the most English of games, that Arlott, the most English of Englishmen, became, by accident, its spokesman on radio.

Cricket had long had its stylish essayists, and Arlott himself was one of them – though some curious reticence restrained him from displaying even one of the 40 books he wrote on that and other subjects, alongside the 10,000 volumes of his personal library at his home in Alresford, Hampshire. He hid his own works in a drawer in his bedroom.

But radio was different. Radio to him was not about statistics or indulgently thanking Mrs Clutterbuck of Shrewsbury for sending 'the team' a delicious cherry cake. Radio was wit and graphic description born of intellect and mastery of the English language.

Arlott revealed such qualities in his apprentice days. Commentating from Lord's in 1947 he watched a South African googly bowler named Tufty Mann tie a Middlesex tail-end batsman named George Mann in embarrassing knots with four successive deliveries. 'All,' growled Arlott, 'what we're watching here is a clear case of Mann's inhumanity to Mann.'

Despite decades of celebrity, Arlott was working-class Hampshire, proud of it and forever grateful to a forceful mother for convincing him that books from the public library were the route to grammar school and that grammar school could lead to anywhere. It did, but it was 11 years before he got his break.

Four of those years were spent clerking in a mental hospital, seven as a policeman in Southampton. He would have you believe that he was the hot cop of the force, but such was his humanity that you couldn't imagine him arresting anyone for delinquencies much short of rape or murder.

While on the beat he wrote poetry and read some of it on the BBC. They thought it original, were intrigued by the rural accent, recognized a remarkable talent and invited him to join the staff as a literary producer. One of the wilder tyros he encouraged was a young, cherubic-looking Welshman. He and Dylan Thomas became close friends and drinking companions, the difference being that Arlott had the constitution to survive the thrashes.

At last he was in the literary circle to which he had long aspired. Cricket, although he loved it and had some modest talent for it, had never occurred to him as offering a career. Anyway he was far more at home with his new, mildly bohemian writing friends than with the crested club ties, easy manners and conventional accents of the inhabitants of the Lord's and Oval pavilions.

But in 1946, still short-staffed so soon after war, the BBC sent Arlott to broadcast ten-minute summaries on the early matches of that summer's cricket tour by India. Arlott had no ambition to join the sports department. He was ecstatic where he was.

But listeners had never heard commentary like it: Kipling, the lowering sun, the British Raj, the history of the ground, the sheer glory of an offdrive crisply hit, the thunderous countenance of a batsman convinced he was wrongfully dismissed, all woven into sentences coloured by arresting imagery, and so intuitively constructed that you could almost hear the commas fall on either side of the subordinate clauses.

It was no conscious assault on sports broadcasting. It was simply the way John Arlott saw it. The style was original, and although he had imitators – notably one South African – no peer emerged in his lifetime.

Arlott was politically Liberal all his life. He would have been an asset in a House where debating standards were already falling from Churchillian to banal, but thankfully for cricket his only foray on the hustings was a disaster. He contested Epping at the 1955 general election and just saved his deposit. His finest debating hour was in the Cambridge Union the night he took on the cricketing establishment in the heated controversy about whether sporting links should be maintained with apartheid South Africa. He was deeply implicated in the row, having been instrumental in bringing a young and then unknown Cape

Coloured cricketer, Basil D'Oliveira, to forge a great career in England.

It was South Africa's subsequent refusal to re-admit D'Oliveira as a member of the England team that detonated one of the most bitter conflicts in cricket history.

The Cambridge Union debate was being reported worldwide. Beforehand Arlott cautiously sipped a sherry, a rare and insipid drink for him. 'They tell me,' he said, 'that I only have to stay sober to win this one.'

When his time came Arlott rose, slipped one hand into a jacket pocket and began to speak. In 15 minutes of flawless oratory he neither raised his voice nor referred to a note. He carried the night, sat down to a standing ovation and an hour later was drinking amiably with Wilf Wooller, his principal antagonist in the argument. Both held strong opinions but both were cricket men.

He had the generosity of many men whose talent is so exceptional that rat races do not exist. He would berate shoddy politicians, crooked statesmen of any hue and rudeness, which he abhorred. But never once did I hear him denigrate a colleague or rival less gifted than himself.

He treated the young as equals. A friend of mine set off to report a soccer match at which Arlott was present and unavoidably arrived at half-time after five goals had been scored. This fact was gleefully included in the report of the man from the *Sunday Times*.

Next morning my friend received a telephone call from Arlott. 'I've just read that spiteful remark,' he said. 'If it lands you in trouble and I can help, just let me know.' The young man and John Arlott had never met.

He was always for the underdog and, amazingly, never quite grasped his own pre-eminence. It was his most attractive attribute.

The night before his retirement from commentating I stayed with him at Alresford and drove to Lord's with him the following morning. He was very quiet, anticipating the fuss that would be made of his last Test match broadcast. He had a couple of fortifying drinks on his way up the six flights of stairs to the commentary position.

Chapter Seven

1991–1992

BOOKIES RUNNING
FOR COVER

*IW liked a bet, and the bookies were very much a part of his
beloved Cheltenham Festival.*

Dateline: **Cheltenham 1991**

DON'T BORE me with Wordsworth's ridiculous daffodils.
The sublime spectacle of encroaching Spring is Cheltenham
Racecourse and a host of golden bookies swaying between Red
Alert and Blue Funk.

At a personal level bookies are good blokes: reformed Gestapo
officers, born-again safe-crackers, potential larcenists who've
sublimated their natural instincts to the dictates of the law.

But, heavens, do they run for cover. For the 75 minutes
between the first and third races of this year's Festival they made
Red Adair look like a novice in the art of damage limitation.

Regrettably this was unconnected with your correspondent's
30 quid on Black Humour at 25–1 in the Champion Hurdle.
So ecstatic was the shrewdly named Black Humour at negotiating
the first obstacle that he became dissociated from J. Osborne at
the second while I was still struggling to get the binos focused.

The panic, of course, was induced by Noel Furlong's first-
race win on Destriero which meant that if his double with The
Illiad came up in the third, his pay-out was worth somewhere
between £8–10 million. This is heavy bread, Lutine Bell stuff,
which can actually affect a shareholder's affections.

What's more, sensing divine intervention in these recessional times, the on-track punters swooped like vultures. If divine intervention also came up this would mean the handing over of maybe up to another £500,000 in used readies on the spot.

Two things then happened in swift succession. The bookies hit the ejector button so that The Illiad's price plunged from 12–1 to 11–2. And The Illiad, beautifully placed, struck the fourth hurdle from home so solidly that it limped home last out of 21 runners.

One bookie actually said: 'Our prayers have been answered,' a matter to which I trust the new Archbishop of Canterbury will address himself the moment he is settled in.

In short, can the punter ever win?

Yes, we can. I know an utterly conservative man who, by applying much of his employer's time to the close study of form books and restricting his bets to never more than £50, has actually paid for his house by betting on horses.

And do bookies ever lose?

Yes, they do. A bookmaker with single-storey premises not far from the Headingley Cricket Ground in Leeds was once visited by a sportswriter of my acquaintance whose knowledge of racing was limited to the rumour that horses have four legs. For a lark this tyro struck a yankee bet, a wager involving the cross pollination of doubles, trebles and an accumulator on four horses in separate races.

I cannot recall the precise prices of the horses but they were so disarmingly absurd as a serious bet – say 3–1, plus 10–1, plus 25–1, plus 50–1 – that the bookie saw no point in laying-off with wealthier members of his fraternity.

This was an error. All four horses won and the poor man, unshielded by some discretionary upper-limit pay-out clause, went straight out of business. It was the one-hit blue-moon job that keeps us all subscribing to the welfare of our friends in the betting industry.

'How many gamblers,' I asked Ron Pollard yesterday, 'have you known who live by betting?'

Pollard, years with Ladbrokes, now semi-retired, author of a book on the fascinating world of chance which is to be launched at no less a venue than the Palace of Westminster in May, is Britain's oddsman emeritus.

He held up one hand. 'Don't count the thumb,' he said. 'Probably four.'

The message is that unless you can match, or at least challenge, the bookmaker's resources sufficiently to threaten thrombosis, you are a certified long-time loser.

Just after World War Two Jack Gerber, a South African multi-millionaire, scared the daylights out of Britain's bookies with his audacity. His biggest coup was on a horse called palpitate which, just before the off, was being quoted at 100–6.

It was then that an entire battalion of Gerber's hired hands simultaneously hit every bookmaker in business. It was too late to press the panic button. Gerber walked away with winnings which, allowing for inflation, made Furlong's Cheltenham winnings this week look like a few boxes of Smarties.

Today a man of this fiscal stature is Kerry Packer, Australia's richest man. I have witnessed Packer raise his index finger to a bookmaker at the Melbourne Cup which, by pre-arrangement, signified the laying of a million dollars on a single horse. I never knew which horse and subsequently, by the impeccable demeanour of both men, never knew the outcome of the negotiation either. That is betting.

Personally I'm having another 30 quid on Celtic Shot in today's Gold Cup at Cheltenham. The price, I know, is drifting.

But Cheltenham without a bet is like being invited to a vegetarian teetotal restaurant. It's about meeting old friends and getting someone to drive you back up the motorway when you've had a drink.

It is not at all like staring at daffodils.

STIRLING MOSS –
BRITAIN'S MAN
IN A MIGLION

Stirling Moss displayed all those qualities of skill, courage and character so admired by IW. Moss never won a world championship but his name remains synonymous with the sport of motor racing.

Dateline: **Italy 1991**

IF YOU are contemplating the grand cultural tour of Italy, reflecting on the genius of the Florentine masters and absorbing the architecture of ancient Siena, I'm afraid I can grant my chauffeur no references.

In fact he's damned lucky to get nought out of ten.

Florence? We went there, did that. Got through the place in six minutes 56 seconds. Would have been quicker but for the crazy road system round that blockhouse with the dome.

Siena? Boy, did we give that a seeing to. If my chauffeur hadn't been mobbed at one stage, we'd have been in and out in under three minutes, leaving only a trail of pollution and a few Renaissance portraits bouncing off walls.

True, he relented just once. Coming over the high mountain pass between these two cities he became quite lyrical about the grandeur of the Almighty's benevolence to the Italian landscape. 'Terrific view down there to the right, old boy,' he yelled into our intercom.

Heaven knows how he saw it. The rev counter was dancing over the 7,000 mark at the time and we were heading north at fractionally over 140 mph.

The din inside the Mercedes-Benz 300 SLR threatened permanent deafness and the vroom-vrooming as he changed down to humiliate another hairpin-bend into utter insignificance was scattering domestic animals in the valleys below.

Stirling Moss doesn't go into these bends like the rest of us. Where we brake, he rams on the power. 'Nothing to it, old boy, apart from experience.'

Some experience. Over the past 25 hours I have just ridden round Italy in the Mille Miglia at his right elbow, mostly on winding country roads, sometimes with a ghastly vacuum on one side, at others with spectators' toecaps protruding out from the verge.

It rained stair-rods for 750 of those 1,000 miles and I can inform you that high-velocity travelling in an open-topped vehicle with only a six-inch high windscreen between you and the elements leaves you with five sets of sodden clothes, despite the alleged waterproofs, and mild apprehension as to the long-term effects of sitting that long in a bucket-seat full of water.

But having thus far been derogatory about my chauffeur, let me say this about the man deemed by many among the motor-sport cognoscenti as the greatest driver in history: there were at least 100 near-misses but there was not a single moment of danger.

Early on, when Stirling pulls out to confront fast oncoming traffic, you reckon the best you can get away with is quadriplegia. But he has done it so many millions of times that you find yourself easing back to your side of the road through a gap which even George Best, on the soccer field, could not have created. Shameful prayer soon gives way to exhilarating enjoyment.

Only when you have accompanied men of this calibre in the art of high-performance driving do you realize that the next Porsche-owning yuppie who whizzes past you at 120 mph on the M1 is a jerk. He has neither the expertise nor the lightning reactions to cope with an emergency. Stirling Moss, though now 61, does. He also has at his disposal two vital assets: fantastic 300-horsepower acceleration and phenomenal works-designed braking.

The odd thing is that as a professional he drives barely 20,000 miles a year. This is probably half the distance accomplished by a London cabbie and one third of that recorded by a long-haul lorry driver. He drives only when necessary. It is his art.

Towards the closing stages of this year's Mille Miglia we hit Bologna at the height of a traffic jam. This is where the artists take over. 'Better go for it, old boy,' said Stirling. He went.

He put the Mercedes into places where no car has driven before. We were through the city's stoppage in under 13 minutes, passing vehicles on Moss's blind side with infallible three-inch clearances. I only know this because it happened to be on the side I was sitting on.

On the big fast curves out in the country he drives to within a precise six inches of the yellow kerb-line at 100 mph-plus for hours on end, wet or dry. He demonstrated under-steering, over-steering and lectured me on the business of lateral-G. I understood none of it.

'I hope you realize,' said an envious Peter Robinson, European editor of the prestigious *Autocar* magazine, 'what a privileged position you are in. There are motor enthusiasts all over the world who would cheerfully pay £10,000 to occupy the seat you are in during this race.'

Stirling received not a penny from this newspaper. We are old friends and I have long been a fan.

He suffers no agitation about the £13 million Ayrton Senna – or the £9 million Nigel Mansell – will make from this year's Grand Prix campaign. Moss stormed that field, too, with 16 victories. He merely spills over with admiration for Senna and speaks no evil about Mansell's lengthening string of bad luck.

'Money never interested me as much as the driving,' he said, 'so when I discovered that someone would actually pay you for doing what you love best, that was it. Do you know, old boy, that I can make as much money in a morning these days signing limited editions of books and mementoes as I did when I won the European Grand Prix at Nurburgring in 1961? I got £600 for that and I was the happiest man on Earth.'

The constant old-boying places him firmly in the fifties era when, before the colossal accident that ended his Grand Prix career, he succeeded the great Juan Fangio as the world's finest driver. His ultimate triumph, though, was here in Italy. It came in the so-called Death Race, the 1,000-mile road competition which in 1957, two years after his greatest drive, was banned by an Italian government shamed by outrage at its carnage.

After 24 races over open Italian roads more than 70 victims – drivers, co-drivers, spectators – lay dead, killed by the manic quest for speed.

The end came when the Spanish Marquis de Portago lost a front wheel off his Ferrari and lurched into the crowd. He and his co-driver were killed and so were 13 bystanders, five of them children.

Two years previously Moss, the only British driver ever to win, stormed home in a record 10 hours 7 minutes 47 seconds at an average speed – through towns, villages and tortuous country by-roads – of 98.98 mph.

More than three decades later the Mille Miglia has been revived. But it is not the same race. These days it is slowed by regulatory stage time-trials and speed-limit obligations over certain stretches.

These are incompatible with Stirling's personality. Driving the same Mercedes-Benz in which he won in 1955, this year he raced up to the verge of the checkpoints with such panache that we had to hang around there waiting for the rest of the field to catch up.

For this the Italians, temperamentally attuned to the vroom-vroom sports provided it is other people risking their own lives, love him like a son. His return this year, 36 years after his famous victory, was virtually a national lap of honour.

He was besieged at every stopping point. He was showered with gifts and extravagant compliments. I watched him sign more than 1,000 autographs. He was interviewed constantly. And he constantly exchanged endearments with voluble Italians.

'God knows what I'm saying, old boy,' he confided. 'I learned my Italian from motor mechanics in the pits and I gather I speak with the equivalent of a Cockney accent. Apparently I use the most appalling swearwords without ever knowing it. But aren't these people wonderful?'

They were. In pouring rain towards midnight on Saturday they still lined five deep in the towns and villages over the last 100 miles of the race to roar him through. Stirling rewarded them with a wave and a couple of basso profundo notes on the throttle.

Had it been flat-out racing Moss would have won by hours in a 300-horsepower car unmatchable for speed. But under the new regulations the result is determined by a points system based on the accuracy of passages through speed-regulated sections.

This is greatly the responsibility of the co-driver and navigator. Since this was my role, and I am virtually innumerate when it comes to mathematical calculations in pouring rain, I take full responsibility for his failure.

'Never mind, old boy,' said Stirling, 'it was terrific fun.'

At the finish line a Japanese lady TV reporter who had followed our progress around the race thrust a microphone into his face and, for the fifth time in three days, asked the dumbest of all dumb TV questions.

'How,' she smiled, 'do you feel?'

'Knackered,' replied Stirling.

The lady sparkled with comprehension and beamed into camera. In a few days thousands of Japanese will be turning up English dictionaries.

My own consolation was a master class in the art of car driving. A class from which I can never benefit, like the thousands who will sit in traffic jams this Bank Holiday everywhere from Blackpool to Brighton.

To us a car remains a metal object capable of conveying us from A to B. In the hands of Stirling Moss it can be raised into an art form, so our journey around Italy may not quite have been as philistine as indicated.

OPEN LETTER TO JOHN McENROE

IW deplored John McEnroe's antics, and expressed his feelings in his own way.

Dear****,

 ****me.*******,****,******* *** ****** ****** Duchess of Kent and Norma Major. ***** *** ******** *****of your own ******* children? ******** not ******* likely, ************, ***** **** **** *** *****. ************ no. ***** **** Harpic. ** ***** ***** castration.

 ***** **** ***** ***** ** ***** ***** *** ********* American Psycho or Julie ******* Burchill. **** ** **** ******* *** ******* **** off. On

second thoughts *** **** your ***. ********** ****
***** ***** in the Gulf and **** ***** Stars and
******* Stripes. **** **, **** ** *********.
********* you ****** **** ** ***** ******
advice? ***** *** ******* yer bike and ***** ***
******** ******* come back.

Yours profoundly sincerely,
Ian Wooldridge

CARL LEWIS WINS THE GREATEST RACE

From time to time IW found occasion to criticize Carl Lewis's character but he was the first to acknowledge his supreme athleticism.

Dateline: **Japan 1991**

THE EARTH stood still for 9.86 seconds here last evening while eight black athletes traversed 100 metres of its surface. It was, by some measure, the greatest foot-race since man learned how to walk.

Before even discussing how an ageing sorcerer named Carl Lewis gunned down his young apprentice friend Leroy Burrell, consider this:

Our own Linford Christie pulled out the most staggering performance of his turbulent life. His 9.92 seconds was by far the fastest he has ever run. No Briton, no European even, has ever matched it. And yet he finished only fourth.

Only? I have never written a greater calumny. It was heroic.

But, in this seismic collision beneath a black velvet sky, it was simply not fast enough. His enduring consolation will be that he actually participated in a sporting drama that outshone its frenetic pre-publicity.

The billing might have been for a prize fight: Lewis, multi-decorated champion and long-time 9.92-seconds fastest man in the world, versus Burrell, the upstart who just 76 days ago in New York had erased him from the record book with a run of 9.90.

One might almost have expected one of those embarrassing eyeball-to-eyeball confrontations so beloved by boxers, with Lewis, aged 30, outstaring Burrell, at 24 a stripling of an heir apparent. No such thing. There is an uncanny affinity between them.

Both grew up in Pennsylvania, both went to the University of Houston, both have the same coach, both are members of the phenomenally successful Santa Monica Track Club, both turned up to speak warmly of one another during the many Press and television interviews they gave last week, and both are partners in a lucrative company that manufactures fashion track-wear for those who think they can run but can't.

More significantly, as they shook hands on the start line last night, each knew he would have to break the world record again to beat the other. What made this race such a landmark in athletics history was that *both* did.

Lewis ran 9.86 seconds to Burrell's 9.88. It was as though six other brilliant athletes in the race did not exist. They embraced at length before heaping adulation upon one another during endless interviews.

I am not, and never have been, an aficionado of Carl Lewis's showboating demeanour but such prejudice was demolished last night by the sheer physical courage of his run. Frankly, by his standards, he was late out of the blocks. At 60 metres he was running fourth and looked conclusively beaten.

The good Lord alone knows from whence he then generated the power to come through the field and win having, ten yards out, coolly glanced left to see where Burrell was. Burrell, one lane over from Linford Christie, couldn't see what was happening. He is blind in his right eye, an affliction which persuaded him to take up sprinting after conspicuously failing at baseball and football.

The race was an American shut-out, with Dennis Mitchell taking the bronze medal one-hundredth of a second ahead of Linford Christie. Dennis who? You would have never known.

Carl Lewis, after breaking into tears, said: 'There was no way I could have done this without Leroy.' Burrell responded: 'Carl has pushed me throughout my career. There is no disgrace in losing to your great friend. I simply have to look forward to Carl retiring but I am a newcomer to all this and I learned a great deal tonight.'

By now the mutual admiration was becoming mildly embarrassing. But suddenly Leroy grabbed a microphone proffered by Japanese TV and said, according to its interpreter.

'Many people didn't think it possible to run this fast without doping but what you have just seen was a proper race.'

Sitting in row two of the main stand was Ben Johnson, the Canadian whose world 'record' at the Seoul Olympics three years ago was obliterated after he admitted to being rocket-fuelled by drugs.

He did not qualify to compete in the World Championships 100m but will run later this week for his adopted country in the relay sprints.

Athletics is a curious sport but it can offer nothing better than the supreme spectacle we were privileged to watch here last night. It was an odd affair but, in 9.86 seconds, I have not seen better.

WARNING SIGNS FOR GAZZA

Like so many footballers, Gazza failed to convince IW of his personal charms.

Dateline: London 1991

UNLESS GAZZA is utterly gaga it must be dawning on even him that pre-eminence in sport requires a government health warning. It can sincerely destroy your life if the early symptoms are ignored.

With a court case for alleged assault still looming over him, with a divorce case for alleged adultery to be defended, with a leg shattered in that lunatic Cup final tackle still under repair, with a future now committed to the fickle madness of Italian football, with reporters whom he has vilely insulted in a mood for vengeance, his young life is certainly smouldering if not quite yet in smoking ruins.

George Best was already in professional middle-age before the demons got him and, anyway, George had charm and brains and had long confirmed an awesome genius. Paul Gascoigne has done no such thing. His career has hardly started and if it ended now he would best be remembered for bursting into tears at the World Cup and two bovine charges at Wembley before being stretchered off with the game barely under way.

Even his role as the icon of the latest rebellious youth cult has been too gauche and insubstantial to suggest his influence is persuasive to any other than witless oiks.

This is sad and reflects badly on his advisers who, in their rapacity to clean up on a commission basis, have either advised him to grab every quid that's going before he explodes or simply

227

given him no advice at all on how to conduct himself to sustain a public persona which, once and fleetingly, was quite appealing.

Instead it has all been fracas at airports, blue lights flashing outside pubs, swaggering arrogance in bars, angry exchanges with the Press and a stream of embarrassing front-page publicity.

The ironic thing is that naughtiness in a prominent sportsman is a highly marketable commodity if skilfully exploited and, before launching Gazza on a path that could now lead anywhere, it would have been advisable for his advisers to have studied what their business counterparts in America did for 'Broadway' Joe.

'Broadway' Joe Namath was a marvellous quarter-back with the New York Jets whose freely available curriculum vitae included the recondite information that he owned a bar on Broadway, drank Johnny Walker Red Label scotch whisky till all hours and, being a bachelor like Gazza, went to bed only when he'd found a lady to relieve his boredom. In a celebrated *Playboy* article he claimed there had been more than 1,000 of them.

Some of this was true. Much of it was nonsense. But, in addition to an astronomical income from football, Joe was certainly the owner of one of the most prosperous bars in the United States and fronted an advertising campaign for Red Label whisky, which was one of the most lucrative ever negotiated for a sportsman. He retired extremely rich, extremely popular and, presumably, extremely satisfied.

The difference was that Joe Namath's advisers traded his 'notoriety' with great acumen. They did not deal in niggardly contracts or demand petty sums for piffling interviews or insignificant public appearances. When they went for the big hit the hit was truly big. At all other times, when convenient, Joe was available, gratis.

I phoned his agents once from London. Joe was not there. They contacted him and he returned my call at his own expense within the hour. Another time I had arranged to interview him after training at Shea Stadium. My taxi got snarled in New York traffic and I arrived, agitated, half an hour late. Joe had waited and his affability matched his courtesy. Publicity in Britain, of course, was of little or no value to him. But that was the manner in which Namath's advisers had trained him to behave.

Is it too late already for such a parable to have effect? Is such a transformation even possible? Or do Gascoigne's henchmen genuinely believe they are doing a good job? And if so, for whom?

Looking at the tangled mess of the young man's life yesterday these questions were surely open to debate.

PAVAROTTI'S HYMN TO THE HORSE

IW provides an unusual take on the great tenor, whose recent death has caused such sadness.

Dateline: Italy 1991

THERE WAS no top table. Nor did Luciano Pavarotti sing. He simply rose mid-room, beamed his famous sunrise smile at the Princess Royal, who was seated on his left, and made the perfect speech.

It lasted 30 seconds and was confined entirely to welcoming his 93 guests to dinner in Italy's Military Academy, once the home of the d'Este family. Cherubs looked down from the distant ceiling. Marcantonio Franceschini painted them there in 1695.

There was champagne at 8.30 p.m. and a floodlit military parade in the courtyard at 1 a.m. 'Never,' said David Broome, the most travelled of the galaxy of horsepersons present, 'have I seen a show like this. In fact, in our world, there's never been one.'

And that was how Pavarotti intended it – for, away from the grand opera houses, relieved of the acclaim that remorselessly attends him throughout his ten-and-a-half months on the road each year, his private passion is for horses.

He owns them, breeds them, prospects for them, caresses them and croons to them. Sadly, he can no longer ride them.

Instead, he promoted the four-day first Pavarotti International Horseshow at the weekend to watch the world's finest show-jumping exponents do that for him over his extensive acres in central Italy.

Everything bore the Pavarotti hallmark: an arena fit for regal jousting, carpeted grandstands, luxurious loggias furnished with glass-topped oak tables, a restaurant with heavy table linen, cut glass and a regiment of sommeliers to decant the finest wines. There were parades by medieval crossbow marksmen and vintage cars. A girls' choir had been flown in from Mexico. The Salzburg Festival Orchestra came down to honour Pavarotti and play one movement of a symphony and a short encore by Haydn.

The first Pavarotti Horseshow cost £2,800,000. The great man didn't pay for it. He lent his land. The rest was financed by commercial sponsors who simply clamoured for the privilege of associating their companies with the maestro's name.

The entire site was being flattened again yesterday but 'The Pavarotti' will be back next year. It is to become a permanent annual fixture on the international showjumping agenda and thus will commemorate the Pavarotti legend when there are only discs and tapes to recall the grandeur of his music. And that pleases him. For each morning, he confesses, he is concerned, if not exactly haunted yet, by his awareness of the impermanence of the human voice. He has no intention of singing on, like his compatriot Gigli before him, when the great resonance has gone.

'You know,' he said, 'there are great similarities between the careers of a singer and a horse. Some jumping horses go on till they are 20 years old. For others, they get to 12 and suddenly they are finished. No one can tell when it is going to happen.

'The human voice is equally unpredictable. Every day I wonder: will I have one more year, or two, or three, or ten? I love, I adore music. I still enjoy travelling the world.

'But I know that it must end. And when it does there will be this . . .' and he waved an arm expansively around the fabric of the costliest horse show ever staged.

'What you see today,' he added, 'is only the beginning.' His modesty, for he is the most gracious of performing stars, restrained him from adding that he knows he has the wealth and the personal magnetism to scale another world.

Pavarotti's passion for horses has been with him for even longer than his marriage with music. 'I fell in love with them when I was a boy on my uncle's farm. I rode them all the time and I rode them, as a man, when I returned here from my tours. I made efforts to ride them whenever I was singing abroad.

'You know, I have kept a record of the best 78 horses I have ridden anywhere in the world. I have them all in a notebook, like a boy who writes down football scores.'

He delayed proffering an explanation why he rides no more. Eventually he did. Well, almost. 'Two years ago,' he said, 'my favourite horse here died. She was an Irish mare called Vagabond. I have never ridden since and I shall not ride again.'

The true answer became apparent when Pavarotti edged his enormous frame from the driving seat of his Mercedes with difficulty and glanced around for a shoulder to lean on in order to hobble the few paces to meet Milton, the lovely grey gelding who is probably the greatest showjumping horse ever bred in Britain.

Milton is 14. Luciano Pavarotti is 55.

Pavarotti greeted Milton like a stage contemporary. He nuzzled him and hummed him a little song. And then, painfully slowly, he struggled back to his car. He walks barely a few paces without support and one could only marvel at his capacity to command either an operatic platform or Hyde Park on a rainy night under such infirmity.

He concedes nothing to it. In his Modena grandstand, he had tables to lean on and moved around to greet old friends with bear-hugs, plant kisses on their wives, hold hands briefly with their daughters, and welcome the president of the International Equestrian Federation, who happens to be the Princess Royal, placate an Italian woman television presenter whose nerve appeared to be cracking, and chat to reporters.

Men wore suits and ties. Ladies wore St Laurent and Gucci. Pavarotti, with a sartorial disregard that can be carried off only by the truly successful, wore baggy black pants, a T-shirt and a zip-up jacket most wives would donate to Oxfam. He was, by some octaves, the worst-dressed man in the place.

It was in this setting that Britain's showjumping team – David Broome, the Whitaker brothers and young Peter Murphy – completed their year's work by winning the Nations Cup. In Modena, Broome agreed: 'The big man won the day.'

He did, too, without singing a note. At the close he handed the microphone to his aged father who proved where the great voice came from. Luciano Pavarotti wept.

NATIONAL HUNT – JUGGLING SPILLS WITH THRILLS

Few sportsmen other than jump jockeys are so consistently required to show the physical bravery that IW so admired.

ABBOT OF FURNESS, at 5–2 on, was streaking it by about 30 lengths when he struck the penultimate fence at Ayr on Thursday and went down in an ugly heap. His jockey, Neale Doughty, lay very still in the biting wind and the path of eight on-coming horses.

'Now,' cried the course commentator, 'We have a race on our hands,' and you couldn't fault him for accuracy. The crowd roared in response for not a few, still bludgeoned by New Year hangovers, had been inspired to back On The Hooch. From obscurity On The Hooch took it up to win at 16–1, thus sending its supporters back to the bars to celebrate their sagacity.

By now, the forgotten Neale Doughty was back on his feet – just. Feeling not much worse than a man who had recently jumped from the third floor of a blazing building, he checked for fractures, found none, but was too badly shaken to ride the last race.

Forty minutes earlier, at Lingfield, Steve Smith Eccles had been less fortunate. Flung from Cazaudehore at the first flight of hurdles, he was kicked by several trailing horses and then underwent an operation for a broken ankle.

On Boxing Day we saw our two premier National Hunt jockeys, Peter Scudamore and Richard Dunwoody, survive horrific falls within a matter of seconds at Kempton Park. Dunwoody was still on the ground when his mount, Desert Orchid, was accorded massive acclaim for running riderless into retirement. Scudamore, having broken his left leg, an arm, both collar bones and his skull in the past, rode on.

That same afternoon a less well-known jockey, Philip Barnard, suffered head injuries when he fell at Wincanton. He died in hospital the following day. He was the fourth jockey to be killed in ten years. Several others in that time have suffered injuries which left them paralysed.

If a similar toll of death and permanent disablement had been recorded in boxing in this country, the clamour for its disbandment would be even more deafening than it already is. So why the comparative silence about the terrible dangers of National Hunt racing?

A difficult question defies a definite answer, but there may be two reasons.

The first is the characters of the jockeys themselves, the second the calculated indifference of a vociferous minority who associate steeplechasing, its practitioners and supporters with the field sports they deem so barbaric.

I confess to being in blind admiration of National Hunt riders. Their rewards, just adequate for its stars and pitiful for the rest, are so far removed from what teenagers can amass for playing three sets of bad tennis with all the physical dangers that entails, as to confirm a streak of mad heroism.

They know, from easily available statistics, that they will probably fall off once in 12 rides and that in one of every 20 of those spills they will sustain a bad injury. The ratio makes the modern matador and Grand Prix driver, whose incomes are astronomical, look comparatively safe.

Courage on this scale can be extremely attractive to those of us who do not possess it. It is the more attractive because they make so light of it.

When Terry Butcher finished a gallant football performance for England with blood congealing from a bandaged head, his manager of the time, Bobby Robson, was moved to say: 'Men have received VOs for less.' He later had the grace to apologize for so ludicrous an emotional reaction, but the point is that such an analogy would have occurred to no one in National Hunt racing.

Its administrators have strived to minimize the dangers with obligatory protective wear, plastic railings which will collapse under a jockey's weight and stricter medical supervision to ban a rider from ill-judged premature return to the saddle. But still, because of the nature of the contest, injuries and fatalities occur.

So why no protests, even muted, from the familiar quarters? Why no hue and cry about human injury and even death from publications of a certain hue which regard themselves as the conscience of humanity? Why no protest marches down to the track when the screens are placed round some unfortunate animal and a single shot rings out?

If the anti-hunt protagonists were as concerned about the sanctity of life – human and equestrian as well as vulpine predatorial – one might have respected their attendance, disruptive though it may have been, at Ayr or Lingfield, Kempton or Wincanton.

Since there was no sign of them it would appear that poor Philip Barnard was less important than a fox. It would seem that National Hunt jockeys may continue to kill and maim themselves unmourned, the unspeakable unpursued by the great unwashed.

It is not remotely true, of course. These are the bravest men and women in all sport, the more so because they are attracted by the challenge and the thrill and not the money, of which there is so little.

Neale Doughty, for example, will expect no extravagant ovation when he appears at Haydock today for five rides. There are plenty who would have criticized his sport and gone home after Ayr to spend a month in bed.

CAPTAIN CONNER KEEPING THE CUP

IW liked to write about larger-than-life figures and few were as upfront as Dennis Conner, the great ocean-racing helmsman, who won the America's Cup four times and lost twice.

Dateline: **San Diego 1992**

DENNIS CONNER doesn't instantly strike you as one of the sporting giants of the era. He has a stammer, a fuse as short as the match and a complexion frequently associated with alarming high blood pressure.

The latter, in fact, is attributable to a number of factors: constant exposure to offshore winds, corrosive salt air, whisky, vodka and good Californian reds. Late at night he is also partial to a Sambuca or three which he doesn't bother to light.

Dennis isn't one for finicky details. Except on a yacht. Get a finicky detail wrong as a crewman under Conner's command and you'd wish you'd signed on for a holiday cruise with Bligh on *The Bounty*.

I had a row with him once. I'd written something about him which was unfortunately reprinted in Australia where we both happened to be in temporary residence. It was like being run down by an aircraft carrier. Dennis doesn't harbour resentments.

He drops all his depth charges, blows you out of the water and then advocates a few reconciliatory drinks.

This is an admirable way to carry on, particularly if the victim feels he has some modest talent for Conner's after-hours hobby. Forget it. At 2 a.m. Dennis is winning the European Cup while you are sliding under the Third Division league table.

The man is a phenomenon. No way would you want him at your shoulder in the trenches. He wouldn't be there anyway. Dennis would have thought the problem through, infiltrated Wehrmacht HQ with a bottle of schnapps and screwed up communications to the point where the enemy were hurling themselves at an innocent haystack. Tricky is the word for Dennis.

Also hero. Hero certainly to the San Diego business community – hotels, restaurants, nightclubs, porno joints, taxi drivers and licensed souvenir stalls – who had been beguiled into believing that the staging here of the 1992 America's Cup would attract millions of well-heeled tourists who would high-spend this nation's ninth largest city out of economic recession.

And also the local 'official' sponsors who, in contributing sums from as little as £1,500 up to £150,000 to associate their businesses with an international sporting event, had likewise been told it was going to bring them the riches of the old Samarkand road.

Very brassed off they were last week. The America's Cup had yielded them nothing. Tourist figures were actually down. The world wasn't watching. Nor was America. ESPN, the only TV channel screening it, was confessing audiences well below 800,000. And, with weeks still to go, the big Challenge Round yet to start, Dennis Conner – crazy Dennis, the only afterguard sailor the Americans had ever heard of – was on the way out.

Conner had a one-boat campaign and £12 million which these days is like entering a family saloon in a Grand Prix.

His American opponent for the right to defend the Cup for

America was Bill Koch – pronounced, locally, Coke – who had four boats and so much money, acquired after suing his own brothers for his late father's petro-estate, that he hoped to get two of them into the best-of-13 Defenders' round starting on Saturday.

Thus, although his two fastest yachts have distinctly different names, *America*[3] and *Kanza*, it would have been Koch v Koch in those races and therefore Mr Koch, fine helmsman as he undoubtedly is, would have been driving America's defender against either Italy or New Zealand in the Challenge Round starting here next month.

This is the kind of affront that brings out the the truly evil in Conner, the boy from the boondocks pitched against an Ivy League Bostonian of inestimable wealth.

In a brilliant sail in light airs on Monday, Conner's *Stars and Stripes* took the start at the pin end and outdazzled Koch's *Kanza* to win a decisive play-off over an eight-leg 20-mile course by 2 minutes 12 seconds. This was like beating Sebastian Coe MP by about 12 yards for the world's 800-metre record he still holds.

If he'd lost, the real America's Cup would have been dead. Koch v Italy or New Zealand in the Challenge Round would have had all the pull of yet another seminar on environmental waste.

This you must understand. Practically no one understands the America's Cup. Its current racing formula, L plus 1.25 to the square root of −9.8 over 0.388, isn't exactly a major topic for discussion in New York bars. Dennis Conner is, Dennis Conner is the Mike Tyson of yachting and he's not yet behind bars.

What's more he's the local boy. He was born here in San Diego on the wrong side of the tracks, learned the yachting game by begging lifts as a crewman on rich men's crafts and soon discovered that he had a Mozartian precocity for it. He is

238

probably the greatest short-race helmsman who ever lived. Never has America's Cup yachting so desperately needed such a man.

Devised in 1851, some years before the Charge of the Light Brigade and a long while before the American Civil War, the America's Cup used to be about gentlemen yotties having one hell of a time drinking champagne and hurling gold bars on to the ocean bed. Pressmen were not encouraged.

Now, like so many other sports, the America's Cup has fallen into the hands of the entrepreneurs. They have assigned a building to pamper the 1,008 media men who applied for accreditation to cover this stunning event. Mid-morning yesterday precisely seven were availing themselves of its facilities.

This America's Cup is a disaster, mitigated only by Dennis Conner's last-minute charge into the Defenders' challenge. So long as Conner is around some credibility survives. Even the taxi drivers have heard of him. Of the America's Cup they know nothing except that it's something going on out there in the water.

When it was staged in Newport, Rhode Island, and Fremantle, Australia, the America's Cup took over the town. Here it is a fringe – lost one street back from the waterfront.

Only Conner keeps it alive. He has a drapery business here somewhere which sells the floral curtains Americans apparently like round their beds. He rarely goes there, consumed as he is by the sea.

He has won the America's Cup three times, lost it once. When he won it back from Australia he was invited to the White House to receive the blessings of the then president, Ronald Reagan. Dennis stumbled on his way to the rostrum and his reply to Reagan's tribute was largely unintelligible.

He is a star. Alone he keeps this America's Cup, so costly now that Britain can't even afford to enter, afloat. He still has to beat off Koch's other boat to defend for America.

He probably will. Dennis Conner is the brinkman in excelsis, a genius who can do it outside as well as inside the bar. At his game he is a giant in the closing quarter of the 20th century.

DAVID GOWER – AN HOUR OF CAMEO

Like most cricket fans, IW was fascinated by the contrasts between the Roundhead and Cavalier characters of two of England's greatest batsmen, and compared their not dissimilar career records.

As DAVID GOWER took guard for England yesterday for the first time in 16 months he was directly confronted by a comforting notice alongside an Old Trafford sightscreen.

'A Career Move,' it said. 'Join the Greater Manchester Police.' He'd probably make a terrible cop but at least there appeared to be some kind of alternative if his contribution to a looming Test match catastrophe amounted to no more than what his detractors call 'another of those bloody cameos'.

They'd be calling for his head again. It's jealousy, of course. At that very moment, the now greying Boy David was within 34 runs of being England's heaviest-scoring batsman in history.

He'd amassed those runs with an elegance and panache conferred on none but the extravagantly gifted but even his most militant propagandists, of whom I have long been one, had to concede there have been moments when he's got out to shots of such apparent absent-mindedness that you feel like shooting him.

So it was hard to tell who was more nervous as he walked in to bat yesterday: Gower or his fan club.

As usual he concealed it with the familiar half-smile. You can never question the physical bravery of a man who charges head first down the Cresta Run as a break from facing the world's fastest bowlers, but this was rather different. The knives that had cut the core from his career were not entirely sheathed.

Well, we saw the whole of Gower's cricketing life reviewed inside 12 balls. The second he nicked wide of fourth slip for four. The third he struck majestically past cover for four. The eighth flashed over the slips for four. The 12th he carved high but eminently catchably to Salim Malik at first slip.

That could have been the end of it for the Cameo Kid: caught napping, bowled fate. The only point was that Salim dropped it.

Gower was 15 at the time but thereafter we glimpsed the glory of his second coming with everything eclipsed by the ethereal cover-drive with which he reached the 34 runs he needed to pass Geoffrey Boycott's mountainous 8,114.

Head to head

	BOYCOTT (1964–81)	GOWER (1978–92)
Tests	108	115
Innings	193	200
Not Out	23	16
100s	22	18
50s	42	39
HS	246no	215
Ducks	10	7
Runs	8114	8154
Ave	47.72	44.31

Boycott was there to watch it. So, at a range of barely 18 yards, was Gower's captain, Graham Gooch. Both have been controversially critical in print of what they saw as Gower's 'attitude problem' but this was a day for burying hatchets.

Boycott later wrung Gower's hand twice, once for television, once for the Press cameras, and neither time quite hard enough to crush his fingers. Anyway, Gower was out by then.

After hitting 50 off 42 balls and then closing down to lunch at 69 not out, he returned to crash the second ball thereafter for four and flash the very next into the wicket-keeper's gloves.

It was a very Goweresque way to go at a juncture when England were still 106 runs short of fending off the follow-on. But a lot of arguments were settled yesterday, not least that, in flow, an hour of David Gower is worth a day without a name.

He has other talents of course: wildlife photographer, underwater car driver, aviator, bon viveur, pretty good writer and TV performer.

After yesterday, though, a career move to the Greater Manchester Police would appear unlikely. A few more years as an England batsman are indicated unless someone up there takes leave of his senses again.

LINFORD CHRISTIE – A DEAD-END KID

IW wrote, 'If he relied on charm, he'd still be running,' but also had something to say in favour of Olympic gold medal sprinter Linford Christie.

THERE ARE ways and ways of getting your own back on a stifling summer's night. One is to go out and beat up an inner city. Another is to go to the Olympic Games and smash the world in the 100 metres.

Thank God that Linford Christie chose the latter.

It is no secret that as a young black man from the Caribbean he did not find London's streets paved with equality. Hopefully his riposte will prove inspirational to others who feel similarly crushed.

It was a run powered as much by maniacal determination as muscle and finely tuned technique.

The face was contorted, the concentration so intense that I don't think he once blinked. On this night, sprinting on a planet of his own, he was unbeatable and his victory margin, by Olympic standards, was absurd.

Americans have traditionally looked on the 100 metres as a banker victory. They have won it 15 times in 23 Games. Britons have won it thrice: Christie on Saturday night, Allan Wells in a final politically boycotted by the Americans in Moscow in 1980 and Harold Abrahams in Paris in 1924.

They made a film about the Abrahams triumph. It was called 'Chariots of Fire'. It was ludicrously inaccurate in many aspects but its central theme – what motivates a man to produce an indomitable performance on the great occasion – was not only uncomfortably true but uncannily prescient about another 100 metres final 68 years later.

Abrahams and Christie could scarcely have been raised in more contrasting environments. The Abrahams were comfortably middle class. Privileged schools, universities and solid professions were taken for granted. But what both men shared was a sense of rejection.

Harold Abrahams was a Jew in an era when anti-semitism was rife if hardly explicit. He was given a hard time at Cambridge where the style of the day was accomplishment without apparent effort. Any visible determination to violate that Corinthian code was derided as vulgar.

Abrahams certainly rocked that comfortable Establishment

243

punt. The nation lauded him when, visibly determined to the point of obsession, he not only won the 100 metres gold at the Paris Games but lowered the Olympic record to 10.6 seconds.

The parallel is inescapable and it is to be hoped that, like Abrahams after his triumph, Christie will now brush some of the chips from his shoulders, enjoy the status he has won for himself and continue to inspire kids to emulate him. In any case, with a good honest agent, he will be minimally £1 million better off by this time next year.

His victory, with the world watching, completed a probably unequalled 14-day period of triumph for British sport in the modern era. The line between strident American-style jingoism and justifiable pride may be rather thin but, for a country reeling under recession and attracting hoots of laughter because of the antics of some of our politicians, our sportsmen have tended to redress the balance in three great arenas.

On the acres of Muirfield Nick Faldo kept his nerve to win the Open Golf Championship from the strongest international field ever assembled. One Sunday later on the Hockenheim circuit Nigel Mansell virtually sealed off the world Grand Prix title from all foreign challenges. Yesterday was Christie's day, even if he didn't want to share it with many.

These are not easy men. They are absorbed in their own worlds, haunted by the demons of failure. Each has come through from an unprivileged background to great riches. They are unforgiving about some of the knocks they have received, particularly from the Press, on the way up.

But charm is scarcely a prerequisite of champions. Charm certainly did not win Linford Christie the blue riband title at the Barcelona Olympics. If he'd relied on charm he'd still be running.

What he did, more effectively than any parson or social worker or pontificating newspaper columnist, was to show the young rioters of Burnley and Blackburn that there is another road to travel. Sport demands no academic qualifications. If you show guts and determination it no longer even requires money.

Linford Christie came from nowhere to hit the top of the pile and remind the Olympic movement that he was what the Baron de Coubertin had in mind when he revived the Games.

He was not thinking about the established professional stars. What he had in mind was the kid convinced the world was against him, that there is no way out.

It isn't and there is. We saw it down 100 metres of Barcelona running track the evening before last and it was simply breathtaking to watch.

Chapter Eight
1993–1996

THE TOLLYGUNGE CLUB

In the early 1990s IW undertook a worldwide tour, writing about less well-known sports as well as the major events. 'Having begun the trail in the Hampshire village of Bashley, watching the local non-league football team,' he wrote, 'I stopped off in St Moritz and Monaco on my way to Calcutta, venue for the first Test against England.' The following episode in his global adventure rounded off his stay in India.

Dateline: **Tollygunge 1993**

IT IS 6.45 on a morning of ethereal beauty. The early sun electrifies the plumage of the blue jays and golden orioles circling above. White egrets, no longer required to sacrifice their feathers to the headwear of viceroys from afar, stroll confidently about.

Yet, this could have been the British India of 1893 and to compound the illusion Naib Risoldar Khaju Khan, late of the 61st Cavalry, green puggaree flying, lance lowered, yelling fit to instil fear into the bravest, sways from his saddle at full gallop, pierces the tiny wooden target through the heart and swirls it above his head.

The lance was invented to kill men. When they practised on wild animals it was known as pig-sticking. Today, it has become the thrilling equestrian sport of tent-pegging and the Naib Risoldar – he proudly retains his military rank of senior NCO – is a legendary exponent of it.

It runs in the family. His grandfather fought in France in the Great War with the Jodhpur Lancers. His father extended the tradition and today, Khaju Khan's own son is serving with the 61st Cavalry, the last fully mounted regiment in the Indian Army.

'We are soldiers and horsemen,' he said. In truth, Khaju Khan is now riding master at the Tollygunge Club on the outskirts of Calcutta. Early yesterday it was a century and many cultures removed from the great concrete stadium down the road where five hours later a new and jubilant India was to celebrate the defeat of England in a cricket Test match.

When the British Raj lowered the Union Jack here in 1946 it left behind 100 acres of England which are more English than England has in recent years become.

You turn off a teeming filthy street into a high-walled world of order, strict convention, impeccable manners and sport: riding, golf, croquet, tennis, billiards. Most of its members are Indians whose accents hint at Oxford or Cambridge, in some exaggerated instances both.

Bob Wright OBE, member-manager, was absent, recovering from a mild heart attack. His wife, Anne Wright MBE, is a delightful lady with a drawing room the length of three tennis courts and five cocker spaniels, one of whom surreptitiously bit my colleague, photographer Graham Morris. In the prevailing atmosphere of stiff-upper-lip stoicism, Graham took it on the calf without complaint.

Anne Wright led us down to the stables, probably the most hygienic place in India outside its five-star hotels, and introduced us to Khaju Khan. So help me, the Naib Risoldar flung up a salute straight out of Trooping the Colour.

Khaju Khan then mounted Starling, a chestnut stallion, and got to work. He is a supreme horseman and the tent-pegging was the proof of it.

Above: IW
admired the
many
achievements
of gold medal
winner Mary
Peters both on
and off the
track.

Right: With
Mark Phillips
and Jackie
Stewart, both
heroes in their
respective
sports of
equestrianism
and Formula 1.

IW found Lawrie Smith to be the most competitive of British ocean racing skippers.

During his world tour in 1993, IW disembarks from a submarine after inspecting wrecks in Pearl Harbor.

IW on board *Virgin Challenger II* in which his friend Richard Branson broke the speed record for an Atlantic crossing in 1986.

Princess Diana presents IW with a Creative Award for Sporting Achievement.

Another favourite gray, the show-jumper Milton, is greeted by the great tenor Luciano Pavarotti at an equestrian show in his home town of Modena.

IW and friends
(*left to right*)
Frank Bough,
Nigel Dempster,
Colin Moynihan
(then Minister of
Sport), Trevor
Bailey, Bobby
Robson, Des
Lynam, Leslie
Thomas, Cliff
Morgan,
Jonathan Palmer,
Stirling Moss and
Ross Benson.

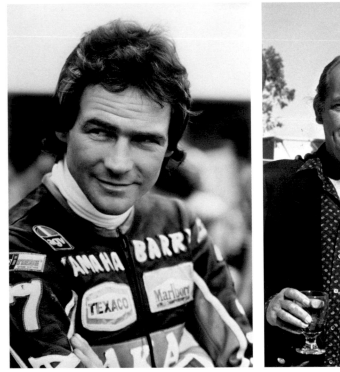

Above left: The name IW gave much-injured motorcyclist Barry Sheene was 'the nuts and bolts man'.

Above right: Frank Bruno – a terrific ambassador for British boxing.

Left: Unlike wife Sarah, IW was not suitably booted for the mud at 'Gatcombe Park'.

The sport has military undertones in that in the old days of ferment, siege and occasional mutiny the cavalry charged enemy encampments, lancing out their tent-pegs at high speed so that the canvas would collapse on infidels either sleeping the heat of the day away or drunk. Fearful slaughter would then ensue.

No more. It is now the highlight at gymkhanas and, as cavalry regiments the world over turn to tanks, is probably a dying art.

Anne Wright has tent-pegged but, then, there seems little in this world she hasn't done. Born in Liss, Hampshire, she was brought to India at the age of one, tomboyed her way on to tiger hunts, had a rifle of her own to shoot, in her own words, 'anything that moved', returned to Europe to be educated at English boarding and Swiss finishing schools and then came back to India and married Bob, who survived being blown up in a tank on D-Day. In the circumstances, it may surprise you that her MBE, received from the Queen, was for her work for the World Wildlife movement.

'I suppose I just got disgusted with the slaughter,' she said. 'Pig-sticking still goes on in some areas but tiger shooting for sport is now totally banned. Since 1972 you can get 15 years in prison for shooting a tiger that's only minding its own business.'

When England cricket teams came here before World War Two, a tiger shoot between Test matches was virtually obligatory. Now the massacres occur only at the wicket.

Anne Wright is always delighted to entertain David Gower, who has just arrived here to commentate for Sky TV and is similarly disposed to the conservation of wild animals.

It is a pity he has not been playing here these past five days, not that the outcome of the Test, one way or the other, would cause a facial muscle to move at the Tollygunge Club. British India still lives in the hearts of many of the members and even those who serve here.

The Naib Risoldar Khaju Khan is the classic example. 'Cricket?' he said, well knowing England's plight on the final morning of the Test. 'It does not interest me.'

He steered Starling back towards the stables and, as we moved back into the chaos and rising heat of downtown Calcutta, a morning of sheer magic was over.

LONE SHARK

IW continued his sporting circumnavigation of the globe by stopping off in the paradise islands of the Bahamas for a spot of deep-sea fishing. A non-swimmer and understandably rather nervous, IW wrestled with a feared denizen of the deep to give Daily Mail readers a taste of the thrills on offer to the winners of a holiday competition the newspaper was running at the time.

Dateline: **Bimini 1993**

JUST INTO the sixth hour, Bob Smith shut down the 300 horse-power twin engines and Bonita II began to wallow steeply on the turning tide. We were 11 miles out into the Gulf Stream, arguably the finest big-game fishing arena in the world.

Point one: if you are vulnerable to motion sickness, don't apply.

Point two: equally, don't enter if you have moral qualms about fishing. It can be a bloody business and your views are utterly respected even though they may hardly be compatible with the predatory cannibalism that has forever been the law of those that live and die beneath the sea.

Point three: having carefully considered points one and two, then come and join us. Bimini is an unspoilt paradise. The natives, white and black, are overwhelmingly friendly. The sea is 10 shades of turquoise. It is so far off the beaten track, despite being only 25 minutes by seaplane from Miami, that inside a day you'll be hard pressed to recall which political party, if any, is running the show back home.

I was diverted to the Bahamas on this world tour – no grim hardship I have to tell you – to establish benchmarks in three categories of sport fishing against which our competition-winning readers, hopefully as naive and unskilled at it as I am, may wish to set their sights.

Cards on the table. Yes, I have deep-sea fished on three previous occasions, never capturing anything more exotic than a 44lb wahoo off Bermuda some dozen years ago. Reef-fishing has yielded only a few insignificant specimens and inshore bone fishing, until yesterday, was an unknown science.

If prospective candidates consult the neighbouring time-and-catch table (on page 254), they will see that in two categories they have virtually nothing to beat. Bone fishing, requiring an experienced angler's touch, frustrated me for three hours until I got the vaguest hang of it. Reef-fishing is largely about luck.

It was Category Three, swaying out there over many fathoms in eerie silence, that enthralled me. I will be ecstatic if a *Daily Mail* reader beats that target because I know that in so doing he or she will have experienced the thrill of several lifetimes.

Cap'n Bob knows his business. He is 71 and has been fishing these waters for more than 50 years. We'd been trolling for ages at seven knots for a wahoo without success when he said: 'Okay, we'll try for a big one now, a marlin or a shark.' You sit there, mildly apprehensive that some invisible force will drag you head first over the transom into the Atlantic.

The Target to Beat

TYPE	TIME	CATCH
Bone fishing	*4 hours*	12 hooked, only two netted ... one of 2lbs and one of 4lbs
Reef-fishing	*6 hours*	Barracuda 3lbs, barracuda 8lbs, barracuda 12lbs, barracuda 15lbs, grouper 28lbs, grouper 35lbs
Deep-sea game fishing	*8 hours*	Hammerhead shark 413lbs

The Wooldridge haul in three different categories

It didn't happen like that at all. After only 20 minutes the pull was quite gentle. But then the reel began to screech out and whatever was down there started to run. He ran and ran and when he stopped, pulling against him was like trying to extricate Excalibur.

Very quietly, to keep the tension down, our fish-wise mate Alton said: 'This one's big. When he isn't pulling, stand up quickly.' And when he wasn't, Alton slipped a fighting harness beneath my hips and clipped two sturdy metal spring clips into rings behind the rod. 'You're okay now,' he said. 'The line will break before you go overboard.' This was somewhat reassuring since I've never learned to swim.

So began a fascinating contest. A few turns of the reel-spool, then a run by your opponent that takes 50 hard-earned yards off your advantage. By ducking the rod-head suddenly and then reeling fast, you can recover a little ground but for ages the fight is stagnant with the line taut between two wills with very different motives. Time exists no longer. It could have been 20 minutes or three hours. You get tired but the splendid Alton, who is not permitted to touch you or assist you in any way, other than vocally, was all concentrated encouragement.

'Hit him now,' he would suddenly say, and you reeled again.

But was it a marlin, the king of the seas? It was not. Even before the dorsal fin broke the surface. Bob Smith yelled from the bridge: 'Shark. Hammerhead.' Head down and praying that having got this far the line wouldn't snap, I saw little of it apart from the odd glimpse of the viciously thrashing tail.

Surprisingly, as I don't make a hobby of killing things, there was no sense of remorse. I don't like sharks and hammerheads, with their eyes spaced out like the wing-tip lights on aeroplanes, are the ugliest of the breed. Inshore he would have grabbed a small child bather for breakfast. A marlin would have been different. But we didn't get a marlin.

This struggle, I was later told, lasted 65 minutes and after Bob and Alton had expertly tied him alongside the boat and towed him in, he was scaled at 413lbs. No big deal. They catch sharks far bigger than that around here twice a week.

So there it is: the challenge that awaits you if you win this *Daily Mail* competition. All I can promise, if you meet the same luck offshore, is an aching back and arms that feel as if they have been elongated on some Inquisition rack.

Bone fishing is an altogether different scene. You skim out in a fast flat-bottomed boat, weave through narrow avenues between mangrove swamps and then wait in gently lapping water, utterly clear and only three feet deep. Even then I couldn't even spot a bone fish, let alone hook one, for the first three hours. Rudy Dames did the casting, frequently dropping the line 100 feet distant with all the accuracy of Eric Bristow. In 30 years he has caught 20,000 bone fish, some 19,500 of which have been thrown back. There was nothing wrong with his form this week. Twelve times he cast so impeccably that we got bites. On the first 10 occasions I'd lost them with insensitive jerky movements. Bone fish have brains as well as fight.

'They're having fun with you,' smiled Rudy. But eventually we netted two, one of two pounds, one of four. They are silver-green and very pretty and both, I hope, are back enjoying their freedom off the shores of Bimini. Reef-fishing is less serene but my haul of four barracuda and two grouper in six hours in prolifically stocked waters is nothing to write home about. Grouper are as tough as street fighters but the barracuda offered less resistance. It was less a benchmark than a target all our *Daily Mail* readers should comfortably beat.

But the shark? Or a comparable or bigger marlin? That may prove slightly more testing. It will certainly provide an enormous thrill for anyone who beats it and thrills are what this competition is about.

CASINO ROYALE

IW discovered that even the once exclusive Monte Carlo Casino had not escaped the effects of recession.

Dateline: **Monte Carlo 1993**

FOR MORE than a century heroes and villains, fools and philanderers, the fabulously rich and the soon-to-be destitute or even dead, have blazed the 70-yard trail from Monte Carlo's Hotel de Paris to the most illustrious casino in the world.

Winston Churchill played here, inscrutably by all accounts. Onassis was a flash investor, much to Jackie's evident displeasure. And in the days before the paparazzi shadowed royalty like leeches a former Prince of Wales – Charles's great-great grandfather, later to become Edward VII – was an enthusiastic punter when affairs of state were not too pressing.

One year he brought Lily Langtry, the most alluring of his mistresses. She wasn't mad about roulette it seems and, according to local legend, Edward attacked the tables with exclusively male cronies in a private salon.

He dined there one evening after gambling. When the pudding arrived on a vast trolley the silver cover was removed to reveal a genuine bonne surprise. There, totally naked, lay the most coveted courtesan in France.

There is no record of subsequent proceedings but I like to think the story is true, if only to suggest the present Prince of Wales is but a novice in these matters.

If you are interested at all in green-baize sport, the Monte Carlo Casino is the cathedral of it. Built in 1863, a baroque masterpiece with exquisite murals and bomb-burst chandeliers, its elegance contrived to keep the hoi polloi at bay and its mystique intriguing to the world.

Did desperate men lose their all here and go away and shoot themselves? Indeed they did. Did anyone really break the bank? I doubt it, but it is a fable the management is in no hurry to refute.

It is true that in 1966 a Briton named Norman Leigh carried £387,000 off the premises in a single week but, even given its relative value 27 years ago, it was a piffling sum by high-rolling standards. Today Kerry Packer will stake that on the turn of a single card. Anyway Norman Leigh was later found dead, penniless, in Portsmouth.

By then the Belle Epoque was over. Its death toll was finally sounded in 1968 when there occurred an event that registered nine on the Richter Scale with the players who would never have dreamed of arriving without black tie or jewels.

The Monte Carlo Casino installed slot-machines. One-armed bandits. The clattering furniture of the working classes on a cheap night out. An abomination that would attract coach parties from unspeakable places. A form of gambling so crudely elemental that even the dimmest in Las Vegas can understand it.

They remain there, admittedly relegated to side rooms to mitigate the profanity, but it still came as a shock to enter a neon-blazing salon named The Double Diamond where if you press the correct sequence of electronic buttons the pay-out – probably in AD 2093 – will be 1.5 million francs for a 10-franc investment.

It was, alas, not the only sign of these vastly changing and recessional times. Laid side by side, the gaming chambers of the Monte Carlo Casino would probably cover an area three times the size of Wembley. Yet at 11 p.m. two evenings ago there were fewer than 200 patrons in the entire establishment.

Yes, there were black ties and dinner jackets but they were all worn by croupiers, most of whom were standing in forlorn huddles round empty roulette, baccarat and chemin de fer tables lamenting the demise of the big spenders. Unlike their London counterparts, the croupiers of Monte Carlo are permitted to accept tips across the tables. Some bought farms or small hotels with them in the lavish old days.

There was action around roulette Table Three, however, though it must be said that James Bonds and exiled Balkan mini-royals were conspicuous by their absence. In fact, we were such a motley lot that I felt somewhat overdressed in suit and tie.

There were polo-necks, open necks, T-shirts, leather jackets and scuffed shoes. None of the 20 of us exactly looked as though he had a country estate to wager against the spinning wheel. Play was mostly random which was probably just as well. One of the most famous telegrams ever sent from Monte Carlo read: 'Cracked the system. Send more money.'

The croupiers are friendly, accommodating and brilliant. They can calculate winning odds as fast as a computer, use their rakes to flick chips the length of the table with mesmerising accuracy and can instantly remember – since, again unlike London or Las Vegas, the chips of each denomination are the same colour –

precisely on which square, line, corner or other territory of chance you have staked your money.

Any win rewarded by a modest tip is greeted with a chorus of gratitude. It's yet another indication, I guess, of just how deeply the world recession is biting. Never mind the trade figures, when Monte Carlo feels the pinch you know it's serious.

It was glorious, though, to sit there among the ghosts of a gracious, naughty, thrilling age. Away from the dreaded slot-machines an atmosphere of faded grandeur still survives.

How did we get on? It is not a question you should ever ask a gambler, but put it this way: I retained my amateur status.

JAMES HUNT – WINNER ON TRACK

This is IW's tribute to James Hunt, a friend for almost 20 years, who died in 1993.

JAMES HUNT was not born to die like the rest of us. It should have been in a Spitfire on the wrong end of a dogfight in the Battle of Britain, or at 190 mph braking too late into a perilous bend at Monza.

Then his pals, and not a few ladies, would have gone down to the pub and obeyed his last will and testament: toasting his arrival in some celestial sports centre where St Peter played golf off a two handicap and the archangels spent their days on the squash courts.

The grief would have been no less, but the end more appropriate. James lived life on the edge, concealing a massive intelligence beneath what many saw as public-school buffoonery.

Only after his racing days were over and he turned to BBC Grand Prix commentating, complementing the multi-decibel excesses of Murray Walker, did the nation understand from his command of English and his fearless appraisals the depths of this man.

Till then he was seen as a playboy, vroom-vrooming his way into the gossip and society columns, attracting women like the Adonis he almost was, and never lost for a happy word.

James almost died early in his motor-racing career when he somersaulted off the Oulton Park circuit and pitched upside down in a lake, trapped by his seat belts. They fished him out eventually and his reaction to the episode was a curious one. He continued to pelt headlong into his own motor-racing career but when his younger brother, David, sought to follow him on to the track, James refused to assist him in any way. 'It's too dangerous,' he said.

Only rarely do racing drivers acknowledge danger but, relaxed one evening, James did. 'Motor racing,' he said, 'is a simple straightforward deal. Spectators come to the track to see someone killed. They will deny it forever, but there's no doubt about it. They were there the day so-and-so died. Well, I find that a perfect contract provided someone's prepared to pay me £1 million a year for taking the risks.'

The day James almost demanded to die was 24 October 1976. It was pelting rain so hard on to the Mount Fuji track, 100 miles outside Tokyo, that James, surprisingly a modulated trade unionist at heart, vigorously informed the Japanese organizers that racing would have to be postponed until the following day.

'There can be no following day,' the intractable Japanese told him. 'Today or never.'

This presented a small snag to Hunt, who had to finish in third place or better in the Japanese Grand Prix to win the world championship. Within minutes he was campaigning as vehemently to get the race reinstated as he had been to get it delayed.

Conditions were so appalling that Niki Lauda, his main rival, pulled off after a single lap muttering 'insanity'. Hunt drove on in blinding spray. He burst a tyre at 180 mph, screamed into the pits where his brother, Peter, and I were standing, and thrashed out again. Half an hour later he was world champion.

Strangely, perhaps, this is not my happiest memory of James Hunt. It comes instead from São Paulo, Brazil, where in devastating heat I was wandering past a window which was suddenly rapped by knuckles and a beckoning hand.

A side door opened and James said: 'Come in here and keep your mouth shut.' Inside was the entire cast of the Brazilian Grand Prix, attempting to relax in the only air-conditioned room on the premises an hour before the start.

Some slept. Some appeared to sleep. Some looked apprehensive.

'B*******,' shouted James suddenly. 'You guys need a bit of fun.' At which point, suitably bribed by James, a Brazilian police band burst in and roused them with blaring military music. The siesta was over and Hunt, laughing, went to his car. It will be my abiding memory of the man who died yesterday. He stood for almost everything British sport lacks at the moment.

COLIN INGLEBY-MACKENZIE – CORINTHIAN SPIRIT

Colin Ingleby-Mackenzie was the sort of man whom IW much admired – one who lived life to the full. A witty, sophisticated man of the world, he was great company and not afraid to have a drink or place a bet.

THE OTHER night in Annabel's a number of cricket luminaries were discussing who, if anyone, could inject some semblance of inspiration into an England team drooping as visibly as Graham Gooch's moustache.

Barely moments had passed before there burst into their company a man for whom the night – it was around 1 a.m. – was still young. Much noise and laughter ensued to the point where a staid former president of MCC was seen involuntarily to slide a few inches down a wall.

It is ever thus in the company of A.C.D. Ingleby-Mackenzie (Eton, Hampshire, the City, Ascot and Aspinall's) who, at 59, has contrived to retain the countenance of a truant cherub and an enthusiasm for living that is sheerly infectious.

He was never quite good enough to play for England but in 1961, aged 27, he left an indelible mark on the game when he captained a journeyman Hampshire team to their first County Championship title in 66 years. The previous season they had finished 12th, so they were hardly on a roll.

The methods he employed to achieve this success veered from the merely alarming to the simply outrageous. He gambled on declarations that gave his senior professionals vertigo, geed them up with promises of exotic relaxation at the close of play and, when asked his philosophy on leadership, replied: 'Iron-fisted dictatorship. I absolutely insist that they get to bed before breakfast.'

It was all in stark contrast to the unrelieved doomsday depression that has enshrouded our England team, their leaders, their selectors and their administrators all this year.

First there was that rude, humourless, catastrophic tour of India with the all too predictable but unwarranted jibes about native food and hygiene. Next came this instant steam-rollering by Australia. To lose the Ashes before the end of July, no matter how well the young newcomers in the Australian side played, is less assassination than suicide. Graham Gooch is a magnificent batsman. His leadership, dogged by that air of slumped resignation, was never more apparent than a cookhouse corporal's. Keith Fletcher, for all his dynamism, might as well have been re-wallpapering his Essex home. The selectors, throughout, have been about as positive as the Tory party on Maastricht. And Ted Dexter, the supremo who once played this game like a god, contributed little more than a number of remarks which suggested he was seriously off with the fairies.

Rarely, if ever, in the history of English cricket have so many willing and bemused players owed so little to a management structure whose strategy appeared to stretch no further than physical jerks at dawn and copping a few extra quid for slapping beer advertisements on players who came and went like suburban commuters.

I have no idea how Colin Ingleby-Mackenzie, given the chance, would have tackled the task as supremo-cum-manager in the England dressing room. But, for a start, I can guess how he would have handled the tabloid Press who were giving Gooch and the team such a daily drubbing.

'Come in, chaps,' he would have said. 'To save you a lot of thoroughly worthy investigative journalism, I'll tell you tonight's programme. The chaps are a bit down now that the Australians are 961 for two so, after a few bottles of champagne in the dressing room, we shall be going to dinner and then on to a nightclub-casino of which I have the honour to be a member. There the England team will have the choice of roulette or watching a live sex show. We'd be delighted if you'd join us and please bring your cameras and girlfriends.'

And then, of course, he'd have a quiet supper with his players, listening, talking, planning, supporting, cajoling, enthusing.

When asked next morning why no one showed up, he'd reply: 'Got this sudden message, old boy. Whole place absolutely riddled with AIDS. I do hope all you chaps are all right.'

It's called leadership and the secret of leadership is that no one sees how it works. The gift is rare for it is as much about imagination as courage.

This weekend our cricket administrators foregather in the wreckage of our national game to attempt to pick up the pieces. None of the foregoing will interest them because to endorse a new way of going about it would jeopardize their own jobs. The only point is how could a certified lunatic, let alone A.C.D. Ingleby-Mackenzie, conceivably do worse?

SUMMERS WILL NOT BE THE SAME WITHOUT BRIAN JOHNSTON

Cricket commentator Brian Johnston died peacefully in his sleep yesterday after suffering a heart attack in December. He was 81. And last night, in seven simple words, John Major summed up his loss. 'Summers will not be the same again,' said the Premier. It was a sentiment echoed by millions of fans for whom – via his BBC radio broadcasts – Johnston was the personification of the game. Behind his schoolboy humour was a professionalism and a kindly nature which made him much-loved by all who knew him.

THERE WERE days at the Test matches when you suspected the BBC radio commentary team were simply praying for rain.

John Arlott, the epigram maker, would retreat to a corner with a bottle of claret, leaving the microphone at the mercy of Brian Johnston.

What followed was a torrent of anecdote and dormitory wit illuminated by the occasional well-rehearsed Bertie Woosterish gaffe.

The nation adored it. They adored Brian Johnston: the clipped inimitable Etonian voice, the essentially English humour, the permanent conviction that the world was a wonderful place even if it was raining cats and dogs outside the window.

'I've always been a frustrated comic,' he said late in the life that ended yesterday, never to be replaced in the uniqueness of his broadcasting style.

Less than a month ago when he collapsed, aged 81, he was heading to captivate a West Country audience with another of his two-hour one-man shows, 'An Evening with Johnners'. He didn't need the money. He was a consummate entertainer who loved an audience.

Actually, he was a mass of wonderful contradictions: a social conformist who affected the sort of brown-and-white co-respondent's shoes worn by his comedian hero, Max Miller; an Oxford BA who denied the remotest intellectual attainment; a man of extreme formal manners who, on receipt of a letter of pompous admonishment for one of his jokes, would reply on a saucy seaside postcard with the inevitable double entendre.

Born on 24 June 1912, at Berkhamsted, Hertfordshire, with several golden spoons in close proximity, his early life took a predictable course: Eton, Oxford, the family coffee business, the Grenadier Guards.

It was a chance meeting during his rugged service with the Guards Armoured Division (which earned him a Military Cross) that so dramatically changed it.

At the time of the Normandy landings, the Guards' mess was shared by Wynford Vaughan-Thomas, the celebrated BBC war correspondent. 'If we both get through this lot,' Vaughan-Thomas suggested to Johnston, 'come and see me sometime.'

Johnston did. Not long afterwards, having survived anything the Panzer divisions could hurl at him, he was back in Britain, microphone clenched in fist, while lying prostrate between rail-way lines as an express train roared over him.

Calmly he described the sensation, live on air, to the vast audience of 'In Town Tonight', a programme for which, week in week out, he performed outrageous stunts. Another was to stand in front of a dartboard while the British champion speared cigarettes out of his lips with six-inch nails. He had found his metier: radio.

All the while, cricket was his passion. Keeping wicket at Eton and New College gave him some knowledge of the game, but it was cricket's code of honour that transfixed him.

He was a staunch guardian of the game's ethics and a resolute critic of the Kerry Packer revolution, which saw both the introduction of pyjama-style uniforms and a serious decline in on-the-field chivalry.

Paradoxically, it was cricket that detonated his only serious clash with his BBC employers. When he was seconded to the TV commentary team, several regarded his perpetual jokes as trivializing the game. They sacked him. Johnners, deeply wounded, returned to radio and the more relaxed atmosphere of the Test Match Special team.

Admittedly, his jokes were remorseless. His favourite practical jape was to address a profound question to a colleague when he had a mouthful of cake. Johnners was big into cakes. He would virtually appeal for them over the airways.

On a single Test match day, as many as six would arrive in the commentary box, their donors knowing that the great man would acknowledge them by name to the listening millions.

His own sense of chivalry was expressed in an extraordinary manner. For 15 years, Brian Johnston travelled all over Britain to interview more than 4,000 mayors, town clerks, fishermen, Women's Institute jam-making champions and assorted eccentrics for his weekly 'Down Your Way' programme. He never missed an assignment through illness or weather.

After 733 'Down Your Ways', he abruptly quit. It was his personal tribute to his predecessor, Franklin Englemann, who had also fronted the programme exactly 733 times before his retirement.

His broadcasting won him the OBE and the CBE, earned by the immense professionalism that he loved to conceal behind the perpetual banter.

Brian Johnston leaves an ever-supportive wife, Pauline, five children, numerous grandchildren and a nation of listeners who hung on to his very last word.

CHELTENHAM FESTIVAL – A MEETING OF FRIENDS

IW loved his annual visits to the Cheltenham Festival for the racing, the hospitality and the company of so many friends, old and new.

Dateline: **Cheltenham 1994**

IT IS NOT a habit of mine to address you from a gentlemen's lavatory at a sporting mecca but the scene in just one of them 20 minutes before yesterday's Cheltenham Gold Cup captured the magnetism of this glorious event.

Twelve stalls, between seven and nine men queueing at each, a few discreetly dancing from foot to foot. Many, after all, had been drinking since dawn. Some had never been to bed.

It was about as comfortable as a wartime troop train or a Tokyo tube in the rush hour. There was no shoving or pushing, much ribald humour and widespread conviction that this just had to be Jodami's year. These were racing men as distinct from the peacock stockbrokers who escort their trophy wives to Royal Ascot.

The crush was no less in any quarter of this magic fold in the Cotswolds. The bars were jammed, the lines for food were out of *Schindler's List*, the jam to donate still more of the house-keeping to Tote or bookie was ridiculous. Outside, the biting wind was like razor blades across the face.

God knows why we keep returning to this compacted mayhem but we do, year after year, because there is no sporting event to compare with it. This year we rushed from Bali, Indonesia, to get here because a year without the Cheltenham Festival is a year without Christmas.

Mutually we leave our brains behind at the Gloucestershire frontier post. Thereafter time has no meaning, money no value. Tomorrow is a distant future of hangover and, almost certainly, at least temporary poverty. We are with like souls, that is the truth of it.

Practically anyone you want to meet is at the Cheltenham Festival. Yesterday these ranged from the ubiquitously sporting Princess Royal to that vastly misunderstood professional footballer, Mr Vinnie Jones. Alas, the Queen Mother was resting after two days of relentless excitement. But she, of course, remains the patron punter of the event. There is a delightful streak of madness in them all.

On St Patrick's Day it was probably the safest place in all England because had the IRA planted a bomb in the mayhem it would have killed as many of their own as of us.

I only wish the bigots of both sides would actually come to one of these Festivals. They might learn a thing or two about tolerance. Yesterday Irishmen, with faces veined like roadmaps, laughed, drank and bet with Englishmen in British military uniforms, one of whom had taken the precaution of tying a label emblazoned with his home address to his epaulette as a precaution against anticipated amnesia. Mr Gerry Adams and the Reverend Ian Paisley were noticeable by their absence. Neither, it would appear, wished to know how well the rest of us can get along together.

Anglo-Irish accord? Come to Cheltenham and you will realize that anything is possible.

The minutes approaching the Gold Cup rank with anything

in sport for rising excitement. It is not so much the money, unless you are a Lloyds victim with his last throw on the race, as the sheer spectacle of it: the bravest horses with the bravest men upon them. It is surpassed only by the sight of them coming off the last bend, faced now by the appalling climb up the cruellest hill in racing. A blemish of spirit, either equine or human, here will be cruelly exposed.

Up this incline we have witnessed many of the great dramas: Burrough Hill Lad, Dawn Run, Desert Orchid. Yesterday Jodami, overwhelmingly the gents' loo favourite, couldn't sustain it.

The noise was deafening but the triumph was French-Spanish-Polish as The Fellow, with his downbeat English name but owned by a Spanish marquesa, trained by a Frenchman and ridden by a Polish-born jockey, finally took his place in history.

There was no argument about it. Jodami came back at him again over the final fence but, after all his near misses, this was clearly The Fellow's day at last.

Sportsmanship reigns supreme at this game. In the face of devastating disappointment, unended after months of planning and preparation, physically exhausted after two circuits around the most testing territory, jockeys have the grace to congratulate their conquerors. They are wild men, many of them, but they engender a degree of sportsmanship long and regrettably lost in so many other professional fields.

Gold Cup day ends in a detritus of torn tickets, men reaching for chequebooks to buy the last bottle, and the occasional scene of triumph. A few years ago here I watched three men, after a successful day, hail a cab for their next venue.

'And where, gentlemen,' said a Gloucestershire cabbie anticipating late-night television at home with his wife, 'would you like to go?'

'Murrayfield,' they said.

'Murrayfield? Where's that?' asked the driver.

'Edinburgh, Scotland,' they replied. 'There's a rugby international being played there on Saturday and that's where we'd like to go.'

They went. They also took the cabbie to the match. Four days later he rejoined his wife in Cheltenham for late-night television.

That's Cheltenham. You wouldn't miss it for worlds. You will cross half the world to get there. Real life is suspended here. You will lose. And you will keep coming back until the great handicapper in the sky decrees otherwise.

KEITH MILLER SET THE CRICKET WORLD ALIGHT

IW was not alone in finding Keith Miller the most glamorous of sporting heroes on the field of play, and during the following years they became close friends.

H E WAS just 24 the day war ended and what he most vividly remembers was the silence. No flags, no high jinks, no drunken revelry. Only the silence across the vast bleak airfield at Great Massingham in Norfolk.

The fighting planes of 169 Squadron were redundant. No more early-evening briefings before the nightly probes over Cologne or Essen. No more empty chairs at breakfast. He'd piloted Mosquitos, always at night, protecting big Lancasters to their targets. Brave men acknowledged fear and he'd known fear all right. He'd crash-landed once and walked away unscathed. But now it was over and he was still half the world from home.

'I simply stood there,' he recalled, 'and thought, "What the hell am I going to do now?" I'd never felt so lonely.'

Home was Australia where in 1941 he and his oppo, Johnny Hosking, had volunteered from the Royal Australian Navy. 'Johnny was far better educated than me,' he said, 'but he failed some test so we told the Navy to stuff it and went round the corner and joined the Air Force.'

At the time he was better known in Australia as a Rules footballer than cricketer but, ironically, it was cricket that possibly saved his life. On a Sunday in 1943, headquartered now at a hotel in Bournemouth, he was invited to play for the RAAF team in London. In his absence the Luftwaffe bombed the hotel at lunchtime and killed several of his mates in a bar in which he would inevitably have been drinking.

These may be black recollections with which to welcome back to this country Keith Ross Miller who, bracketed with our own Denis Compton, was the most charismatic cricketer I ever saw. But there is no doubt it was war that put the rest of his life into perspective. Every moment was to be lived, no 'incident' on the cricket field worthy of discussion a moment later.

Merely to watch him come down the steps at Lord's, grinning broadly, Hollywood-handsome, tossing back that mane of hair, dragging on his batting gloves with his teeth, afraid of nothing, ready for anything, inspired a generation of schoolboys into pathetic imitation. Our mothers didn't swoon in those days but they swallowed hard.

Miller's lonely desolation on VE-Day was soon over. He was invited into an International XI to play England in the Victory Tests of 1945 and no greater series has ever been staged in this country.

'The reason,' says Miller, acknowledging the terrors of a war that claimed so many adolescent lives and shaped the characters of those who survived, 'was that we didn't give a bugger whether we scored a century or a duck. We were alive.' Miller, in that Victory series, plastered the English bowling all round the grounds. In a huge innings at Lord's he shrapneled the wall above the radio commentary box with the second biggest hit ever seen on the ground.

He bowled, too. 'What does this chap bowl?' queried Bob Wyatt, former England captain, who had never heard of Miller. 'Don't know, sir,' came the reply. Miller loped in off a few strides and bowled Wyatt first ball.

That Victory series of 1945 established him and he was set on a career for Australia unparalleled in cricket. It was not merely his capacity for dismembering an attack or a burst of fast bowling that could turn a Test in six overs. It was the style of the man, the huge *joie de vivre* that related sport to real life and always saw him turn up late for nets before the Lord's Test in full morning dress. He'd just come back from the opening races at Royal Ascot.

He never questioned umpires or fell about embracing colleagues at the fall of an opposition wicket. 'I guess you don't do those sort of things,' he said, 'when you've known what it's like to have a Messerschmitt up your ass.'

Earthy, handsome, adored by women, an inveterate gambler, a society catch – Lord Mountbatten once sent a car to collect him at close of play at Southampton so he could partner Princess Margaret at dinner at Broadlands – he earned barely a penny from the game to which he contributed such esoteric distinction.

Unlike so many old-timers, it doesn't bug him. He is full of praise for the young Australians who have just up-ended West Indies, well knowing they earned more from a brief Test series than he did in his entire life for Australian cricket.

'But I'd like to see all cricketers being a bit more generous to one another,' he said. 'If Compo took 50 or 100 off us,

I'd always go down the wicket and congratulate the old bastard. Compo would do the same to me.' Keith Miller and Denis Compton have been friends for life. Forty years on they speak every week on the phone, mostly swapping horse-racing tips.

This week they are together again. Today they will be at The Oval for a celebrity match to commemorate not so much VE-Day as the tumultuous unofficial Test series of 1945 which followed it, matches which convinced Keith Miller that he truly had something to contribute in what remained of his life.

Miller, statistically, is 75 now but he's packed so much into a life that could have been extinguished in his early 20s that in reality he's about 120. 'What a bastard,' he said, struggling out of a taxi with the stick that has to support his recent surgery.

'Was that really Keith Miller?' asked the taxi driver. 'Yes,' I confirmed. 'Christ,' he said, 'have I got something to tell my son.'

I've had something to tell my sons about Keith Miller for years. It was about the day I absconded from school in 1948 to watch the great man bat for Australia at our local county ground. In a single over he struck three sixes out of the premises.

Many years later, as a fledgling cricket reporter on this newspaper, I met Miller for the first time in the bar on the same ground. 'Mr Miller,' I said – 'Keith,' he reprimanded – 'do you remember hitting three sixes in an over on this ground?'

'No,' replied Miller, 'all the bloody grounds look the same to me now. Have a drink.'

Profligate of talent, generous of spirit, occasionally outrageous of conduct, unfazed by acclamation and indifferent to any form of authority, Keith Miller is back not only to endorse today's match at The Oval but remember his friends of the RAF and RAAF who didn't make it beyond their early 20s. 'Poor bastards,' he said. You have to understand the Australian language to appreciate his tribute to the men without whose sacrifice you and I would not be waking up to freedom this morning.

FRED PERRY PLAYED TO WIN

Fred Perry was the only truly great English tennis player, having won Wimbledon three times (1934–36) and having also taken the three other major championships – US, French and Australian.

Dateline: **London 1995**

WE SANG all the big-hit hymns at Fred Perry's glorious memorial service in St Paul's Cathedral yesterday but the main event was a singles match between Tony Trabert, American ex-tennis champion, and Rudyard Kipling, composer of heroic verse.

In the pulpit, Mr Trabert, being an American, was not everyone's choice to deliver the valediction on the greatest British tennis player who ever lived. Trabert won 6–0, 6–0, 6–0 because, with humour and great affection, he cut through all the cant.

Kipling wrote two immortal lines in his famous poem 'If'. They read:

If you can meet with Triumph and Disaster . . . and treat those two imposters just the same.

This tosh, though nobly written, is inscribed above the portal through which every Wimbledon finalist has to walk before his or her appearance on Centre Court and is just about as appropriate in the context of modern tennis, where triumph means many millions of dollars and disaster means just a few million fewer, as at the Normandy landings. In short, this one you have to win.

The poem has four verses, each read in turn by Virginia Wade, John Newcombe, Pete Sampras and Martina Navratilova, standing in for the injured Steffi Graf.

It is a stirring poem from another age but to anyone who knew Fred Perry, the son of a Socialist MP from the wrong side of the social tracks, it was about as absurd an evocation of his fighting spirit as anyone could muster.

Fred wanted to win everything, which is why he took the men's singles title at Wimbledon in 1934, 1935 and 1936 and won Davis Cup after Davis Cup for Britain. Off court in his later days, he was the most considerate encourager of both young tennis players and young journalists.

So yesterday when Trabert, the American who won Wimbledon in 1955, slipped into the witness box of the pulpit we heard some truth.

Perry, badly injured on one occasion, asked a certain opponent to go easy on him in a match he knew he was going to lose. His opponent ignored the supplication. Perry, now fully fit, obliterated him 6–0, 6–0, 6–0 at their next meeting. Roused, Fred Perry could be the bastard *in excelcis*.

Until that story, the ceremony was misguidedly beginning to make a paragon out of a man who had to blow away layers of social prejudice even to be recognized.

'Fred,' Trabert said, 'was a rascal, a terrific man who could be a little sarcastic and loved to needle you.'

That was Fred. Losing Kipling-wise, treating disaster as a mere imposter, was not his style.

There were lots of reporters bustling around St Paul's wanting to know why the Duchess of Kent, the loyalest of royal tennis patrons, sent only a representative. The Press representative in charge said he did not think she attended memorial services of 'ordinary' persons.

So be it. Fred Perry was about the least ordinary British sportsman I have ever met because he won world titles when it was almost indecent for a scion of the British working class to do so.

Fred Perry was a friend and mentor and it took Trabert, an American, to get his real value through to a vast British congregation.

TIP AND MR PALMER

Other journalists focused on Arnold Palmer but IW introduced his readers to the other half of a great partnership.

Dateline: St Andrews 1995

A 500-YARD STROLL separates the Dunvegan bar from the Road Hole at St Andrews and such were the demands on the great man that it took us half an hour.

Some, knowing this will positively be his last Open Championship, merely wanted a brief chat. Three asked him to pose for photographs. Five requested autographs and each time he signed, not with some imperious scrawl but with careful calligraphy. He had a kindly word for all of them until someone shouted: 'Hey, Tip, when does Arnie get in?'

'Mr Palmer,' corrected James Anderson with Jeevesian hauteur, 'arrives tomorrow evening in his private jet.'

James Anderson is Arnold Palmer's caddie. They've been together for 35 years but private friendship does not permit gratuitous informality. Over a drink he will call the master Arnold but on the course, with packed galleries craning to catch the legendary word-play between the most famous star-caddie partnership in golf, it is still strictly 'Sir' or 'Mr Palmer'.

Nor would Palmer ever dream of calling Anderson Anderson. It is always 'Tip', the nickname which by a momentous misunderstanding brought them together in the first place.

This week they work together for a last time neither had honestly expected. At 65 Palmer had been ruled out of this year's Open Championship by age limit, but with estimable pragmatism the Royal and Ancient merely changed the rules to get Palmer back one last time, and the first thing Palmer did was instigate a chain of messages from America saying 'Get me Tip'.

This can be a complicated business. Tip has neither phone nor fax in his St Andrews cottage. He has no need to tout for trade. But the message got through and Tip metaphorically came to attention and went into training. Tip, like most of Scottish caddie masonry, loves a drink. 'Mr Palmer has always been aware of that,' he said, 'but he also knows that when I work for him I cool it.'

Anderson is 63 and some of the biggest galleries ever seen will follow this partnership, total age 128 years, around the Old Course for at least two rounds, four if Palmer makes the halfway cut. It is an experience none should miss for this is golf from another age, a duo from another stage.

Typical exchange:

'How many yards, Tip?'

'Seven iron, Mr Palmer.'

'You'd better be right, Tip.'

'I am, Mr Palmer.'

Palmer hits a seven iron into the heart of the green and asks: 'How many yards, Tip?'

Anderson replies: '173, Mr Palmer, but I didn't want to put you off.'

Palmer, to crowd: 'He doesn't need me out here at all.'

So it goes on, hole after hole. It's not Laurel and Hardy because an Open Championship is a deadly serious business but it's huge theatre, a seemingly telepathic relationship between the multi-millionaire who made modern golf what it is with his bravura go-for-broke hitting and a lugubrious Scot with deadpan humour.

Telepathy, of course, doesn't enter into it. Tip Anderson simply knows the Old Course at St Andrews. So he should. Since the age of 14 he has caddied round it slightly more than 10,000 times.

With professionals and low handicap players one round is a walk of 3.5 miles. With hackers it is more like five. Give it an average of just over four and you find that he has walked some 46,000 miles round the Old Course, getting on for the equivalent of twice round the world.

It is in the genes, too, since his father was a St Andrews caddie for 40 years and it was that which inadvertently led to him becoming Palmer's Man Thursday.

In the late 1950s the Americans had all but deserted the Open Championship. In 1960 Palmer, the new American shooting star, decided to enter. He cabled St Andrews asking for the services of the most experienced caddie in town. 'We've got you Tip Anderson,' they replied. The confusion arose because Tip's dad was also known as Tip, so called because between his assignments as a caddie he picked up pin money chalking the tips of billiard cues in an Italian fish shop which had installed a couple of tables to attract custom. When the call came Tip Senior, who had never heard of Arnold Palmer, sent his son, who had inherited his father's nickname.

'*You're* Tip Anderson?' exclaimed Palmer as he met the

28-year-old outside the R and A clubhouse. 'I was expecting a much older and more experienced man.'

'Aye,' replied Tip Junior. 'That's my father. You've got me instead.'

The frosty start hardly improved when their first practice round was played in a high gale that made accurate clubbing difficult but then everything gelled. In the Open itself Tip Junior handed Palmer the clubs and Palmer, on his first visit to Britain, hit them with blazing intensity. Palmer lost to the Australian Kel Nagle by a single shot but by then the rapport had been established. Palmer trusted Tip, Tip adored Palmer for his style and impeccable manners.

The following year Anderson carried for Palmer at Royal Birkdale. They won the Open. The year after that Anderson carried for Palmer at Royal Troon. They won the Open.

Christmas cards, family joys and sorrows were exchanged. Invitations for Tip to visit the Palmer home in Pennsylvania were issued but Tip didn't go. He has never left Britain or been in an airplane in his life. He was simply Mr Palmer's man for the Open.

They last appeared together at St Andrews in 1990, when Palmer, on level par, missed the halfway cut by a single shot and flew off into the sunset on the wings of nostalgia. But it wasn't over and this week their last hurrah together is a bonus for those of us who believe golf must be something more than automatons playing to computerized yardages.

Tip Anderson didn't hit a golf ball himself until he left school at 14 but by 16 he was junior champion of St Andrews, which means, in this academy of golf, that if he'd ever been given a handicap it would have been around four or better. He makes light of it. 'Never good enough,' he said, 'which is why I stayed with caddying.'

Have master and man ever had a row out there on the course?

'Never,' said Tip. 'We have had exchanges of opinion but obviously Mr Palmer is the boss and there was one occasion when he was absolutely right.'

It was back in 1960 on his first appearance at St Andrews. Coming to the fearful Road Hole, the 17th, Palmer drove immaculately in the first three rounds and asked 'What now, Tip?'

Each time Anderson said: 'Six iron, Mr Palmer.' Each time Palmer hit it flush into a notoriously placed green in two and then three-putted for bogey fives.

In the final round he refused Tip's protestations and struck a five iron which flew over the green into the road. Palmer chipped back and putted down for four. 'There's no accounting,' said Tip mysteriously.

But there is some accounting. Caddies today work on percentage systems with their golfers. Never in 35 years has Tip Anderson discussed money with Arnold Palmer. 'I receive a cheque,' he said, 'and it is always extremely generous.' The amounts? Thumbscrews could not induce him to divulge anything.

'Mr Palmer,' said Tip Anderson, 'is a gentleman.'

FRED TRUEMAN – A BOWLER IN A MILLION

For a dozen years or more I have had his portrait above my writing desk. When energy and inspiration are reaching zero, I can still see him pounding in off that frightening run and the blood begins to surge again.

FRED TRUEMAN always took an enormous psychological advantage into the Test cricket arena. It was the conviction that all foreigners are rubbish. Mind you, it didn't stop there. He felt exactly the same about most Londoners, anyone who voted Labour, all homosexuals and vegetarians, the entire hierarchy at Lord's and practically every cricket writer except John Arlott. Xenophobia for Fred started where the 30 mph limits ran out at either end of his native mining village of Maltby in Yorkshire.

I exaggerate, of course. But, then, almost everything about Fred is exaggerated, including himself. He has attracted more apocryphal stories, mostly about social clangers and alarming undiplomatic incidents, than any English sportsman, living or dead.

Happily, Fred Trueman is still with us. At least he was late last night when those of us who truly love the old booger were still celebrating his 65th birthday at the Park Lane Hilton. Early on Fred was in a slightly subdued mood. You could tell that because he didn't address the Prime Minister as 'Sunshine', a clever device when you can't recall someone's name.

But there are two things you could never exaggerate about Fred Trueman. The sheer theatre of watching him come down that parabola of a run, hair flying, with an action second only to Ray Lindwall's in modern cricket is one. The second is the intensity with which he played for his England. It was our England as well, of course, but Fred never accepted that. 'Listen, Sunshine, I'm the poor bastard out there doin' it.' Modesty has never afflicted him. He wanted to entitle his autobiography *The Greatest Fast Bowler who Ever Drew Breath* because he believed it. And for a few years at the zenith of his long career he was perfectly justified.

At Edgbaston in 1963, rain had so disrupted the Test that no result was conceivable against a fortress of West Indian batting. We were still playing cards when Fred came on to bowl on the last afternoon. We soon stopped. Fred took six wickets in 24 balls. England won by 217 runs with three hours to spare.

I first met him on the *Canberra* sailing down to Australia for the Test series of 1962–3. Fred immediately announced he was brassed off. Gordon Pirie, the renowned British long-distance runner, was also aboard and had been co-opted to organize some strenuous exercises for England's cricketers to strengthen their legs. 'Just look at 'is legs,' snarled Fred. 'They'd bloody break off before he'd bowled three overs. He's a nutter.' Trueman's suspicion proved right. The moment we arrived, Pirie, shocked that cricketers actually drank beer, sold a story to an Australian newspaper that the England team were a bunch of drunks.

It was a bizarre assembly. England's manager was the grand old Duke of Norfolk, who took an instant shine to Fred because he'd never met anyone like him. There was also the Rev David Sheppard, who'd been temporarily released from saving souls for the even greater calling of opening the England batting.

In the Melbourne Test, in enormous heat, Fred toiled unchanged for 90 minutes at the obdurate Bill Lawry, luring him from leg and middle stumps eventually to nick one into the slips. At last it worked. The catch flew to Sheppard, who dropped it. There have been many versions of the exchange that followed but the most accurate was that Trueman advised the now Bishop of Liverpool to imagine it was Sunday and keep his hands together. Actually, I've cleaned up the text for family consumption.

Fred could be outrageous, never more so than on that Saturday morning against Australia at The Oval in 1964 when he was chasing the then unknown target of 300 Test wickets. Early on he bowled so erratically that Ted Dexter, his captain, was forced to take him off. Just before lunch Dexter stood at the Pavilion End dithering about who next to put on. Trueman made up his mind for him. He snatched the ball out of Dexter's hands and said, 'Watch this.' With his last two deliveries before lunch he claimed his 298th and 299th Test victims. Never before had a vast Oval crowd reassembled before lunch was over. They were rewarded with Fred's 300th wicket. He didn't dance around and there were none of the high-fives of the present era. He just put his hands on his broad hips and grinned.

I recalled the ovation last evening as the great, the good, the not-so-good, showbiz people, his former captains, icons from other sports, statesmen, politicians, men he has had terrible rows with and his great oppo, Brian Statham, gathered at the Hilton to celebrate the fact that, in spite of everything, Fred Trueman had made 65. Statham's top-table presence was particularly welcome. In harness with Fred, he bowled so accurately from the other end that frustrated batsmen tended to take liberties with Trueman and lost their wickets. More recently, when Statham hit a bad patch in business, Trueman was the first to organize a fund-raising event. Naturally, if you even mentioned this to Fred he would invite you to perform a function requiring considerable imagination and much dexterity.

He has never compromised. Many will complain that he has

become something of a grouch in his recent years as a radio cricket commentator, that he finds very little that now happens on the field comparable with the achievements of *his* day. The problem is that, apart from the fielding department, he is quite right. Fred could be awful. Fred could be truculent, bombastic, impetuous and argumentative. He could also be generous and very kind to fledgling reporters. The bottom line is that Fred bowled his guts out for England. It was why England honoured him in London last night.

CARRYING THE OLYMPIC FLAME

The crowds roared to greet the arrival of the Olympic flame in Atlanta, ferried to the city by, among others, IW, who shared his memories of the part he played in the longest relay of all.

Dateline: **Atlanta 1996**

IT HAD BEEN lit on Mount Olympus, Greece, flown westwards across the Atlantic, carried a zigzagging 10,113 miles through 42 American states and now, on the 84th and final day of its journey, it was blazing a fiery path down the hill to the BP filling station on the corner of Peachtree Road, Atlanta, Georgia.

There was only one prevailing thought in the mind of the 9,811th runner in the Olmpic Torch relay chain: 'For God's sake don't drop the bloody thing.'

Well we didn't, though in the maelstrom of the change-over anything might have happened. A quick embrace from runner

9,810 – a plump, matronly lady charged with emotion – and we turned and ran at the head of an extraordinary cavalcade.

There were escort runners at either shoulder, two flanking police motor cyclists, a fleet of police cars with blue lights swirling and klaxons blazing and, just ahead, out-rider cops clearing safe passage and assuring that some maniac didn't dart from the pavement to snatch the Torch in a moment of excitement or inebriation.

Most extraordinary of all was that this happening occurred at shortly before two o'clock in the morning and the streets were still jammed with thousands of spectators cheering, clapping or simply roaring.

Not, I add, for the scarcely athletic figure who was breathing rather hard by the time he moved uphill, but for the symbol he bore in his right hand. It weighs three-and-a-half pounds and you have to watch it because it can set fire to your hair.

It had been like that all day. The Torch began its final leg at 4.45 the previous morning on Stone Mountain, an ironic landmark since in the dark days of Atlanta's deeply racist past, this was where the Ku Klux Klan nightly set ablaze its notorious fiery cross.

By mid-morning, when the Torch reached the metropolitan outskirts, the crowds were six and seven deep and spilled out into its path so frequently that its scheduled progress was severely slowed. I was assigned to start my 600-yard stretch from the petrol station at 11.49 p.m. In fact, I took it at 1.53 a.m. precisely.

For that I was grateful. The scorching heat of the day had slackened but the humidity was still stifling and my heart went out to the marathon runners who will be pounding these same streets a few days from now.

Another irony of the Olympic Torch Relay from Greece to the host city of the quadrennial Games is that it was conceived by about as nasty a bunch of thugs who have ever lived. The

Nazis dreamed it up for the Berlin Olympics of 1936, allowing the flame to be carried only by bronzed, strapping, handsome men striding through avenues of swastikas as fine Aryan trail-blazers of the new master race.

Conspicuously that was not the case during the Torch's route across America. The young have carried it and so have the old. Fat ladies and emaciated men have carried it, many of them nominated by their own townsfolk for outstanding social work among drug addicts and young offenders.

One teenager, severely crippled in a car accident and seemingly condemned to a wheelchair for life, was entered by his local community five months ago as a target incentive.

'You have never seen anything more moving,' said a lady organizer who has accompanied the relay throughout. 'He took the torch and staggered and struggled and fought his way on foot down his section. It had been shortened slightly and it took him half an hour. The whole town turned out to watch and cheer him on and when he finally got there, I tell you this, I have never seen so many people in tears.'

In my own assembly of runners there was a jolly woman whose charity fund-raising for her district is legendary. It was later I discovered she has recovered from two bouts of cancer and is now in a third spell of remission. One of my escorts was Mark Tallent, a sales manager. His pregnant wife, Amy, was with him. So were his sister, Beverley, his brother-in-law and their two kids, Kasey, aged seven, and Kayla, five. They were still there to greet us when we returned at 2.30 a.m. a classic close-knit family.

I have written as cynically as anyone about the commercialism and devious politicking of the Olympic movement in recent years and do not retract a word of it.

This was, nevertheless, a valuable insight into the sheer joy and enthusiasm that the Games can bring to a community. I am grateful that they allowed an Englishman to participate for those were 600 yards of life's passage I shall never forget.

All day yesterday, the flame wound its way round Atlanta's packed streets until, near nightfall, it was passed into the hands of its 9,993rd and penultimate runner. His name was Al Oerter, an all-American discus thrower who won the event at four successive Olympics.

Then, to a roar that split the heavens, it was borne into Atlanta's Olympic Stadium.

Some will claim that it has been unextinguished since it was lit from the sun's rays on Mount Olympus, Greece, by two alleged virgins all those weeks ago.

It isn't *quite* true but at least your correspondent had the fortune to pass it on in good condition.

CLIFF MORGAN – VOICE OF THE RHONDDA

In the 1950s Cliff Morgan was the great fly-half for both Wales and the British Lions – and later he had an equally remarkable career as a broadcaster.

THE DANGER in writing about legends aged 66 is that the reader is suddenly alarmed that he's plunging into an obituary notice.

Fear not and hallelujah. This morning, as on most Saturday mornings these past nine years, the Voice of Trebanog will be introducing the BBC's 'Sport on Four'. It's a little gruffer now from all those Silk Cut, but the unmistakable cadences of the Rhondda link us through arguably the most sensible programme on radio sport. There is no striving for Burtonian resonance or Dylan Thomas rhetoric. Clifford Isaac Morgan is no professional Welshman.

The second Christian name is no surprise when you know a little of his boyhood. There were no ball games on the Sabbath and even the Sunday newspapers lay unopened until Monday. It was classic valley culture: chapel, choir practice on Wednesdays, the zinc tub by the living-room fireside when Dad came back from the mine, fish and chips if the housekeeping ran to it on the eve of pay day. The home reading syllabus was the Bible, Shakespeare, *David Copperfield*, *Pears Cyclopaedia* and the *Western Mail*. It was a frugal, very happy home.

To this living room one morning came two men bearing £5,000 in large white fivers and a post-dated cheque for a further £2,500. Cliff Morgan had never seen a £5 note. Now 1,000 of them would instantly be his if he signed to play professional rugby league with Wigan. The cheque could be cashed after he'd stayed with Wigan for six months. At the property prices of 1952 he could have bought eight cottages down his street.

Cliff's mum cooked the visitors bacon, eggs and black pudding for breakfast and said Cliff wasn't going anywhere.

Well, he was but it was to play for glory and no money as an amateur for Cardiff, Wales and the British Lions as the most brilliant international outside-half of his generation. When, eventually, the reflexes slowed and the cheering died, he was a national idol. And financially broke.

Desperation was the springboard to such a remarkable career in public life that his autobiography *Beyond the Fields of Play* is not only obligatory reading for the rugby union players who can now run Porsches and domestic staffs but parents who remonstrate when their kids get a good clip round the ear when they run amok at school. The Rhondda taught resilience and, by heavens, Morgan has needed that.

He chose freelance journalism, a precarious field at the best of times, sheer quicksands when you have less business sense than a parrot on a stick. Morgan has no business sense at all. While less celebrated 'personalities' would claim anything from £1,000 to £3,000 plus expenses to speak at a dinner, Morgan would drive to some outlandish rugger club after an exhausting working day to speak for nothing. Memorial services, weddings, reunions, Cliff was your man. He once flew down to Sydney, Australia, to present some sportswriting awards and was back inside four days.

Cliff has great contacts. As chairman of London's Saints and Sinners Club there was huge curiosity as to whom he would produce as his speaker for the annual lunch. He wheeled in Princess Anne, the only woman ever to address this esoteric assembly. All for no money, of course, but Morgan doesn't bitch about that in his book. He simply admits he's a man who can never say No. Only two days ago he gave the main address at the funeral of his great friend and Welsh rugby international colleague, Clem Thomas.

His rise and rise in broadcasting was phenomenal: BBC sports organizer in Wales, editor of BBC TV's 'Grandstand', editor of ITV's 'This Week', Head of BBC Radio Outside Broadcasts and, to crown everything, 11 years as Head of BBC Television's Outside Broadcasts.

It wasn't a smooth passage. When he took that last job he could hear the doors slamming against him as he walked down the corridor. BBC TV is the original home of jealousy, professional intrigue and thwarted ambition, however warranted. Who was this bloody little Welsh rugger player, this miner's son, who'd leapfrogged them all?

The pace throughout was so unrelenting that there had to be a price. On the way up Cliff Morgan was commentating on a rugby match in Germany when he had a stroke. The left side of his body was paralysed and his speech was impaired. They were so broke that Nuala, his wife, had to borrow the money for the air fare to reach his bedside.

The recovery was long and tough and that was when Morgan discovered who his friends were. Among them were David Coleman and his wife Barbara, and Henry Cooper. There was a letter from Richard Burton, then filming in Budapest, which concluded: 'Should you need anything as mundane as money, you have only to ask.' Jack Solomons, boxing promoter, sent a cheque for £2,000 with the message: 'You may need this during the time you will be out of work.'

Cliff asked Burton for nothing and never cashed the Solomons cheque.

When the next cash crisis came it concerned the fees to maintain the private educations of their two children. Cliff sold his car and Nuala sold her engagement ring. Their son is now a surgeon and their daughter works in medicine.

A couple of years ago, parking his car outside his London home, Cliff was mugged, badly beaten and robbed. He makes no mention of it in his book. 'Never thought about it, really,' he said yesterday. 'I don't suppose it would interest many people. You don't want to go around whingeing all the time, do you?'

There is a lot of rugby in his book as well. But essentially this is a story about genuine family values, not those as projected by politicians. Cliff's mum must have been a terrific woman and his dad a saint.

HOLYFIELD BEATS TYSON

IW takes a typically individual stand on one of the greatest upsets in recent boxing history – in 1996, the apparently invincible Mike Tyson was defeated by Evander Holyfield. In the re-match Tyson infamously bit off part of Holyfield's ear.

Dateline: **Las Vegas 1996**

To THE END, as the shock waves were still reaching out to the ends of the earth, it was more like a bizarre ecumenical prayer meeting than the inquest into, arguably, the biggest upset in sporting history.

Mike Tyson came in dressed like a 1930s stockbroker: immaculate dark suit, neatly folded white handkerchief peeping out of the top pocket, stiffly starched collar, discreet grey and black tie. Only the face bore testimony to where he'd been exactly an hour earlier. There were four livid vertical weals down his forehead, an ugly bruise on his right cheekbone and a gash over the left eye, which was rapidly closing.

'Praise be to Allah,' he said.

Evander Holyfield wore a baseball cap and T-shirt.

'Thanks to Jesus Christ, my Lord, my Saviour,' he said. 'I won because I believe in Jesus Christ and can get over anything.'

Well they weren't exactly the immediate reactions you expected from two men who'd just spent 10 rounds and 37 seconds attempting to bludgeon one another into their respective hereafters – Tyson converted to Islam during his prison incarceration for rape – but then absolutely nothing happened as expected on this astonishing night in the Nevada Desert.

Don King, fight promoter and also Mike Tyson's manager, didn't expect it. Had he done so the match would never have been made. Tyson himself didn't expect it because he regarded himself as invincible. The Tyson camp didn't expect it since they'd been strutting around here like turkey cocks. The book-makers didn't expect it because of the sheerly insulting odds they laid against Holyfield.

Last Wednesday you could have got 22–1 against him. True, those odds shortened to 11–2 an hour before the fight because of the rush of money from speculators who, in my wisdom and immense knowledge of the noble art, I recently described as 'demented' if they were to invest a shirt button on Holyfield beating the Iron Man, let alone inflicting palpable metal fatigue in the process.

In this I was hardly alone. Twelve of America's leading boxing writers were canvassed for their predictions. All 12 picked Tyson, only two believing the contest would go beyond the sixth round. As far as I could determine only the uncanvassed man from the *Boston Globe* got it almost on the nail. He'd forecast a Holyfield win in the ninth and his newspaper actually published this lapse into either alcohol or dementia.

His prediction was a sporting earthquake registering 10 on the Richter Scale, all of which was much less shocking than actually witnessing it happening.

There was no question of Tyson being in anything less than peak physical condition as he was, allegedly, before his only previous defeat to Buster Douglas in Tokyo. Nor was there any hint that the sheer atmosphere of menace this man creates merely by walking down to the ring had diminished.

With Holyfield neatly dressing-gowned in his corner, Tyson strode in expressionless, already stripped for action. Throughout the announcements and the singing of his own national anthem, he prowled diagonally back and forth across the ring like some jungle animal delineating his inviolable territory.

In his previous four post-prison fights this fear factor was desperately effective. One opponent virtually dropped unconscious at his feet with fright. Frank Bruno, after crossing himself a dozen times, at least survived two rounds 50 seconds in a contest that earned Tyson another £20 million.

It was money for old rope and Tyson clearly reckoned on another killing this time, metaphorical or otherwise. Only this time the fear strategy didn't work. Holyfield, four years his senior, with three poor fights behind him and said to have suffered some heart disorder, wasn't scared of him at all. Only later and at considerable length did we discover that this was because Jesus was also with his seconds and cuts men in his corner.

'I prayed to Him throughout my sixteen weeks in training and I prayed to Him up there in the ring,' said Holyfield, 'because I knew what I was facing.'

As early as round three, though, it became apparent that Tyson had no such contractual arrangement with Allah. He ripped into the fight, abandoning his own massive knowledge of scientific boxing, bent only on summary execution.

Holyfield's riposte was not entirely Queensberry Rules. Since again and again, close in, he trapped Tyson's arms beneath his own in an orgy of holding. Indeed, the referee Mitch Halpern spent about a quarter of the fight untangling them from knotted limb embraces.

Suddenly in the sixth, Holyfield had Tyson on the floor and you sensed that now a reign of terror was ending. And so it did, with utter savagery in the 10th, as Tyson, now with vacant eyes, staggered to regain a tenuous balance and then in the 11th, when he was driven across the ring by eight successive blows that left him defenceless. Tyson defenceless? We assumed honourable retirement would come before such an absurd notion could cross our minds.

There have, of course, been many Fights of the Century, some much better than this in the days when there were rich seams of heavyweight talent. But in an era when the sport of boxing itself is on the ropes, when it is manipulated by cartels whose only concern is amassing vast fortunes from television, Holyfield's defeat of Tyson will take its place among them. Tyson the invincible was honourably defeated and with great grace he was the first to admit it.

Boxing will forever intrigue me. For weeks leading up to potentially big drawcards, it stages Press conferences and photo opportunities at which two fighters, almost invariably from similar poor backgrounds, will slag one another off with vile insults. It is all part of the publicity game, rarely worth the newsprint it's recorded on.

And it is invariably exposed as it was here after Holyfield–Tyson, when it becomes clear that smashing the living daylights out of one another generates an affinity born of all the mutually inflicted pain.

In defeat, Tyson reached across formally to shake Holyfield's hand. 'You fought a hell of a fight,' he said. 'I have no excuses and have great respect for you.' Holyfield was equally gracious in response.

However I felt a little uneasy about the introduction of all the religious incantation. Tyson's reference to his new faith was brief enough but Holyfield droned on and on about the spiritual assistance he had received from his corner.

He had 'Jesus Is Lord' printed across the front of his baseball cap and informed all those of us who'd completely written off his chances that it was his duty to forgive and love each and every one of us.

The benediction is gratefully received but the memory of the fight will last a great deal longer.

Chapter Nine

1997–2000

THE TRAGIC DECLINE OF MUHAMMAD ALI

This is one of the saddest pieces IW ever wrote. Despite Ali's illness, now described as 'Pugilistic Parkinson's syndrome', Ali has nevertheless continued to travel the world and his financial situation has stablized.

Dateline: New York 1997

I T IS NO longer possible to interview Muhammad Ali. The mind still functions in the wreckage of his body but he cannot speak. Only a sudden widening of the eyes conveys his comprehension of a conversation. Occasionally he attempts a sentence but it emerges merely as a garbled whisper. From time to time he lapses into sleep, snoring loudly. Then an involuntary jerk of the head awakens him and he smiles apologetically. The hands flutter incessantly, the body trembles and when he labours to his feet to walk in short, shuffling steps, you fear for him because his gait is forward-leaning and perpetually you think he is about to fall. But he doesn't and in confounding you he turns and grins.

Thus Muhammad Ali at 55. Thus the supreme athlete of our generation, arguably of the 20th century. Thus the man deemed by *Time* magazine to be the most instantly recognized human being in the world. Thus The Greatest, the man whose dazzling virtuosity within the prize ring was matched only by his articulacy and outrageous showmanship outside it. And now this: the speechless broken victim of both the treachery and brutality of professional boxing.

I should have wept for this man whose precocious emergence I witnessed as a young reporter when he danced to an Olympic gold medal in Rome in 1960. I should have raged in recollection of his downfall that terrible night in Las Vegas in October 1980 when, in the three last rounds of his fight-too-far, the young Larry Holmes moved in and remorselessly slammed 30 steam-hammer blows to Ali's head. And I should have screamed obscenities against the iniquities of those who bled him of vast fortunes in the intervening years. At least $40 million remains unaccounted for. But I did none of these things for the great man who clambered from his chair and slowly raised his arms in an embracing bear-hug. You reckon, in our game, that you can become impervious to emotion but it isn't true.

Inside that body, now three stone heavier than in his fighting prime, behind the now bloated face, the spirit remains intact. Indeed it has been so rekindled that Muhammad Ali is about to embark on a world tour that will include visits to 11 European cities.

Many will regard his mission as a vicarious peep-show, the shameless pedalling of a human wreck barely able to string three coherent words together. But that is to forget the moment at the Atlanta Olympic Games last summer when this man emerged from the shadows high on a gantry and the world held its breath as Muhammad Ali's shaking hands fumbled with a burning torch to ignite the Olympic flame.

'That,' said Lonnie, 'is when he knew the world hadn't forgotten him and he needs people to stay alive. Meeting people is his lifeblood.'

Lonnie, real name Yolanda, was five years old when she first met Ali, then a brash 20-year-old named Cassius Clay. She could hardly avoid it. The Clay family lived just across the dusty street in Louisville, Kentucky. The families were inseparable friends and the young, already famous, boxer used to bounce her upon his knee. By the time Lonnie was 17 she knew beyond all doubt that she would marry him.

'Don't ask me how or why,' she says. 'I just *knew*. It was a long wait. Ali's first wife was Sonji, whom Lonnie never met. His second wife was Belinda, of whom Lonnie speaks with high regard. His third wife was the glamorous Veronica, upon whom Lonnie has no comment. There were seven children of these unions and Lonnie was always aware that there had been more than a few other dalliances along the way.

'My relationship with him was entirely different,' she says. 'I was fourteen years younger but as I grew up we became great friends. He never flirted with me but he always took me out to lunch or dinner when he came back to Louisville. He was kind and full of good advice, particularly about my education.

'The funny thing was that I wasn't even very interested in his boxing. I only saw him fight twice and I wasn't really aware of what had happened in that Larry Holmes fight until a couple of years later. Then he came back to see his mother and he took me out to lunch. For the first time I noticed that his voice was slightly slurred and that sometimes he stumbled as he walked. I also knew that something was going wrong with his third marriage.'

Ali paid for Lonnie to graduate in business studies at a California university. In July 1986 Ali and Veronica were divorced. The following November he and Lonnie were married. 'It wasn't all that romantic,' said Lonnie. 'He didn't go down on one knee or anything. He simply said: "Better get across to Louisville and get a licence."'

It was then she discovered the murk, the turmoil, the charlatans, the flattering deceivers, the hangers-on, the retinues of free-loaders, the bent publicists, the bought-off journalists and some of the utterly corrupt promoters of the boxing world.

Despite their enduring friendship she had been unaware that Ali's sheer profligacy with money was petty cash compared with the vast sums that had been ripped off him after he had been seduced from his Southern Baptist upbringing by the Black Muslim movement. Boxing for Allah was an expensive business. In 1978, his unparalleled career in boxing now in decline, he was so broke that he outraged his Muslim masters by turning to a *white* man for rescue. That man was Barry Frank, New York chief of Mark McCormack's IMG sports management organization. 'Muhammad was in such bad shape that we had to do a deal with the First National Bank of Chicago even to buy him a house,' Frank recalls. 'But we knew we couldn't fail to market such an enormous personality. Stick with us, we said, you'll be right for the rest of your life. But there is one unviolable stipulation. You look good, you speak wonderfully so you must never step into a boxing ring again.'

Two years later a rising promoter named Don King offered Muhammad Ali $10 million to fight Larry Holmes at Caesars Palace in Las Vegas. Ali took the bait. Watching the closing three rounds of what then was still a 15-round world heavyweight championship was the most sickening 11 minutes I have spent in a lifetime watching men or women in physical combat. Blow after blow slammed into Ali's head. Viewing big fights on television is to have no comprehension of the devastating power of the hitting. A single one of those punches would have killed the likes of me but such was Ali's bravery and pride that night that he would not go down and such was the referee's sycophancy to a blood-baying crowd that he would not stop it.

It was the end of Ali in more ways than one. Barry Frank telephoned him to say that his contract with IMG had been torn up. 'The deal,' he said, 'was that you never fought again.'

'Sorry,' replied Ali. 'I couldn't resist the money.'

No balance sheets exist to reveal exactly how much Ali received from the promised $10 million but, when her turn came at last, Lonnie did not marry a wealthy man. They were not broke. They had a four-bedroomed farm house and 88 acres in the fruit-belt of America's Mid West where, from his out-house office, Ali still personally signs replies to every fan-mail letter sent to him. He received more than 6,000 letters in a single week after his dramatic Olympic Games appearance in Atlanta.

'I didn't go blind into this marriage,' said Lonnie. 'I soon learned the score. I knew he was hopelessly vulnerable to being exploited and I knew it was my duty to maximize his legacy. His legacy was his fame and we saw just how enormously that fame was remembered at the Olympics.

'Muhammad came alive again that night. He wouldn't go to bed. He just sat there cradling the Olympic torch and I knew then that he had to get out and meet people again to stay alive. It is beautifully quiet where we live, but it's too serene for him. He loves the limelight, attention, adoration, people . . . so we decided on a new course of action.'

From time to time, as Lonnie relates all this, her husband opens his eyes and nods endorsement. He becomes inarticulately profusive when she talks of Asaad, the son they adopted six years ago. 'He loves him,' says Lonnie, the wife-daughter-mother figure of a stricken idol. 'If he had his way we'd have adopted an entire orphanage of kids. He loves them. He loves everyone and that's been half the problem.'

Ali rolls his eyes.

Lonnie also rolls her eyes, but in a different way. The gesture says: 'See what I am lumbered with.' But visibly she loves the boy from across the road to distraction. Her shark-antennae are operating and she's too intelligent and shrewd to allow her husband to get caught again.

Six weeks ago, through Howard Bingham, the most steadfast friend Muhammad Ali has ever had, Lonnie contacted Barry

Frank to re-open the contract that had been broken off after Ali had fought Holmes.

'Y'know,' says Lonnie, 'I'm aware I was placed on this earth simply to assist Muhammad Ali. It's no big deal, but I gave up my own career at twenty-five to look after him. I was brought up strictly Catholic and have converted to Islam because that's what he wanted and I now believe fatalistically that certain things are ordained. I am probably living proof of that.'

Quite what Muhammad Ali will get up to during his forth-coming world tour is not clearly defined. Certainly he will open events and new buildings with Lonnie as his mouthpiece and maybe that's what it will amount to. But, as the Atlanta experience proved, thousands will turn up merely to get a glimpse of him. Perhaps by then Ali will have perfected his remaining party trick. It is an astonishing performance that appears utterly to contradict his impaired physical balance. He rises, turns his back on you and appears to levitate six inches from the floor. The eye has been decieved, of course, because what he has actually done is balance his entire bodyweight on the ball of his right big toe. His demonstration in front of me was not entirely successful but at least I got the gist of it.

'How in Allah's name can he manage that?' I ask Lonnie. She shakes her head and laughs. 'I don't know,' she says, 'but all his life Muhammad has been an inspiration to people.

'First of all it was to young people to excel at sport. Maybe now it is time for him to inspire the disabled of the world to rise above themselves. His religion has taught him to accept his condition. He believes his condition now was ordained for him from birth.'

It sheds a new light on what so many of us regard as one of the great human tragedies of sport. But was it really ordained that Ali should break a contract to take that fearful beating in Las Vegas? Was it really ordained that he should be fleeced of successive fortunes? 'I don't know,' said his remarkable fourth wife. 'But I can tell you one thing. It was ordained that he would marry me.'

Muhammad Ali smiles at that. He had one trick left. He slowly reaches for my left arm, rolls my fingers into a fist and steers the fist towards his nose to simulate a punch. It was a British left fist, remember, that felled him for the first time in his fight career – the fist of Henry Cooper.

Was Muhammad trying to tell me something? Was he sending a message to his British fans of old or a personal greeting to Our 'Enry?

Tragically, as about so many things in the life and times so far of Muhammad Ali, we shall never know.

MARY PETERS – THE ENDURING ICON

IW remained a great admirer and close friend of Mary Peters, helping her to write her autobiography and producing a number of articles on her athletics career and on her untiring work for a better Northern Ireland. Here he reports on a visit made at the time of Princess Diana's funeral.

Dateline: **Belfast 1997**

O N THIS, in some respects the most extraordinary day in our nation's modern constitutional history, I write of another woman who has also had to balance engulfing acclaim with a private life of great but unspoken sadness.

Such catchpenny titles as Queen of Hearts and Princess of the

People do not become her and she would not welcome them. Yet yesterday, in the space of a few hours, I watched her bring sheer joy to two elderly and infirm pensioners and then utterly bewitch a class of 26 awestruck nine-year-olds.

'Do you still run?' a little girl asked her. 'I do,' replied Mary Peters, 'but not as well as I used to. But one day when you are very famous I will tell everyone about the day I first met *you*.' The little girl's face puckered in deep thought. Who knows, another inspirational seed may have been sown.

Mary is very tactile with people, involuntarily hugging old and young alike. She can also be as tough as leather, swap earthy stories, excoriate those she knows are bleeding sport by sheer avarice and, at the same time, be extremely sensitive.

Yesterday, for example, she was really disturbed about the dinner for 508 guests being held in her honour in Belfast last night to commemorate her legendary gold medal victory at the Munich Olympic Games exactly 25 years and two evenings previously.

'Am I doing the right thing?' she kept asking. 'The whole of sport, almost the whole of Britain, is shutting down.'

We did not proffer any answer as presumptuous as that Diana, Princess of Wales, would have wished her to continue. We simply pointed out that some of those guests were travelling from the far corners of the earth to be with her and she should not let them down.

The feat that Mary Peters achieved over the two-day, five-discipline women's pentathlon in Munich in 1972 was prodigious, the more so because she was never remotely favourite. In bookmaking terms she was probably 5–1 at best but that was to fail to recognize a steely inner motive. Yes, she was running for herself. But she was also running for Belfast, a city that had been home to her from the age of 11 and with which she had established a deep affinity. In 1972, at the height of

The Troubles, Belfast was a bleak, grim place. 'I desperately wanted to give them a happy day,' she recalls.

She did precisely that with an amalgam of adrenalin and guts. She ran the fastest hurdles of her life, the fastest 200 metres of her life, hurled the shot farther than she ever had and jumped higher than ever previously. Four personal bests under extreme pressure on the ultimate sporting stage gave her the gold medal and set Olympic and world records.

Today, an Olympic gold is worth minimally £1 million, mostly far more, in sponsorships and endorsements. Then it would probably have been at least £250,000. Mary Peters made not a penny. Well, she did, but she gave it all away. She decreed that it would build a new running track on a derelict site on the edge of the city. We were there yesterday with the children from Year Five at St Bride's School. The Mary Peters Running Track is now one of the most beautiful mini-amphitheatres in world sport. It has never been touched by terrorism.

Mary has never considered it a sacrifice and there is no hint of rancour when she says: 'You know, that gold medal actually cost me money. I got hundreds and hundreds of letters after Munich and the postage in replying to them put me out of pocket. It was four years before I could afford to buy an old banger, a Morris 1100, for £400.'

Today she zips around in a nippy Tigra, sponsored by Saville's Auto Village, who reckon there's good mileage in having her name, albeit discreetly, along the doors. But such perks have been a long time coming and there have been financial and personal stresses in the meantime that she has stubbornly concealed from a world, which now sees her as a statuesque, vibrant and still-beautiful woman of 58.

For 20 years she worked 12 hours a day to wring some kind of living out of her own health club, but Mary is no business-woman. She sold the club earlier this year. 'I have my little cottage and my little car and I couldn't be happier if I had a million in the bank,' she said. But that is not entirely true.

The Svengali of her years as an international athlete was Buster McShane, a dynamic figure who started life as a 14-year-old riveter in Belfast's Harland and Wolff shipyards and became an uncompromising, domineering athletics coach who once struck Mary during training. But the affinity was unique. Without Buster she knew she would never have won in Munich. Six months later, after a drink in the Belfast Arts Club, he drove his Jaguar into a stone wall and was killed instantly. More than 10,000 people surrounded the crematorium on the day of his funeral.

Later, during the difficult business years, she was to rely heavily on the advice of another friend, Deryck Monteith, a former Irish rugby captain and Northern Ireland boxing steward. He was a robust, humorous figure but a few years into their friendship he was stricken gravely ill and Mary was to help nurse him through his last painful months.

She has never married. 'Three men have asked me,' she says, 'but nice though they were, none of them was right. Anyway, I don't think any of them would have put up with my hectic lifestyle. Marriage is certainly not out of the question. Yes, I have many friends but there is a loneliness in my life. Still, I've learned to be pretty independent.'

Independent and always on the run. For the past 18 months she has been president of the British Athletic Federation. She is a member of the women's committee of the International Amateur Athletic Federation. She is deputy chairman of the Northern Ireland Tourist Board and president, vice-president or chairman of a dozen other sporting or charitable bodies.

And she still has time to care. Yesterday we drove the 27 miles out to 26 Tandragee Road, Portadown, an address of great significance in her Olympic story. It was here, long before the days when prospective Olympians expected grants and hand-outs from some lottery, that Mary and her father built a sand-pit for long and high jumping and laid a concrete circle for shot-putting in the field behind their first house in Northern Ireland.

The door was opened by Maria Wright. Her none-too-well husband, Leslie, was inside. They had never met Mary before. Inside five minutes they were old friends. Mary had made their day, their week, possibly their retirement years. She has this warmth, this instant rapport with old and young, with anyone from any station of life. Where, this week, have we heard so much of this magical quality before?

On the way back to Belfast she dropped in to see her bank manager, Brian Malcolmson. He went to the strongroom to withdraw a box. It contained Mary's gold medal and her CBE. She collected the medal. 'I won't wear it,' she said, 'but it's surprising how many people still like to see it.'

Not in Belfast, it isn't. She, too, is an icon across class and religious frontiers and thank God this inspirational woman, a proclaimed atheist, is still alive.

QUEEN MOTHER REINS IN THE JOCKEYS

A staunch monarchist, IW was happy to salute the late Queen Mother.

IT WAS the picture that any paparazzo would almost have died for. The scene: a Chelsea restaurant towards the end of a gregarious lunch, table still laden with bottles and coffee cups. The protagonists: two whooping young sportsmen and one digni-fied elderly lady revelling in their uninhibited zest for life.

What the hell's going on here? Very simple. Two of our bravest and greatest jockeys, John Francome and Willie Carson, are instructing Her Majesty Queen Elizabeth the Queen Mother in how to play spoof, a pub gambling game requiring three coins, minimal intellect and maximum cunning.

No photograph and no record of how the game ended exist. However, it may be assumed that the Queen Mum, an experienced punter, got the gist of it quickly. It is rumoured, obviously wrongly, that a little inside information may have helped her pick up a bob or two when the betting industry had the temerity to make a book on how one of her grand-children would be named.

Such is her passion for racing that all of 30 years ago she had The Blower, the sound commentary service that preceded today's televised Racing Channel, installed in Clarence House.

It is why, now nudging 100 years of age and limping slightly after her second hip operation, she will receive a tumultuous reception at the Cheltenham Festival today. The masses have a wonderful, unspoken protocol about this. They give her one huge ovation and then leave her in peace.

I have one abiding memory of this remarkable woman and it has nothing to do with her determination to stay in London throughout the German Blitz and get down there to the East End the following morning to walk through the rubble and comfort the bereaved.

It is far less important but it concerns a chap I had a drink with on the eve of the Cheltenham Gold Cup in 1984. His name is Stan Riley, a lovely man in a well-worn sheepskin who had lost a small fortune in pig farming, but then had a bright piece of lateral thinking.

Dr Beeching had shut down miles of British railway tracks. Stan bought up the wooden sleepers over which the trains would no longer run and paid 12 pence each for 26,000 of them. He sold them later for £7 apiece. 'Enough of this,' he determined, 'we shall now go into National Hunt racing.'

Stan and his wife bought a horse called Burrough Hill Lad. After a terrible fall it was sent to Jenny Pitman for schooling, recovered brilliantly and was second favourite for the Gold Cup.

Stan's unease was palpable. 'All those cameras, the television and Queen Mother presenting the Cup,' he said. I was with a retiring, kind man who actually struck me as though he'd rather lose than endure all the fuss.

Burrough Hill Lad came up that terrible escarpment like the Bullet Train next day and took it by six lengths. Stan, still in the same sheepskin, went down to the winner's circle enveloped in grim-faced unease as the crowds and cameras closed in.

Suddenly, the throng parted and the Queen Mother came in to present the Cup. She identified the problem instantly. From around 15 paces distant she had her hand thrust out, beaming happiness for him, and a moment later the two owners were engrossed in animated horse chat. Stan Riley will never forget what the Queen Mother did for him that day and, for that matter, nor shall I.

She has, of course, been a prolific winning owner in her many years and has suffered the most appalling disappointments, none more so than when Devon Loch, seven lengths clear with only 80 yards to run in the 1956 Grand National, went down with all four legs splayed out like a shattered card table. Her concern that day was less for its jockey, Dick Francis, who quit riding on the spot to become a millionaire novelist, but for Devon Loch.

She came to the London Press Club once and insisted on having a go at snooker. At 88, she was still lowering herself into the River Dee in Scotland to maintain another passion, fly fishing.

Never mind the new Cool Britannia, with its notions about how the royals should now melt into the background.

The nation will wish the Queen Mum yet another happy Cheltenham and maybe some enterprising unit will nominate her for Sportswoman of the Year. She'll turn up, make no mistake, provided there is a gin-and-tonic at hand and maybe a game of spoof when it's all over.

Some lady.

HOUNDING THE HUNTERS

Six years after this article was published the law against hunting with dogs was passed by means of the Speaker invoking the Parliament Act after the Lords had rejected it. As a libertarian, and an opponent of class legislation, IW was appalled.

THE MOST dangerous sporting event I have ever reported – and this includes the Cresta Run, grand prix motor racing, downhill skiing and heavyweight boxing – was the Melton Hunt Club Ride.

This is contested by horsemen and horsewomen over high hedges, tarmac roads, stone walls and deep ditches across four and a half miles of natural Leicestershire countryside. It makes the Grand National look like any other steeplechase.

Unfortunately, the year I covered it, my story was removed from the pages of the *Daily Mail*. Just before edition time we learned that the father of the winner, who was also competing, had broken his neck and died in hospital.

A few days after the funeral I spoke to his son. 'Your article never appeared,' he said. 'We withdrew it out of respect for your family,' I explained. 'You needn't have done that,' he replied, 'my mother was also killed in the hunting field.'

This doubtless will be music to the ears of the Labour MP for Worcester, Michael Foster, who was deliriously happy yesterday that our Prime Minister had pledged ad-lib on television that fox-hunting is to be outlawed during the life of the present parliament.

Mr Foster, a former student of Wolverhampton Polytechnic and lecturer in accountancy at Worcester College of Technology, had been frustrated since last year when his Private Member's Bill to kill fox-hunting was rejected. Now here was The Boss endorsing Mr Foster's claim to political immortality by banning a pursuit that has been going on in England since King Rufus was killed by a hunter's arrow in the New Forest and has thrived for the past 300 years.

Considering his own reported interest in fishing in an earlier life, Mr Foster's concern for all creatures that God made strikes me as being rather subjective. Maybe he is concerned that horseback humans are too precious to risk breaking arms, legs and necks, but I suspect that is not the case. I reckon this is a nasty outbreak of Old Labour-style class warfare.

If that is so, here is a cross-section of those who were out with the Cottesmore Hunt one day last winter: the field master, for a start, was a woman, and there were farmers, housewives, a roofing contractor, a pawnbroker, a jeweller, a motor trader, a solicitor, a doctor and a journalist. Not a corpuscle of blue blood between them. I must declare a personal interest here. I hate horses. I love betting on them, particularly at National Hunt meetings, which is why I regard them as feckless, unreliable and stupid. I have only ever sat on two of them and was scared to death both times.

But I revere the jockeys who ride them professionally and admire the amateurs who ride in the Melton Hunt Ride and to hounds and simply can't comprehend why Mr Blair, with Ulster, Serbia, John Prescott and much else on his hands, should choose to lumber himself with another confrontation that is going to cause him grief.

Yesterday I spoke to Michael Clayton who, after a tumultuous career reporting violence in Vietnam, Cambodia and the Middle East for BBC television, became editor of *Horse and Hound* and transformed it into the biggest-circulation equestrian magazine in the world.

'Destroying hunting,' he said, 'would be the equivalent of destroying skiing in St Moritz.'

Personally I'm more concerned with the future of the Christmas card industry, with its traditional views of hunting packs, and also the nation's chickens, who regularly get torn to pieces by foxes before Mr Foster can eat them in some Worcestershire Indian restaurant while pontificating about how the rest of us should conduct ourselves.

Hero and friend Stirling Moss drove the Mille Miglia with IW at his side.

This stunning publicity shot of Steve Davies and Stephen Hendry was taken by photographer Ted Blackbrow in 1990 during a snooker tournament in Dubai. IW could not resist writing about it because he had personally come up with the idea and designed the image.

IW regarded his good friend Peter Alliss as the voice of golf.

IW pays up at Aspinalls – he had made a £1,000 bet with Charles Palmer, that London would not host the 2012 Olympics.

For IW, as indeed for many Test umpires, the great leg-spinner Shane Warne was a most appealing cricketer.

When Michael Parkinson interviewed Shane Warne, IW rated it as the best he'd ever seen.

Henry Chappell with his step-uncle at Sydney Harbour.

Youngest son Max accompanied his father to Pamplona.

IW's great friends Christopher Morgan, Sir Brian Williamson and John Curtain join him in Pamplona.

IW aged four.

Oldest son Kevin and grand-daughter Lucy.

Ian enjoying time with his young boys at home in Ealing.

IW and Sarah discover that they were not the first Wooldridges to visit the Australian outback.

Grandson Henry Vaughan in Australia with his mother, Carla, and father, Simon.

'Woollers' and close friend 'Benaud' – neither ever addressed the other by his first name – enjoy another glass of chardonnay.

Triple family honours – IW, his nephew Mike Wooldridge and Mike's wife Ruth have all been awarded the OBE.

IW, Sarah and her son Jorge, photographed by Mark McCormack in his marquee at the Wimbledon championships.

Sarah (suffering from a broken ankle) and Veronica, IW's first wife, both accompanied him when he collected his OBE at Buckingham Palace.

IW and Sarah relax at home.

After spending the afternoon at New Milton's sports ground, watching the local cricket team play, Sarah unveiled this memorial to IW.

ALLISS THROUGH THE LOOKING-GLASS

And then there was one . . . Richie Benaud, the authoritative voice of cricket, had moved to Channel 4. Murray Walker, the shriek of motor racing, had decamped to ITV. Jimmy Hill and Bob Wilson, the football gurus, gone. Then the final stunning blow: the abdication of Desmond Lynam, the coolest hot property the BBC had underpaid for years. But as their portraits were stripped from walls, one remains. Peter Alliss, not for want of alternative employment, is still with the BBC to interpret golf for the masses. Hugely popular, as a recent *Sportsmail* vote proved, there are Reithian attitudes in this avuncular figure, as revealed in the frankest interview he has ever given.

WHEN 16-year-old Henry Alliss brought some school friends home the other day he introduced them to his father thus: 'This is Dad. He shouts a bit, but he's okay really.'

Shouts a bit? Could this be the hidden alter ego of the honey-tongued BBC golf commentator whose brief flash of irascibility during this year's Open Championship deluged *Sportsmail* with the biggest response to any poll it has ever conducted?

More than 2,000 readers wrote in. And by a seven-to-one consensus the verdict was: 'Lay off Alliss. He represents standards of behaviour our country is fast losing.'

The dissenters called him pompous or reactionary, sometimes both.

Alliss replied to his accusers with a smile. 'I quite understand that,' he said. 'Anyone over fifty in Britain today is regarded as a dinosaur. If you still stand up when a woman walks into the room they think you're completely daft.'

It was the hottest day of the year when we met at Wentworth. He was wearing a jacket and tie and was 10 minutes early for our interview. He is so punctilious about such matters and much else that it seemed appropriate to invite him to list the things he dislikes most in the 69th year of his very public life.

He was up and running in a flash: 'Graffiti, vandalism, bad manners, road rage, riding bicycles on pavements, very bad language on television, rude and uncontrolled children, parents who let their children run riot, inconsiderate people who slam hotel doors at unsocial hours, poor teachers, schools with no discipline, all-night television, excessive nationalism and almost everything now regarded as politically correct.'

So what *does* he like?

'British humour, solid stone houses, orderly queueing, good manners, fish and chips, fair play, dogs, discipline, honesty, Scotch whisky, kindly eccentricity, pine trees, rhododendrons, bikinis, Bournemouth, Cadbury's chocolate and coal or wood fires in wintertime.'

Young Henry Alliss, the youngest of Peter's six children from two marriages – one, Victoria, died tragically at the age of 12 – clearly has a rigorous agenda to live up to.

'Well, I suppose I've shouted at all of them from time to time,' says his father, 'and if you ask them whether I was a disciplinarian they'd probably say I was dramatically so.

'But so what? They don't go around abusing things or people. They all come home as often as possible. The house is always full of laughter. Is that so bad? And isn't it nice when someone comes up to you and says: "I met a couple of your kids the other day. They were charming."'

The house is approached by a longish drive in six acres of land in Hindhead, Surrey, and has six bedrooms and two full-time gardeners. It is closer to London's airports than his beloved Bournemouth and Alliss still commutes almost three months each year to commentate in America, as well as following golf all over Europe.

His idea of relaxing when at home is to have a few friends in for dinner. The hospitality is legendary. You don't drink the latest supermarket bargain.

The chatelaine on these occasions is his wife, Jackie. She is small, dynamic and hugely protective of her husband's reputation. She is also a JP on the Surrey bench at Guildford, is a governor of a local school, runs a charity to raise funds for the detection of tumours and, for relaxation, pilots her shared small private plane. She is currently on holiday with some of the Alliss children at their other place in southern Spain.

None of these manifestations of middle-class comfort was attained from a silver-spoon upbringing. Peter Alliss, son of a fine professional tournament golfer Percy, left grammar school at 14. Well, at 14 and three-quarters actually, but still too young to contemplate university or the conventional professions.

'There was another contributory factor to the way I think now,' said Alliss. 'I was brought up in the Second World War years when nothing could be taken for granted, not even your life, and nothing could be wasted.

'You didn't leave lights on all over the house. You had one bar of chocolate a month. And even after the war, when you took a girl out, you had to get the last bus home at 10.30 or trudge 10 miles. These days, driving lessons at 16, a gift car at 17 and a gap year falling around the Far East before going to university seem to be regarded as a birthright. I simply don't understand it.'

At 15, Alliss won the prestigious British Boys' Golf Championship, became an assistant to his father at the Ferndown Golf Club in Dorset, left for two years' National Service and returned to become a professional tournament golfer. He played in eight Ryder Cups, 10 World Championships and every Open Championship until 1974.

Becoming a television commentator never crossed his mind.

'Extraordinary how these things happen,' he said. 'In 1970 I'd played pretty well in a tournament in Dublin and on the plane coming home I was probably on a high and regaling my neighbours with stories about the hilarious things that can happen to you in Ireland.

'A few weeks later I was approached by Ray Lakeland, a northern BBC chap who produced sports programmes on rugger, rugby league, cricket and golf. Ray said: "I was sitting just behind you on the plane back from Dublin the other day. I heard everything you said. Why not come and have a go at television?"'

Alliss did. At first, short comment inserts into long transmissions, then, after his final Open Championship appearance in 1974, an invitation to join the full commentary team headed by the magisterial Henry Longhurst, a classicist in the economical use of the beautiful English language in such an hedonistic medium as television.

Longhurst, a short, squat man, hated appearing on camera. For the next 14 years Alliss fronted TV's *Pro-Celebrity Golf.* For the second time in his life he was a national figure.

Never has he fallen into the celebrity trap that destroys so many febrile TV front-persons before they've learned some three-syllable words from the dictionary.

'By choice,' said Alliss, 'I would prefer to arrive at and depart from golf tournaments by submarine.'

He comes up with ad-lib phrases like that all through his golf commentaries. 'I have never thought where they come from,' he said. 'They just happen.'

He is as uncompromising about golf as he was about the upbringing of his children. On TV, he briefly criticized Frenchman Jean Van de Velde, who made such a hash of the last hole of the Open Championship at Carnoustie, and makes no apology. 'I have seen amateur players at St Andrews and Gleneagles go out there and take air-shots off the first tee. What in God's name are they doing there?'

Alliss, unashamedly, does not like the second rate.

His youngest son, Henry, is named to honour three of Peter's greatest friends: the late Sir Henry Cotton, supreme golfer; the late Henry Longhurst, emeritus of the English language; and Henry Cooper, the Cockney rough diamond who became the first man to horizontalize Muhammad Ali and, with his lovely wife Albina, has richly contributed to British public life.

'You know what all these three very different men had in common?' queried Alliss. 'In their own very different ways, they had style. They epitomized our country at its very best.'

Thus an insight into the mind of Peter Alliss, a man who deplores what is happening to our country. His greatest credential is that he is no commercial fat cat. He has earned his every penny the hard way.

HOW DOLLY CHANGED THE COURSE OF HISTORY

IW had always been an opponent of apartheid and made his views known in many of his earlier articles.

SHOULD it be the elegance of Peter May, Colin Cowdrey or Graeme Pollock? The inspirational belligerence of Vivian Richards or Ian Botham? The genius of Garfield Sobers or the defiance of Ken Barrington? Or even the stupendous 70 with which Ted Dexter blew the tracks off the West Indies' juggernaut on that glowering day at Lord's in 1963?

The canvas is so infinite, the opportunity to watch such a galaxy of batsmen in their prime so enviable, that to nominate the greatest innings one has ever seen is an impossible assignment. Instead, I choose an innings that was probably the most *significant* played in modern Test match history.

There was no inkling of the crisis that was to engulf cricket when the fifth and final Test against Australia began at The Oval in 1968. England batted first and Colin Milburn, Cowdrey and Dexter were all soon out. As so often, it was characteristically John Edrich who ground it out. At the close he was 130 not out and England were 272 for four.

Late in the proceedings he had been joined by Basil D'Oliveira, who was 24 not out.

Early next morning, before leaving for The Oval, Basil phoned his wife, Naomi, who was at home in Worcester. She said she hadn't slept all night.

'This is a big day for you,' she said. It was as if she sensed that this August Friday could tear not only their world but the world of sport apart.

D'Oliveira's response was interesting. 'Don't worry,' he said. 'Just drop everything. Get the neighbours to look after the kids and pull up a chair in front of the television. I'm going to bat all day.'

He didn't. He merely scored 158.

It was an innings seemingly of carefree exuberance, totally out of context with the grim warfare of Ashes battles. From time to time he plunged down the wicket to smash Australia's bowlers back over their heads so that, at his century. John Edrich came down the pitch and told him to calm down.

But on he went as though some unseen spirit were guiding him. Or maybe it was just that a man named Nelson Mandela, incarcerated on Robben Island, South Africa, was wishing him well.

D'Oliveira was born in South Africa with a vast talent for cricket. Unfortunately, as a Cape Coloured – which meant his skin was probably lighter than my wife's after a Caribbean holiday – he had no sporting future there under the apartheid regime. His destiny was downgraded train seats, loos and buses and low-grade non-white cricket. As his fame grew he could not even converse with white journalists in their hotels. They had to meet him in the car park.

One white journalist outraged by this was John Arlott who, on his first and only visit to apartheid South Africa, was confronted by an immigration form requiring him to declare his race: caucasian or black? Arlott wrote 'Human'. He arranged for D'Oliveira to come to play in England, first in the northern leagues and then with Worcestershire. He was so good that on naturalization he was soon in the England team. Also, he was a blithe spirit who was hugely popular with fellow cricketers and crowds alike.

But in 1968 his form had not been consistent. He was dropped by England until a spate of injuries to other players saw him recalled for the final Test – the last big match before the England team to tour South Africa in the coming winter was to be announced.

It was unthinkable that D'Oliveira, back on form, having taken a crucial Australian wicket in England's victory at The Oval, having averaged more than 50 in his first 10 Tests, could be omitted from the all-rounder position in the party.

As if to endorse his claim he scored 128 for Worcestershire against Sussex on the very day MCC's selectors met to name the contingent to fly to South Africa. D'Oliveira was not in it.

Many lies have been told about what happened in the Lord's committee room that day. But two things had already occurred.

Through the all-white old-boy network, MCC had been informed that any England team containing D'Oliveira would not be acceptable in South Africa on racial grounds. And D'Oliveira himself had been offered a bribe worth £48,000 by a major South African tobacco company. What the emissary, named Tienie Oosthuizen, didn't know was that his telephone conversation had been tape-recorded.

Basil's exclusion plunged MCC into the biggest furore in its history. It was savagely attacked by Press and public. Members resigned. But then an escape hatch was opened.

Tom Cartwright, chosen ahead of D'Oliveira as the touring team's major all-rounder, was injured and had to withdraw. D'Oliveira was now chosen as his replacement. His enduring dream of returning to his native country as an equal member of the human race was about to be fulfilled. Or was it?

Just 24 hours later, speaking at a National Party conference in Bloemfontein, the Orange Free State epicentre of the rabid apartheid policy, Mr Johannes Balthazar Vorster, South Africa's prime minister, spat out a diatribe against MCC's eventual inclusion of D'Oliveira.

'There was an immediate outcry because a certain gentleman of colour was omitted,' he ranted. From then on D'Oliveira was no longer a sportsman but a political cricket ball, forced back into the team by leftist and liberal politicians with pink ideals. Under no circumstances would D'Oliveira be allowed into South Africa to play for England. The MCC immediately called off the tour.

Thus, in the footsteps of the Olympic movement and FIFA, the world football governing body, they virtually completed South Africa's sporting isolation.

South Africa is such a sports orientated country that I shall always believe this, even more than trade sanctions, hastened the end of the apartheid era and that Basil D'Oliveira, unwittingly, was an important catalyst.

Twelve years later I was in Port Elizabeth, South Africa, covering one of the so-called rebel cricket tours. Strolling into the
pavilion to get a drink mid-afternoon, I saw a heavily jowled
man, tie loosened at the throat, sitting at a table cluttered with
empty glasses and filled ashtrays.

He was no longer South Africa's prime minister, but that was
less to do with his pro-Nazi proclivities during World War II
than his involvement in a local political scandal. Regrettably, I
have to report that my interview with Johannes Balthazar Vorster
was the briefest I have ever had with anyone.

As I wrote at the outset, Basil D'Oliveira's 158 at The Oval
was not the greatest Test century I have ever seen. But I doubt
if there will ever be another which will so turn the world on its
head.

ATHERS HAS TAKEN
IT ON THE CHIN

*IW was intrigued to find Michael Atherton an unusually
complex and highly intelligent sportsman.*

As you would expect of a man who once batted nigh on
11 hours to save a Test match for England, Michael Atherton isn't backing away from the huge controversy he has detonated in the very heartland of English cricket. Nor is he claiming
to have been ambushed by some rascally interviewer out to cause
trouble.

'True,' he said, 'the question came out of the blue but all I
did was answer it perfectly honestly. If my opinions are held to
be provocative, too bad. I'm not backing down.'

The question was: how did Atherton view the future for a County Championship that has been in existence for 136 years?

His reply, in effect, was: 'It doesn't have a future. It's a dead duck.'

The reaction at Lord's was much the same as it would have been in the Vatican if he'd declared that Papal Infallibility is tosh. There were dark murmurings of excommunication but as of yesterday morning the Gestapo hadn't called and even his county employers Lancashire hadn't been on the telephone with even the mildest rebuke.

They won't be able to catch up with him for the next 10 days since he's now in a private Caribbean villa with his girlfriend, but on his return his argument – realistic economics versus romantic heritage – will be hard, if not impossible, to refute.

'Last season,' he said, 'Lancashire finished second in the County Championship. That's not a bad track record. And do you know how many spectators watched them throughout the season? Just 7,700. That works out at barely more than 200 a day.

'And what's happening now? The English Cricket Board have decreed a seven-Test summer with the sixteen best English players contracted to them, which would take them out of the county game. How, with attendances like that, can the counties conceivably support four hundred full-time professionals?

'This isn't something I've just thought up. I've held these opinions for years and I'm amazed that simply by saying them in public all this business has snowballed. Surely I'm allowed to express an opinion?

'We're not talking here about an exclusively English problem. All over the world people are no longer watching domestic first-class cricket yet they're still flocking to Test matches and one-day internationals to support their national teams. Obviously we can learn something from that.

'No, I don't have all the answers and I don't think we'll get them while we have all these unwieldy committees with their contradictory views. We need a few strong men to sort it out. There is a strong case for semi-professionals to reduce the wage bills, one-day cricket and floodlight matches. I'm not in the business of talking cricket down. Cricket has been my life and I'd love to have some input in the way it goes from here. I guess I'm less constrained by history and tradition than many of them.'

Never was there a derogatory word about the men at Lord's or the Victorian attitudes that sustain a form of a game which is palpably defunct.

Michael Andrew Atherton is a very interesting man, much misunderstood, even maligned, by those whose only acquaintance with him is via his surly countenance and snapped dismissals of provocative questions at televized media conferences at the end of a hard day's play in the Test arena.

'Why do we need them?' he asks. 'They have just watched six hours or more of tribalistic cricket and are entitled to knock the hell out of us if we have done badly or praise us if we have done well. Why do they need an England captain to tell them what happened? Don't they watch the game?'

Few remember that Atherton has captained England in more Test matches than any other cricketer. He names Jardine, Hutton, Illingworth and Gatting as his top England captains since the early thirties because they were all winners.

Early on, at Manchester Grammar School and then Downing College, Cambridge, and Lancashire he was such a consistent winner that he earned the nickname Fec, an acronym for Future England Captain. His ascendancy did not coincide with a golden era of English cricket and, as often as not, he was left to dig out England's reputation with innings of stubborn defiance, the greatest of which was his undefeated 185 while ducking, diving and hitting anything the South Africans could hurl at him in

Johannesburg in 1995. He took it on the chin, the chest, the forearms, the helmet and what is colloquially known as in-the-box for 10 hours and 45 minutes. It was the fourth longest innings played by an England batsman and, in my submission, entitles him to say a few words about the critical future of the English game without retribution.

A fascinating facet of Atherton's character is that the very last thing he wants to talk about is cricket. You name a book, he's read it. You recommend a film, he's seen it.

After England had been massacred in the Cape Town Test match the other day, he did not play golf but took a boat out to Robben Island to see where Nelson Mandela had been incarcerated for all those years.

'Did you know,' he asked, 'that Mandela slept there on a bare concrete floor with only a bucket to piss in?' I didn't.

You would never know whether Atherton votes right or left. He is an honours history graduate with an uncluttered mind and, aged just 32, has much to offer the game.

Nothing has changed of course. Writing in *Wisden*, A.G. Steel, also of Cambridge and Lancashire, stated: 'Cricket is in the very direst peril of degenerating from the finest of all summer games into an exhibition of dullness and weariness.'

Steel wrote those words in 1900. A century later Michael Atherton might just be the man to do something about it.

THIS ISN'T THE
BEAUTIFUL GAME

IW identifies football's several failings.

PARDON the impertinent intrusion. The truth is that asking me to greet the new football season with anything remotely resembling enthusiasm is like asking St Francis of Assisi to preview next year's bullfighting in Spain.

For God's sake, we've still got two Test matches to play against West Indies. The Olympic Games are just around the corner. The summer has hardly started. Yet here we are already analysing which bunch of wily dagos will beat which other bunch of wily dagos to the Premiership title about halfway through next year's cricket season.

It is not that I hate football. I used to play it. For three years I reported football for this newspaper, getting zonked with Jimmy Greaves, dining well past midnight with Jimmy Hill, listening with huge respect to the wisdom of Bill Nicholson at Spurs, watching that fantastic Real Madrid-Eintracht Frankfurt match at Hampden, ghost-writing the great Matt Busby's column for a season, loving those legless nights in the Ipswich boardroom when the Cobbold brothers owned the friendliest club in Britain.

I can no longer understand what is happening in a professional game which has clearly lost its marbles. The transfer fees are ridiculous. Players' wages, now bordering £55,000 a week, are an obscene insult to eminent brain surgeons, let alone nurses and school teachers.

Half the players in the Premiership have surnames I can't even pronounce. Clubs with less than £50 million to spend in the slave market openly admit they have no chance. Towns without a decent hospital hear *nouveau riche* club chairmen pledging squillions for a new left-back.

On television Mr Wenger, of Arsenal, conveys deeply self-protective pessimism with a relentless hangdog expression, while up at Manchester United, Sir Alex slides his lips over a few clichés to interviewers too scared to ask him a penetrative question before he goes off to write a few more venomous addenda to the latest reprint of his massively lucrative auto-biography.

Indeed, I admit to becoming somewhat paranoid about what many of its current librettists describe as the 'beautiful game'. It isn't a beautiful game at all. It is an absolute rip-off now, utterly controlled by hardly known agents who, since the Bosman ruling, make a 10–15 per cent killing every time their clients move from X to Y.

Today Liverpool. Tomorrow Real Madrid. Next month Everton or Milan. If you can't see through that little game you were certainly born yesterday.

The rip-offs multiply: websites to broadcast players' illiterate opinions, television contracts that wipe good matches off the screen unless you subscribe to obscure channels that require a quick tenner off your credit card. And then there are the prices you are expected to pay at big grounds. Take your kid and two of his mates to a decent match for a birthday celebration, buy them a soft drink and a hot dog and you're set back £200. And that's before you've visited the souvenir shop where the mark-up prices are criminal. Well, you have to pay the players somehow.

Football in Britain is now totally out of control.

Just look at our recent attempt to bring the 2006 World Cup to England. It was doomed from the moment the ridiculous Tony Banks was put in charge. Seconded, for want of a better word, from his duties as Minister of Sport, he plunged into the fray, confident that with Sir Bobby Charlton and Sir Geoff Hurst at his shoulders, he would pull off a coup. Even the ennobled former strikers couldn't save him in a campaign that wasted £10 million and the rest.

And FIFA, the world governing body of the game? By the day it becomes more like the International Olympic Committee, with smiling elderly men filmed embracing one another with diplomatic hugs while just waiting to stab one another through the neck. Meantime, all of them are living high on the hog.

Then there is the jargon. What, for example, is the left-sided player of whom there appears to be such a paucity in the English game? Does this mean we have no native-born footballer who, if he is only on £20,000 a week, can kick as adequately with his left foot as his right?

I don't understand it, just as I don't understand so many of those gentlemen who call the interminable football radio phone-in programmes via mobiles while driving down congested motorways on the return journey from some match. 'Ullo, Dave, we was brilliant today.' What has this 'we' business got to do with someone whose only exertion was to negotiate a turnstile?

Anathema? Well, I guess you could call it that. Strangely enough, the very same sports editor who commissioned me to write these considered views on modern football was the same man who was inordinately generous to me during the last World Cup.

He kindly financed me to travel to Bhutan, a tiny kingdom high up in the Himalayas alongside Mount Everest. Why? Because Bhutan, by royal decree, had no television. It was the only country on earth that had no idea the World Cup was in progress.

Bhutan's national sport is archery. What bliss.

COLIN COWDREY – A TRUE GENTLEMAN

Now that sledging appears to be an accepted part of cricket, the example of sportsmanship epitomized by Colin Cowdrey shines ever brighter.

FROM THE very font, he was destined to be a cricketer. At his christening in the tiny church among the rolling hills of southern India, they named him Michael Colin Cowdrey. And before the week was out, his father had written to Lord's putting his name down for future membership of MCC, the Marylebone Cricket Club.

He was to fulfil that destiny, from schoolboy prodigy to Test batsman of exquisite elegance, far beyond his father's wistful imagination.

He could play every shot in the manual, but no batsman in history has ever surpassed the beauty of his cover drive, struck with colossal power yet without apparent effort. Timing was the trick.

His death, at the cruelly early age of 67, leaves much undone. He was advancing to a career in public life as Lord Cowdrey of Tonbridge when ill health struck him down.

There were times when his own privileged upbringing bore him down like guilt and he was determined to strive to generate sporting opportunities for inner-city kids bereft of apparent hope. Thus he leaves a heritage of good intention, a frustration which reflected the greatest frustration of all in his career.

The prize he wanted above all others eluded him. This was to captain an England team to Australia. The job went to Ray

Illingworth instead, and Illingworth won the Ashes. They remained on speaking terms, but only just.

Colin Cowdrey was four years old and toddling around his parents' tea plantation north of Bangalore in India when his cricket education began.

They had a staff of six to attend a family of three, and one of them, a teenager named Krishnan, did little more than bowl to Cowdrey on the lawn. Thirty years later, Krishnan continued to write to Cowdrey at his home in Kent and still addressed him as 'Dear Little Master'.

Before sunset in those idyllic last days in India, Colin's father would return from work and instil an ingenious discipline on his tiny son. He would set the stumps tight up against the side netting of their tennis court, thereby restricting Colin to play only off-side shots. An adopted mongrel dog named Patch retrieved the ball.

'It was the most valuable thing that ever happened to me,' recalled Colin. 'The natural tendency of infant batsmen is to try to slog everything to leg. My father would have none of that.'

Thus were born the elegant off-drives and late cuts that 20 years later were to dazzle cricket audiences around the world.

The war years were miserable. Cowdrey's parents remained in India. Colin was sent to boarding school in England and didn't see them for seven years.

Introspective, shy and lonely, cricket was his salvation. From preparatory school he went to Tonbridge. Aged just 13, he went straight into the Tonbridge first XI, and at Lord's – the youngest batsman ever to play there – scored 75 against Clifton.

He captained Oxford University and then, at 21, was chosen to join Len Hutton's 1954 England team to Australia and made his maiden century in Melbourne.

A less sensitive man may have shrugged off the blows that were now to fall upon him. Colin couldn't. Returning from that seven-month tour of Australia and New Zealand, bronzed and slim, he was called up for National Service in the RAF. Two weeks later he was discharged because, according to official documents, 'of a long history of foot trouble'.

The hate mail poured in. The Press attacked him. In Parliament, Sir Gerald Nabarro accused him of dodging the column.

'I agree that it must have looked pretty suspicious to the public,' Cowdrey said, 'but I can assure you that my discharge was not due to any high-level string-pulling on my part.' What exacerbated the furore was that immediately after his return to civvy street he scored a century for MCC against Oxford University at Lord's, made 139 for Kent against Northants, and then 115 not out and 103 not out in a single match against Essex.

After he was badly knocked about by the South African fast bowlers Heine and Adcock in the third Test at Lord's, he received a letter saying: 'Serves you right. If there's any justice you will get hit like that for the next two years.'

Cowdrey was distraught. He replied personally by hand to all his accusers who had appended names and addresses.

Aged 22, an amateur earning nothing from cricket apart from basic travelling expenses, he was a slave to his upbringing and education. Today's £50,000-a-week footballers would have laughed and tossed those letters into the waste bin.

It was an episode which he never forgot – for all the subsequent brilliance in his career, his knighthood and his peerage.

It was a career that featured more than 7,000 Test runs, with a century in his 100th Test match, 107 first-class centuries, his captaincy of Kent to the county championship in their centenary year, becoming president of MCC in its bicentennial year and the first elected chairman of the International Cricket Council.

But Cowdrey was forever wary of a modern world which he never fully understood.

He was generous, kind and invariably courteous, the quintessential Englishman of the old school, an almost Victorian upbringing, which revered Crown, Country and Convention. In fact, I believe he was one of the few true Englishman we had left.

Only once did I see him depart from this mode of behaviour and it was when he captained England to West Indies in 1968. After three drawn matches England won the fourth Test in Trinidad and proceeded to Guyana, where a draw would win England the series.

In the second innings, Colin scored 82, having laid down his bat in the crease to rush to the lavatory, which earned a six-minute delay in the proceedings. England drew the match after a tense last over and thus won the series.

At the time, I wrote in this newspaper: 'England have set the pace throughout the tour only because Colin Cowdrey, at 35, has become more professional than any of the professionals beneath him.

'He is the classic exception to the rule, the smooth man who has deliberately acquired rough edges. In the process, he has undoubtedly alienated a few cronies who believed the sun shone out of his Oxford cap.' I was wrong about that. This was Colin's finest hour, victory in the Caribbean. But I still believe he cheated with that unscheduled lavatory break. It was most unlike him, but years later he didn't win the captaincy to Australia which he so desperately wanted.

This was probably wise. Ray Illingworth, a pugnacious Yorkshireman who despised the soft south, delivered the goods after a vicious Test series. I don't think Colin would have stood up to the unrelenting pressure.

Michael Colin Cowdrey was the product of an age which no longer exists. A recent biographer, Mark Peel, has described him as 'the Last Roman', and the description fits.

But in writing 97,000 words of his official biography, *MCC: Autobiography Of A Cricketer*, I discovered an indecisiveness which may explain why he never became a permanent England captain.

From the outset, I explained that any words he spoke would go into the book. With his vast inside knowledge of the game and its leading exponents, he spoke at length, leading to profiles of such icons as Sir Leonard Hutton and Sir Donald Bradman.

It was only later that I discovered he was sending the resulting chapters to the subjects concerned, seeking their approval.

Eventually we arrived at the D'Oliveira affair. Basil D'Oliveira had been offered an enormous bribe from a South African commercial source to declare himself unavailable for a forthcoming cricket tour by England to South Africa in the late sixties.

D'Oliveira, a South African-born Cape Coloured then playing for England, spurned it. Colin knew every detail of the machinations employed by the British government in an effort to avoid a political crisis and public outcry.

One morning, he rang me to say we should meet a certain person who wished to discuss the chapter I had written about it. He picked me up without disclosing our destination.

It was the Foreign Office. We drove there in silence and were met by the then Foreign Secretary Sir Alec Douglas Home. His party had not been in power at the time of the crisis but Sir Alec had been President of the MCC. He was utterly charming but quite ruthless. 'Colin,' he said, perusing the relevant chapter, 'did I really say this?'

'You did, sir,' said Colin. 'Well, since you can't write shorthand, I think we should excise it,' said Sir Alec, producing a pen and drawing a line through three critical paragraphs explaining the British government's disgraceful attempt to keep the South African tour alive. The three paragraphs contained information which has never been revealed to this day.

'I'm terribly sorry,' said Colin as we left. But it was the end of our literary collaboration. He sacked me from writing the rest of the book and the project was finished by Tony Lewis, an excellent journalist and also a former England cricket captain.

There were no hard feelings. But I had learned a great deal about the indecisiveness which had lost Colin Cowdrey the captaincy to Australia. The ruthlessness he had displayed in the West Indies was no longer there. He prevaricated, as some gentlemen of a certain upbringing do.

He remained a close friend until his death yesterday. A superb cricketer, a man of uncompromising values, has quietly left the field of play.

BRAVE STEWART DESERVES RECOGNITION

Could IW's timely public reminder have played a part in the deserved award of Jackie Stewart's knighthood in the following birthday honours list?

Dateline: London 2000

GONGS galore for sport and the good folk who make us laugh, deliver milk and see our school kids across the road in safety.

But tell me this: why no knighthood for Jackie Stewart? They won't, of course. They never do.

Was it because of premature gossip column speculation that he would get one? Was it due to some malevolent feeling that he is too close to the younger Royals? Do they still hold it against him that for a few years he domiciled himself in Switzerland? Or was it sheer ignorance of what he has achieved for British industry let alone his impact on motor racing, both on and off the track?

Jackie won't thank me for writing this. In fact, he might go hopping mad. Nonetheless, we really must question an arbitrary honours system which sends Sebastian Coe and the late Colin Cowdrey – both similarly outstanding sportsmen – to the House of Lords, yet leaves plain Mr Stewart in the pit-lane, if not quite the pits.

Only yesterday, in an excellent profile by Jane Kelly in this newspaper, he recalled the carnage of his racing years when drivers died like flies. 'Thirty years ago,' he said, 'if you raced for five years there was a two out of three chance that you would die.' He did not name the man who did more than any other to reduce that terrible death toll.

That man was Jackie Stewart.

Thrice world champion, he used his fame and forceful personality to compel race promoters to introduce safety measures, whatever the cost. Once, two days before a grand prix, he persuaded his fellow drivers to go on strike if the track was not better protected for the sake not only of the drivers but the spectators. The changes were implemented and the race went ahead.

He is a dynamic perfectionist. An ex-champion shot, his shooting school at Gleneagles in his native Scotland is testimony to his insistence on efficiency and discipline. There, with a galaxy of Royals and celebrities on hand, he raised fortunes for charities. As a consultant to the Ford Motor Company, he was hugely respected for his input over more than 30 years.

Could it be that what weighed against his preferment was that, because of his driving skill and commercial acumen, this son of a Scottish garage proprietor is now sincerely wealthy? It is said, for example, that when commissioned to address business conventions or seminars for young high-fliers, his fees are very high.

Well, I'll add something to that.

Some years ago, before an Australian Grand Prix in Adelaide, I was approached by the convener of a lunching club to ask Stewart if he would address them. Somewhat apprehensively, I asked Jackie what his fee would be.

'Are they well off?' he enquired. 'Pretty,' I said. 'Then I'll do it,' he replied. He held his audience spellbound for more than half an hour.

Every dollar of his fee went to a boys' club he supported in London's East End.

This is neither a eulogy nor a lament, just an off-beat observation about this morning's New Year Honours List which rightly celebrates the prestige so many sportsmen and women have garnered for our country.

Chapter Ten

2001–2004

ACTIONS SPEAK LOUDER THAN WORDS FOR WOMEN SAILORS

The extraordinary achievements of Britain's female sailors were hailed by IW, whose approach to women's sport was that of a male but not of a male chauvinist.

F EMINISTS who rant and rave from rostrums and write bitter books about the uselessness of men may now retire to the powder room.

Here, in order of appearance, are four British women who just do it: Naomi James, Clare Francis, Tracy Edwards and Ellen MacArthur. All of them, either single-handedly or as crew skippers, have sailed around the world in such perilous circumstances that they make me feel like crawling shamefully away into some darkened corner to read *avant garde* poetry.

Dame Naomi blazed the trail in 1977. Francis, now also an outstanding novelist, was the first woman to captain a Whitbread-Round-The-World yacht. Against superhuman odds and the scepticism of all old salts, Edwards then raised an all-female crew to do precisely that.

Now, as you read these words, MacArthur is out there, mid-Atlantic, engaged in one of the most epic sporting duels of the new millennium. With still 3,000 miles of the 24,000 miles Vendee Globe non-stop circumnavigation to go, she is sprinting bow-to-transom against France's Michel Desjoyeaux, a hugely experienced single-handed sailor, to be first home, probably in 15 or 16 days' time.

Two days ago she was fractionally ahead. Last heard of she was six miles behind. These are distances in huge ocean racing which equate to about 0.1 of a second in 26-mile marathon foot races.

MacArthur is 24, comes from landlocked Derbyshire and stands knee high to a Shetland pony. She is now in the 84th day of a challenge in which no one gave her a hope, a view seemingly vindicated when she lagged 600 miles behind Desjoyeaux as he turned North from Cape Horn for the long run home. Now, amazingly, she is breathing down his neck.

She is utterly exhausted. Four times she has shinned up the 90-foot mast of her 60-foot yacht *Kingfisher* to release trapped sails. During one 48-hour stretch of her passage into the Doldrums, where incoming weather system information about windshifts requires immediate tacking, she slept for two-and-a-half-hours.

In radio contacts she does not make light of her sheer agony. She is cold, hungry, alone and nervous but is in there fighting for a British victory.

Some woman. As, of course, was Edwards, whom I first met dockside in New Zealand when she was boat-bumming as a cook in the Whitbread Global Race and calmly informed me that, by the next time round, she would have raised and financed an all-woman crew.

Being male and courteous, I bought her lunch and advised her to forget such an absurd idea. Women, I insisted, would never do it.

For months she bombarded me with phone calls pleading for publicity that might help raise the cash. Eventually she charmed the late King of Jordan and the Royal Bank of

Scotland into financing her venture, which led to her bringing her boat, *Maidens*, back in triumph.

I read Tracy's autobiography, *Living Every Second*, in two sittings. This 430-page volume reminded me that, while I love Tracy Edwards like a daughter, the last thing I'd want is her as a third wife. She's far too tough for me.

That goes, I guess, for many men who'd admit, like me, that they are too scared to submit to the terrors and privations of round-the-world racing. Make no mistake, we have unstinted admiration for these women who prove their valour in real danger instead of squawking about rights to breast-feed their children in the House of Commons.

We are with Ellen MacArthur every nautical mile of her way to the finish line. This small message will be delivered to her today and I hope it brings encouragement.

THE ENIGMA OF THE DON

IW had never warmed to the personal qualities of Don Brad-man, the man he acknowledged as the greatest batsman of them all.

Dateline: **Adelaide 2001**

A GENTLEMAN of the cloth claimed from the pulpit of St Peter's Cathedral in Adelaide last evening that 100 million Indians would be clustered around their television sets watching the live transmission of the memorial service for Sir Donald Bradman, who died last month at the age of 92.

It is not for a sin-stained layman to question the unique channels at his disposal to issue such positive TV audience ratings

343

in advance. But I have to say that, had he backed national predictions that minimally 20,000 would turn up in person in Adelaide, his church roof fund would now be in the red.

The beautiful little twin-towered cathedral was packed to standing-room, well above its 1,740-capacity. But merely 250 yards away, the equally lovely Adelaide Oval, which had installed two giant TV screens to accommodate the anticipated overflow, free of charge, was a desolate spectacle. At a generous estimate, 1,500 people turned up.

True, unseasonably early autumn rain squalls and half-mast flags blustering flat out around the arena did not encourage Bradman idolaters to leave their homes, even for a final hurrah to the local man who just happened to be the greatest cricketer who ever lived.

This, too, was pointed out from the pulpit by the priest, who explained that in a poll taken at the end of 1999, Bradman won the votes of precisely 100 out of 100 'experts' as the finest player of the 20th century.

Frankly, this was both patronising and tautologous. We already knew that, and it was far more accurate than all that business about 100 million Indians, however exultant they might be over their recent series victory over Australia, paying homage to The Don.

I now seem to spend my life going to memorial services for people I've admired – Colin Cowdrey's is at Westminster Abbey on Friday – but this one, I confess, baffled me. Bradman had laid down the ground rules for it before he died and his family complied with his every wish. They were anomalous, to say the least.

Among the VIPs present were John Howard, Prime Minister of Australia and a self-confessed cricket freak. He was not invited to speak and neither was Bob Hawke, the former Australian Premier. Bradman insisted there was to be no political spin on the occasion.

Although the service was to be telecast live, Australia-wide by the national TV channel and fully screened two hours later in a replay on Kerry Packer's Channel Nine, only six print reporters – five Australian and one English – were permitted entry into St Peter's.

There was even a family squabble about who should be the lead commentator on the live broadcast. The Bradmans had wanted Ray Martin, a Packer man, because he had conducted the last major TV interview The Don ever gave, an exchange so anodyne that it was obvious the questions had been submitted in advance to avoid controversy.

Amazingly, Packer allowed Martin to work for the opposition channel, which confirmed that Bradman's wishes reached beyond the grave. But ABC, the national network, would have none of it. It stuck with its own man, Tony Squires, normally the jokey host of a sports panel. I have no idea what fist Squires made of it because I was in church at the time.

Admirably, Bradman had insisted that the congregation should include one representative each from more than 150 minor cricket clubs across the South Australia State. In their blazers and club ties, they mingled proudly with the cast of an autograph hunter's dream.

There, alongside them, were fellow cricketers like Sir Vivian Richards and Sir Everton Weekes of the West Indies and the Nawab of Pataudi from India. England was represented by Roger Knight, secretary of MCC.

Sir Alec Bedser, career-long Bradman opponent and friend, would also have been there had his twin brother Eric, from whom he is inseparable, been up to the long journey.

Also present were six of the nine living members of The Invincibles, the Australian team Bradman captained to England in 1948 without a single defeat.

Keith Miller, the swashbuckling larrikin who Neville Cardus

described as the Australian *in excelsis*, was not well enough to attend. It was rumoured at the time that Miller, an ex-Royal Australian Air Force night-fighter pilot in World War II, hardly saw eye-to-eye with Bradman's scorched-earth policy on that tour.

Thus, last evening's commemorative service was shadowed by nuances of the great man's enigmatic character. He decreed that it should be a community occasion.

This it was, largely dominated by members of his own family. His granddaughter Greta extolled his kindness and generosity and sang in a duet from Andrew Lloyd Webber's *Requiem* with a friend, Emily Roxburgh.

Tom Bradman, a grandson spoke with marvellous clarity about the happy family home.

Slightly less clear, in his opening sentences, was Don Bradman's son John, who knew that, eventually, he would have to explain why he decided in mid-youth to change his surname by deed poll to escape the stranglehold of his father's brilliant reputation. I have rarely felt more sorry for a public speaker. John grasped a glass of water at the outset, afflicted by an ultimate nightmare known as dry mouth.

He swallowed hard, got into his swing, told some loyal supportive stories and then explained why, in his father's declining years, he reverted and changed his name to Bradman again.

'I don't remember him once yelling at me,' he said. 'He never lost his temper. As a family we discussed the change of name business. He said: "Don't do it for me." Well, I did.'

Thus a Bradman family rift was healed in public but it wasn't quite over yet. Towards the end, after Richie Benaud had given a marvellous rundown of The Don's genius as a player, strategist and selector, Sir William Deane, Governor General, chose gratuitously to raise a point that has long intrigued biographers. What did Donald Bradman do in World War II?

Well, after enlisting for the Royal Australian Air Force, he was transferred to the Australian Army, from which he was discharged as unfit just before leading possibly the greatest-ever Australia cricket team methodically to destroy England by county and country. During that fallow time he became a member of the Adelaide Stock Exchange in 1943.

Even after death, the man remains an enigma. He was the greatest, no question about it, and his genius was encapsulated by one of the most perceptive cricket writers who has ever set quill to paper.

'Bradman,' wrote R.C. Robertson-Glasgow, 'had one eye on the heavens and the other on the ledger book. In the whole game he was the capitalist of skill. Poetry and murder lived in him together. He would slice the bowling to ribbons, then dance without pity on the corpse.'

This, I believe, was the true epitaph to the man who we assembled from around the world to commemorate.

He was the hardest and most brilliant sportsman the world has ever seen.

TIGER WOODS HAS CHANGED GOLF

Little has changed since IW's article to challenge his view of
Tiger Woods.

Dateline: **Augusta 2002**

AT HIGH noon at the Augusta National Camp Golf Club
yesterday, the consensus was that only one of three factors
could conspire against Tiger Woods winning the US Masters.

These were an overnight close family bereavement, a car crash
or wrongful arrest by a myopic local cop.

Well, he won, and with it the staggering achievement of four
Major championship victories in succession after one of the most
thrilling afternoons golf has ever seen.

But win or lose, one result was guaranteed: the biggest audience
ever to watch live golf on television in America.

TV executive Dick Ebersol said: 'Even when Tiger plays in
an ordinary weekend tournament, the audience shoots up by an
extra million. With all the history hanging on these final 18
holes, we're confidently expecting an extra three million.

'The only sportsman you can now compare him with is
Muhammad Ali. Tiger has become the most instantly recognized
athlete in the world today.'

His impact on the sport is so immense that he attracts not
only already dedicated golf fans, but casual viewers fascinated
by the young black man who, in four years, has turned the most
conservatively traditional of games on its head.

Blacks are now tuning into telecasts of a sport which, until
recently, was predominantly a pastime for the white and wealthy.
So are women.

Naturally the television companies, their commercial advertisers and particularly Nike, the sports equipment manufacturers who perceptively signed Woods on an exclusive $100 million contract in 1997, are ecstatic. Ironically, so are Woods' fellow American tournament golfers.

Apart from those in immediate contention for yesterday's Green Jacket and the $1,008,000 purse that went with it, all were hoping, if not actually praying, for a Woods victory.

The tough Hal Sutton, tied in 25th place and a doomed 10 shots off the pace yesterday, was both generous and philosophical.

'I want him to be the best there's ever been because he's driving the game,' he said.

He didn't actually admit that the rest were hanging on Woods' flying coat tails, but that's what he meant.

Little wonder. In 1996, before Woods turned professional, the cumulative prize money from 45 events on the American circuit was $69 million. This year it has almost trebled to $185 million.

Even last year, 45 US players each took home more than £1 million.

Last year, Sutton outfought Woods to win the Players' Championship by one shot, but there were no hard feelings because he was well down the field here in Augusta.

'Most other American sports are spiralling downwards,' said Sutton. 'Golf has taken off and believe me it's down to one man.'

This unprecedented boom, even at a time when the American economy is trembling, has reached every level of the game.

Flying over America now you expect to see nothing more than neatly mown fairways and sand bunkers. It has 17,100 golf courses and 10 new ones are being opened every week.

Alongside arts and science diplomas, eight universities are

now offering degrees in golf. More than 1,400 students are already enrolled in courses which embrace playing, agronomy, clubhouse management and, for the dunces, caddying.

Woods is too self-contained and intelligent publicly to attribute any of this phenomenon to himself. He has a nine-man management team to handle his business affairs and two discreet bodyguards permanently in attendance. Tiger, with those hooded eyes, simply plays the golf and, after some indiscretions in the early days, avoids all controversy. Celebrity in America has its perils.

If the pressure of incessant public curiosity and scrutiny does not force him into early retirement, I believe we are witnessing the career of a man who, at 25, will become the wealthiest sportsman of all time.

After watching sport for more than 40 years, I, too, believe he stands at the shoulder of Muhammad Ali.

WHAT VAUGHAN MIGHT HAVE SAID

Bored by the predictable responses of players and managers at Press conferences, IW had some gentle fun at their expense.

THE UTMOST congratulations this column can bestow go to Duncan Fletcher, England's cricket coach, for refusing to allow Michael Vaughan to be hauled before a Press conference at The Oval on Thursday evening.

All day, this young man had concentrated his way to 182 not out with an innings that would have inspired the late Neville Cardus, the greatest of all cricket writers, to reach the heights of his purple prose.

Cardus wasn't all that hot on facts and statistics but no writer, ever, has so captured the mood, the heat, the atmosphere, the glory of a wonderful day's cricket.

The last thing Cardus would ever have done would have been to scuttle over to the dressing rooms at close of play and ask Vaughan the most imbecilic of all opening Press conference questions: 'How do you feel?'

Apparently, the game's sponsors, npower, another of those commercial concerns which deem it smart to dispense with capital letters, were incandescent. So incandescent, in fact, that they are now negotiating to lop £1 million off their sponsorship fee.

Vaughan, they'd assumed, was now one of their employees. It was cricket's *duty* to drag him before the media.

It wasn't at all. Post-action Press conferences provoke more problems than almost anything that happens on the field of play. An unguarded aside by Michael Atherton, when he was England captain, detonated a huge diplomatic incident on the sub-continent. A question to John McEnroe at Wimbledon once actually caused a riot.

Moreover, they are rarely enlightening. Cliché follows cliché and, when you listen to the monotone drone of most of them, you are liable to fall asleep anyway. At least Sir Alex Ferguson's gum-chewing usually renders his latest utterance unintelligible.

However, to appease npower, whoever they are and whatever they do, here is what Vaughan *could* have said had he been hauled in for interrogation:

Michael, how do you feel?

Predominantly with my right hand, but it would largely depend on the object under surveillance. For example, if I were examining a bolt of cloth for a new smoking jacket, I might use both hands.

What was going through your mind as you approached 100?

The awful dilemma in which Prince Charles finds himself

about whether or not to allow Camilla Parker Bowles to join the Countryside March on 22 September.

Were you disturbed by the Indians persistently appealing?

I find all Indians appealing. I find India appealing. There is terrible poverty there, of course, but I recall with delight my visit to the Taj Mahal.

Your straight driving has improved immeasurably. To what do you attribute this?

Probably because I passed my test first time when I was 18 and once danced with Stirling Moss's elder sister.

You are already being compared with greats like Hobbs, Hutton and Bradman. Does that inspire you?

I was just as inspired when Molly Holroyd, our village postmistress, received the MBE, if that's what you're driving at.

How do you plan to spend your evening now you are 182 not out?

On my way to Annabel's, I dropped in at the British Museum Reading Room, where Karl Marx used to eat his sandwiches. He's buried in Highgate Cemetery, unlike Trotsky, who collided with an ice-pick in Mexico.

What do you think Nasser Hussain might say to you if you return to the dressing room tomorrow having just missed a double century for the second time in three Tests?

He would probably ask me when I thought Mrs Beckham would get pregnant again so that David could sew another new name on his football boots.

Are you now looking forward to taking on the Australians this winter?

Not if those celebrity drop-outs are still hanging around but, in other circumstances, yes. They say that Sydney has now mostly been cleared of jungle in preparation for the return of Mr and Mrs Richie Benaud.

Mike, this is a Press conference. Are you going to answer any questions seriously?

I thought I had. Out of respect to English cricket and our precious npower sponsors, I have done my best to help you write about anything other than the usual bilge.

BODYLINE WAS A BLOODY-MINDED ASHES TRIUMPH

The events of the Bodyline Tour remain as fascinating and controversial as ever.

YOU DON'T become an honorary Australian until one of that convivial mob confers upon you the ultimate accolade: 'Welcome back, you Pommie bastard.'

This may grate on refined English ears but you have to understand the background. Australia's aristocracy – an oxymoron if ever there was one – now comprises the descendants of those who arrived on those shores in leg irons with First Fleet.

They were mostly sheep thieves, pickpockets and prostitutes, who'd been sentenced to deportation from England instead of being hanged. Down the generations, this act of generosity has generated an historic and healthy rivalry between our two great countries.

This will be hugely evident in Brisbane tomorrow morning when the latest Ashes Test series breaks out in a cacophony of one-eyed partisanship. To me, this is the ultimate sporting rivalry. I once sat near an England player so consumed by nerves that he made three trips to the bathroom to be sick while waiting to go in to bat.

The Australians, on the field, in pavilions, from hospitality suites, in the stands and on the grassy slopes of what they call the outer, want not just victory but utter Pommie humiliation. That's how it always has been and this epic sporting confrontation will lose all meaning if it loses that intensity.

So how do you counter this Aussie aggression? Well, to the gentleman who's just called you a Pommie bastard – he's probably driven out in the rush hour to pick you up at the airport anyway – you retaliate with a few staccato Anglo-Saxonisms and lead him to the nearest bar. You buy the first drink and refuse a second because he is driving. This makes him feel bad because Australians are punctilious about sharing bar bills.

It is all about mind games with Australians, which is why I deeply regret that a pre-publication copy of David Frith's *Bodyline Autopsy* was not flown out to Nasser Hussain, England's present captain, before hostilities start tomorrow.

Frith writes only one cricket book about every two years, because that's how long it takes him to research the subject. This one is about the most tempestuous cricket series ever played, the battle in Australia when in a preliminary match exactly 70 years ago this week, England rattled up a mere 634 for nine declared (H. Sutcliffe 154, M. Leyland 127, D. R. Jardine 108 not out).

Note Douglas Jardine's contribution. No one could accuse him of being a Pommie bastard. He was a Scot of orthodox parentage who was chosen to lead England in Australia when they seemed about as likely to win the Ashes as Hussain's team are from this morning.

The phenomenal Don Bradman was up against them. Jardine evolved a tactic to scare the wits out of Bradman by ordering his bowlers to aim straight at his throat with a packed leg-side field. But that was the least of his stratagems. He wanted his Australian opponents to feel socially inferior, insignificant, unworthy of his presence.

He often wore a multicoloured Harlequin cap and white choker to the wicket to rile them. He looked down his great, hooked Roman nose to revile Australian reporters as vermin. When he had been barracked for slow scoring on one occasion an Australian, Stork Hendry, sympathized with him. 'All Australians,' retorted Jardine, 'are uneducated and an unruly mob.'

'Well, in that case,' replied Hendry, 'you can go to buggery.'

In a drinks break during an earlier match, Hendry, then 96 not out, was warned by an England player that his interval drink, on Jardine's orders, had been spiked with whisky. 'They don't seem to like you very much out here, Mr Jardine,' the player said to his captain. 'That,' replied Jardine, 'is . . . mutual.'

A few writers began to delve into Jardine's background. One, Frank Devine, attributed his perversity and arrogance to his education as a Wykehamist.

'When Jardine was a pupil at Winchester,' he wrote, 'it was at its ghastliest, hurrying students through so that they could make it to the Western Front. Dreadful food and plumbing, discipline verging on sadism and an attitude of superiority to non-Wykehamists were among the school's hideous aspects.'

While Jardine's scorn for Australians was paramount, that early Spartan discipline made him equally contemptuous of anyone in his own touring party who had the temerity to question any aspect of his captaincy. Not even his tour manager, Pelham Warner, was spared.

'One early disagreement,' recalled Bob Wyatt, 'ended in a first-class row in which Jardine was extremely rude to Warner and from that moment their relationship was profoundly unhappy. When he took against anyone, Douglas could be insufferably offensive, adopting an air of cold disdain.'

Once, in a match before the Test series even started, Bill Bowes, the Yorkshire fast bowler who along with Harold Larwood and Bill Voce was to spearhead the bodyline assault, dared to suggest a number of field-placing alterations.

Jardine went berserk. 'Anyone who plays under me,' he snapped, 'does as I say or he goes home.'

'Right,' said Bowes, 'I go home.'

That evening, Jardine summoned Bowes to his presence.

'Did you mean what you said?' he demanded. 'Are you prepared to be on the next boat home?'

'Yes,' replied the unflinching Yorkshireman.

There was a dramatic pause. 'Well that's marvellous, Bill,' said Jardine, realizing he was about to lose one of his key practitioners in the assault on Bradman. 'Shake hands, forget it.'

Bowes stayed on to complete a tour that today would be a tabloid reporter's dream. Rows, scandals, drunkenness, crowd uprisings mounting as the Ashes series reached the crescendo where Australia actually contemplated ceding from the Empire in revulsion at Jardine's ruthless tactics.

Oh, happy tour. In Coolgardie, a stopover on the arduous train trek across the Nullarbor Plain, Tommy Mitchell playfully pulled a goldminer's cap down over his eyes. A second later he was looking down the barrels of two pistols the miner had pulled on him.

Racism? No shortage of it. In Melbourne the Indian-born Nawab of Pataudi, playing for England, was barracked with the words: 'Hey Gandhi, where's ya goat?' At which the elegant prince stared his aggressor in the eyes and replied: 'Ah, so there you are. Would anyone lend me a piece of rope?'

Even richer pickings came with the rumour that Gubby Allen, another of Jardine's battery of fast bowlers, was actually the son of Pelham Warner. Apparently, on a much earlier tour, Warner, described then as 'a carefree young bachelor', had taken a considerable fancy to a married Australian lady named Pearl. The argument about Allen's authentic parentage, since he'd been born in Sydney, was still raging 55 years later.

Badmouthing, far in excess of today's mere sledging, persisted throughout the Test series. Outraged at hearing his prime bowler, Larwood, called a 'bastard' on the field, Jardine stormed to the Australian dressing-room door to demand an apology.

It was opened by Vic Richardson, grandfather of Ian Chappell, a later Australian captain famed for pithy remarks to incoming English batsmen. Richardson stuck his head back into the dressing room and yelled: 'Hey, which of you bastards called Larwood a bastard instead of Jardine?' There was some doubt about whether, on that occasion, it was meant to be a term of endearment.

We live in calmer times. Nasser Hussain, an excellent captain, will undoubtedly be a more diplomatic spokesman throughout the series. And anyway, he does not have a fast-bowling armoury of the kind Jardine deployed with such antagonistic fervour to put the fear of God into this Australian team.

England won that 1932–33 series 4–1, almost certainly due to Jardine's utterly uncompromising captaincy.

A curious thing happened in England's second innings in the final Test in Sydney with the rubber long dead. Still, 54,000 were packed into the ground soon after breakfast. They had come to see Australia's fast bowlers kill Jardine and that was clearly their intent as they bowled straight at him, inflicting bruise after bruise.

Towards the end of his life, in his bungalow in Sydney, Larwood told me what occurred.

'Mr Jardine,' – note the respect that survived after 50 years – 'never flinched. He took everything they could fling at him, never once complaining, though he was black and blue.

'He'd reached 24 before they got him out and then, as he

turned and walked away from the wicket, that crowd rose as one man and applauded him all the way back to the pavilion. That's Australia for you.'

Larwood reached into a box he had brought from his bedroom and produced a precious memento. It was a silver ashtray inscribed with the words: 'To Harold, from a grateful skipper.'

I am grateful to David Frith's immense research for unearthing some of these extraordinary tales in the most brilliant sports book I have read for years. It is his magnum opus, a tour de force, and, as I said, it could have been a source of inspiration for Nasser as he goes into battle against the Aussie bastards while we sleep.

THE FULL MONTY

IW has always chronicled with affection the contrasts in the character and career of one of the most talented British golfers of his generation.

FOR SEVEN years he was the undisputed heavyweight champion of Europe. His performance in the most recent Ryder Cup was a masterpiece of golf, self-discipline and inspiration. According to the newspapers he has stockpiled £25 million.

You might reckon that most men at 40 would regard that as having made a suitable impact on his profession and life itself and stop torturing himself. If he were a footballer, a tennis player or an athlete there'd be no alternative but Colin Montgomerie is none of these things.

Colin chose golf. It might even be said that golf chose him by blessing him with such inordinate talent. It did not, however, endow him with Kipling's ideal characteristic: an ability to cope with triumph or disaster just the same. Easier said than done, of course, especially in high-performance sport around which the critics hover like vultures. But Colin is particularly vulnerable.

During our occasional encounters I have invariably found him charming but, then, I have not had to seek out an interview with him when he has just taken a 77 or missed a cut. On these occasions Ernie Els he is definitely not.

He can stride past reporters, shoulders slumped, hangdog of expression, face black as thunder, anger visible in every movement. Maybe it's just as well he doesn't choose to speak in these moods, though occasionally he has. He once turned on a group of American spectators, for whom he has small regard, and said: 'The only thing worse than losing is having to spend another day in your country.'

Occasionally, having observed the conduct of small, vociferous sections of American golf galleries at Ryder Cups and even the US Masters at Augusta, I thoroughly empathize with that observation. But it was a disastrous remark, now embedded in the files of newspaper cuttings and will continually be resurrected in future unflattering profiles.

This is not a profile, either flattering or unflattering, because I do not know Colin Montgomerie well enough but, like thousands of his British admirers, I am deeply distressed by the unhappiness that now seems to have enveloped his life.

I refer not to his failure ever to have won a Major championship title – the ultimate prize is still a frustrating mirage – but to the apparent chaos of his domestic life that caused him to fly home from the China Masters before hitting a shot, in an attempt to save his marriage.

In this he failed and within a few days announced his second separation from his wife, Eimear.

This is no agony uncle column and I neither know nor wish

to know the details, but Monty himself has been surprisingly open about what led to the breakdown. In his autobiography, *The Real Monty*, he said: 'I saw myself as a good husband. I was neither a womanizer nor a drinker and I always hurried home at the end of every tournament.'

But he accepted blame for his 'obsessive' approach to golf. 'It was golf, golf and more golf. I look back on my behaviour now and wince.'

Yet there was even more to it than that. It was about *winning* at golf, indeed winning at *anything*, and I take the liberty of quoting an anecdote written by the admirable Lewine Mair, who ghost-wrote Colin's book and probably knows the inside story of the marriage turmoil far better than any other straw-grasping journalist.

Apparently Olivia, Colin's eldest daughter, had been playing Monopoly with her father, and returned to tell her mother: 'I've had to let him win again.' To which Eimear replied with resignation: 'That's your father. It's just the way he is.'

Well, that's how Don Bradman was at cricket, mercilessly annihilating to the point of humiliation any English county team that stood in his path in his invincible tour of England in 1948. He, too, was obsessed.

Bradman's marriage to his wife Jesse survived happily for more than 50 years, which suggests that it takes two to tangle in these matters.

I have witnessed dozens of marriages break down, not only in sport but sportswriting, not excluding one of my own, mostly due to long absences from home in the pursuit of something called success.

Colin Montgomerie has enjoyed enormous success and there are those among us who hope he will relax a little and carry on. For the moment this is a sad story but who knows what the future holds?

ENGLAND WIN RUGBY WORLD CUP

Rugby, whether Union or League, was not one of IW's usual subjects but the manner and style of England's World Cup win against Australia gave him the greatest pleasure.

HAD A fiction writer submitted it for publication it would have bounced back with a sarcastic rejection slip. Handsome, modest hero wins World Cup with last kick and extra time on zero?

Too fanciful by far, old boy. Just a little more plausibility please.

And yet that's precisely how it was when after 99 minutes and 40 seconds of gut-wrenching emotion, John Eales, a former Australian captain, graciously acknowledged that his country had just been beaten in the greatest rugby match ever played.

Beaten by what? An England team that out-dazzled Australia in every department? Certainly not. An England team that had eliminated errors by sure handling? Ridiculous. England made more blunders in this game than they had in two previous internationals strung together.

So how come they won? I will tell you exactly.

By absolute discipline, iron-willed determination, ruthless management over a three-year build-up, total team unity under a hugely respected captain and the genius of a 24-year-old goal kicker who has no ambition to roar around the celebrity circuit in one of his three Ferraris or pose for pictures on Elton John's yacht.

For these attributes a frustrated Australian Press deemed them dull, old and boring.

In which case, please Lord grant English sport a plethora of dull, boring geriatrics who manage to avoid being arraigned on the front pages of the Sunday tabloids for snorting cocaine through £50 bank notes and subjecting teenage trollops to mass priapic initiation rites.

For only the second time in 37 years English streets were largely deserted as millions gathered round television sets in pubs, clubs or at home to watch an England team win a World Cup.

Thanks to the time difference between Sydney and Greenwich, a breakfast-time screening in England meant that many youngsters would have had their introduction to rugby, a sporting code with seemingly arcane rules, colossal violence and much blood.

When they saw George Gregan, the Australian captain, lifted completely off his feet, then carried and catapulted 10 yards through the air, some may have wondered why the perpetrator wasn't red-carded and probably banned for life.

It was because that devastating tackle was utterly fair. That's rugby.

When they saw Jason Robinson hurl himself across Australia's line for England's only try they may have found it strange that he didn't pick himself up, rip off his shirt and then run half the length of the field, arms flapping like a demented duck before disappearing under an ecstatic mob of team-mates.

Well, in rugby, they just don't do that sort of thing.

When Jonny Wilkinson won the World Cup for England with that final brilliantly planned dropped goal, they may have expected him to have turned and executed an elaborate V-sign in the direction of the Australian Press, who'd been on his back for the previous six weeks.

He was hugely elated – his mother back in England was shopping in Tesco at the time – and England's captain Martin Johnson actually smiled in public for the first time in about two years. There was joy but no obnoxious triumphalism. That's rugby, too.

When this titanic World Cup final ended there was the ultimate tribute to the game. Despite their bitter disappointment, Australia's captain and coach could not have been more genuine in their congratulations.

All the Pom-baiting nonsense stirred up by Australian newspapers was forgotten. The ludicrous idea that an England victory or Prince Harry turning up in a red-rose shirt would hasten Australian voters into a referendum to transform their nation into a republic was seen as the utter poppycock it always was.

Australia is a superb sporting nation, arguably, per capita, the strongest in the world. Quarters are never given or asked for when they meet what many still quaintly see as the Mother Country.

After the horrendous beatings they have handed out to us on the cricket field, this was England's turn. And rugby gave it to us. We should examine a little more closely how this was achieved.

For some fatuous reason there were class-warfare agitators on radio talk-ins yesterday still maintaining it is the manifestation of public school and Oxbridge exclusiveness. Utter rubbish.

This may have been so back in the thirties, but to suggest that such snobbishness has survived the transformation into a decade of professionalism, the breaking down of Hadrian's Wall between rugby union and rugby league, is to reveal not only prejudice but blind ignorance.

Come to the *Daily Mail*'s Schools Rugby finals at Twickenham each spring. They are mostly terrific kids from state schools.

It is probably a cheap shot to keep comparing rugby's virtues with the shambolic disorganization of English football, whose economic disasters are matched only by the fact that before a player is selected it is advisable to check up whether he is on a rape charge, awaiting the result of a drugs appeal, on bail for a racial indiscretion or serving 100 hours of community service for a motoring offence.

But Clive Woodward, coach of England's victorious World Cup team, would tolerate none of that.

He demands the best for his players, takes no notice of amateur administrators in striped ties, has no star system in his squad and chooses his team, however it might dent a few egos, entirely on how he envisages the strategy demanded on a given day.

His demeanour in Australia, a country whose noisy patriotic eccentricities he knows well from having lived there, was outstanding.

He met the inevitable barrage of anti-Pomism with laconic humour, knowing it is nothing more than hot air. He has emerged the winner. Believe me, Australia will respect him for it without reservation.

In short, I believe Woodward did even more than Johnson's implacability and Wilkinson's stupendous kick to win this sporting bauble for England.

Bauble? Well, in the context of the world we live in with dreadful massacres being reported almost hourly, the Rugby World Cup is little more than a temporary diversion. But it can be more than that.

We live in a world threatened by mad religious anarchists and a country dragged to its knees by politically correct zealots who believe that children should not be humiliated by defeat. In other words, don't bother trying.

England's rugby team fought on Saturday, by God they did, and how I would like to see their victory videoed into every

English school this week. This was England, my country, at its best.

Thank you, gentlemen, for reminding us that from time to time some of you can rise above our national lethargy and cantankerousness and beat the world.

Chapter Eleven
2005–2007

BULL'S EYE IN PAMPLONA

Over the years IW paid frequent visits to run with the bulls at Pamplona. No longer able to travel, he still wrote on the subject. This is the last of those articles.

ALAS, I must guiltily admit that there is a definite connection between running with the bulls at Pamplona and strong drink. I have done 'the run' 23 times over the years: never drunk, because that would be absurdly dangerous, but always fortified by sufficient rough brandy to quell the nerves.

Yes, there are nerves. As yesterday's extraordinary pictures from Pamplona showed, this is no ordinary sporting endeavour. Limbs can be gored, bodies trampled over and even lives lost amid the exuberance and chaos of this ancient Spanish festival.

No amount of machismo can save you from the force of a charging half-ton bull that has you in its sights. Eight people were gored on Monday and 15 more injured in the crush.

To many, it is a barbaric ritual – not only for the unfortunates who end up in hospital with shattered limbs and torn flesh, but for the majestic beasts whose furious last dance before death so delights the crowds.

Certainly, the Pamplona run seems an anachronism in our age of animal rights, EU regulations and the Health and Safety Executive. Perhaps that's why it's more popular now than ever.

Every year the crowds get larger – thousands of thrill-seekers for whom the danger of Pamplona is not so much a threat, as a celebration. I have shared their excitement and their fear – a fear that becomes visibly apparent about five minutes before the run begins.

A hush descends over the thousands jammed into the narrow streets as the bulls are gathered before the start.

Everyone is waiting for the bangs of two firework rockets: the first signals that the first bull is on its way, the second announces that the sixth and final bull is also free to exact its revenge on the human race during its few brief minutes of liberty.

The timing between these two signals is critical. If the bangs are less than three seconds apart, then that morning's run – one of seven during the course of the festival – is likely to be as tame as a day of gentle birdwatching.

It means that the herd of bulls are moving as one group, proceeding the 900 yards through the streets and into the bull-fight arena – where all will meet their deaths in that evening's *corrida* – as tamely as a flock of sheep.

What presages real danger is when these two rockets are 30 seconds or more apart. This means that the bulls are segregated, bewildered and angry and quite likely, as they did on Monday morning, to turn back on themselves and into the throng of revellers who are following them on foot.

I have seen men killed and gravely injured in these circumstances . . . and also one miraculous escape.

One year, I watched as a middle-aged American businessman, trapped on his buttocks in a doorway, was confronted by a bull that was about to kill him.

There was no one within 30 yards to attempt a rescue until, suddenly, a Basque teenager burst from the crowd and waved a folded newspaper beneath the bull's eyes to distract his focus from his quarry.

The bull turned away and I will forever believe that an American life was saved that day. I asked the man afterwards whether he had sought out his rescuer in the aftermath and suitably rewarded him. It had never occurred to him. The idiot replied: 'I've always believed that fortune favours the brave.'

In truth, it doesn't require much bravery to run with the Pamplona bulls, particularly among the thousands who crush to the top of the Estaveta, the street that dips down directly into the bull ring and offers a comfortable exit from all danger.

The crowds start sprinting from the moment the first rocket is fired and are mostly in the arena behind the safety of the barricades before a bull arrives.

The greater thrill is to bide your time at the side of the street, waiting until the bulls are 10 yards away, and then hurling yourself into the noisy chaos.

Much kudos is afforded those who can run some distance with one hand firmly planted on the flank of a bull. Occasionally this may amount to a 20-yard dash, or – on a good day – 100 yards, before you peel off, hoping sincerely that another of the bulls is not on your tail.

Madness? Perhaps. But also a moment of unadulterated excitement.

Down the years I have taken two of my sons to join in the throng, not as some initiation rite, but for the sheer enjoyment. I admired them as they dodged and ran their way to safety.

One of my sons was trapped between two bulls for a 150-yard sprint. His face shone afterwards and he never drew another sober breath that day. It must run in the family.

But it is when the bulls are fresh at the start, and frequently belligerent, that the run has real significance.

The Basques are the best at it. It is their national sport and they train like Olympians, running two yards in front of the leading horn knowing there will be a painful awakening, or even none at all, if they make a slip.

One such runner is the great Ferman Echeverria, who many

years ago spoiled one of his own 'runs' to educate me in how to keep out of trouble. He taught me how to 'read' the bulls, carefully watching their every move for signs that would indicate which side of the street they would charge along.

I was never hit by a bull and was injured only once, falling over an American and hitting my head on the pavement.

There have been exemplary foreign runners, too, none more welcomed by the Basques than the glamorous Matt Carney, an ex-American Marine veteran of Iwo Jima, who knew no fear. He was badly gored one year and the locals so loved him that they sent a noisy band to his hospital bedside to cheer him up.

Such local fame was shared by one of America's greatest literati. Before he shot himself in despair that his writing powers were failing, Ernest Hemingway returned to Pamplona each year to be lionized for virtually internationalizing the Pamplona festival with his novel, *The Sun Also Rises*.

Hemingway relished the acclamation, holding daily congress with hangers-on outside bars in the plaza, expounding on the virtues of human courage.

This did not sit well with his compatriot, Matt Carney, to the point that one day he approached the great writer and said: 'Hemingway, you've never run with the bull in your f***ing life.' And threw a glass of red wine in his face.

Well, all manner of things have happened in Pamplona, few of which explained why I returned there year after year. There is a theory that middle-aged men go in pursuit of lost youth and young men in search of maturity.

That's too profound for me. I went because you were surrounded by like-minded friends at one of the last sporting hurrahs in the world. It was totally amateur. There were no prizes and there was no sponsorship.

I ceased going five years ago. No longer could I sleep in

the street until dawn broke, ready for a few drinks before the run.

Drugs and pickpockets prevailed. And, more pertinently, my legs were no longer quick enough to get out of the way.

SHANE WARNE – KING OF HIGH THEATRE

During more than half a century of writing about sport, IW became good friends with a number of his heroes. Shane Warne, the great legspin bowler, was both hero and friend.

IN ITS millennium edition, after the profound deliberation you would expect of such a conservative authority, *Wisden* announced its nomination of the five greatest cricketers of the 20th century.

The first four were Sir Donald Bradman, Sir Jack Hobbs, Sir Vivian Richards and Sir Garfield Sobers.

The fifth? Title-less, and likely to remain so, was an Australian larrikin who only considered a career in cricket at the age of 19 when his ambitions to become an Australian Rules football star were thwarted by lack of speed and bulk. Glory be for cricket.

I first set eyes on Shane Warne when he was bowling in the nets alongside the Sydney Cricket Ground. It was mesmerizing. He bowled on and on for the sheer joy of it: enormous legbreaks and googlies interspersed by mysterious deliveries yet to be defined.

That he was subjecting his spinning fingers and right shoulder to needless overwork never seemed to occur to him. It revealed

373

a certain recklessness that was not only to transform big cricket at a time of crisis but also to illuminate, sometimes to his detriment, his erratic personal lifestyle.

Scene Two: Shane's arrival on the international stage, which will be replayed on television long after we are all dead.

Old Trafford, Manchester, 1993. Warne is handed the ball to send down his very first delivery, not only in the match but the series and his first in Ashes cricket. It was so abjectly wide that Mike Gatting contemptuously disdained him. Until, that is he looked back and discovered it had ripped across him and struck his off stump. Gatting's facial disbelief confirmed that it had come from Mars. Typically Warne: a dramatic high-theatre start. But the significance of that single delivery must never be underestimated. For two decades Test cricket had been dragged down by a plethora of intimidating fast bowling, particularly by West Indies and Australia. Now, at last, spin bowling – and wrist-spin bowling at that – had been resurrected.

Shane, 35, has an irresistible personality, a constant broad grin – except when umpires reject his latest frenetic appeal – an instinctive ability to amuse people and the kind of natural gift for insubordination associated during two World Wars with Australian fighting men, the bravest of the brave, yet volubly intolerant of some of the more formal conventions of military life.

This has landed him in several scrapes. A run-in with bookmakers, a period of suspension for taking a diuretic, the lowest of sport's banned substances best left well alone, and a series of domestic upheavals after which, each time, he expresses contrite remorse.

I have one imperishable memory of him when at the height of his much publicized national campaign to give up smoking, he met my wife and I outside a Test ground in Australia where all tobacco was banned. 'For God's sake,' he gasped, 'have either of you got a fag?'

Another vignette. When his autobiography was published in England and he was asked to publicize it on TV and radio interviews around the nation, he rejected planes and trains and asked if he could be loaned a Ferrari to drive himself to each assignment.

This was granted and his initial jerky progress in a 150 mph car down the traffic restrictions of Kensington High Street will long be remembered by pedestrians who scattered out of his way.

A one-off, Warne. In his 2000 *Wisden* citation it suggested the predictions that he could take 600 wickets in Test cricket were 'fanciful'.

Today, as he appears at Old Trafford for the third Test, his wicket toll stands at 599. Huge acclaim, from the entire world of cricket, awaits him.

If *Wisden*'s selection of Warne as one of its five greatest cricketers over 100 years required any endorsement, it comes from Richie Benaud, himself a great wrist spinner in the doldrum years when it was going out of fashion.

'Warne,' said Benaud some years ago, 'is the finest leg spinner of all time. He is on track to break the record for the highest number of Test wickets ever taken.'

Old Trafford awaits that landmark to be achieved this weekend and I hope when it happens, my countrymen in this now tumultuous battle will arise as one man and woman and acknowledge an astounding accomplishment.

THE ASHES PROVE BIGGEST SELL-OUT

IW's illness prevented him from covering his beloved cricket on a day-to-day basis but the public response to England's challenge for the Ashes in 2005 gave him enormous pleasure.

CRICKET's most famous poem was almost a still-life portrait of an age of English elegance: a breathless hush in the close, last man in with 10 to win. Doubtless cucumber sandwiches afterwards.

Contrast that with Old Trafford – no, not that Old Trafford – in Manchester two evenings past. No breathless hush this time.

Maelstrom. Cacophony. A constantly roaring full-house. Not only that. More than 10,000 had been turned away early morning at the gates, another 10,000 halted at the commuter railway stations to be warned that there was no hope of getting in.

Across the nation, those who couldn't cram around television sets had transistors clamped to their ears. In my home, constant to-and-fro phone communication with friends in Australia who were sitting up all night to watch the climax on TV.

'Bloody marvellous, isn't it,' said my mate Laurie Sutton, 10,000 miles distant in Sydney, 'that we can watch this together.'

Ten to win was the least of it. Australia's last two batsmen had to survive 24 balls to draw. Inspired by a stupendous captain's innings by Ricky Ponting, they achieved it. Americans, who demand a positive result in any sporting contest, however contrived, would not countenance a five-day battle ending without a winner.

Well, this one demolished that outlook. It was every bit as gripping as the Birmingham Test, a mere week earlier,

376

described by many a critic as the greatest Ashes confrontation ever played.

'Cricket's back,' claimed many headlines. Not entirely true. Cricket has never been away. What has happened is that this enthralling series, now level at 1–1 with two to play, has confronted a brilliant all-conquering Australian team of the past decade – but now approaching its sell-by date – with a vigorous English squad whose star players have at last been unshackled from the dreary treadmill of county cricket, with its daily abundance of second-rate players before an audience of one retired vicar and a pensioner or two.

County cricket must always have its place, since it is the classroom where the Trescothicks, the Strausses and Vaughans study for their elevation to a central-contract system under which they are reasonably paid and bond into an élite force, fiercely competing for an England place. It has transformed the selection process, once little more than a pin jab at names featuring prominently in newspaper listings. For heaven's sake, England once had four different captains in a single summer.

Much of this development I warmly attribute to Lord Ian MacLaurin, who, in his brief reign as English Cricket Board chairman, began to oil the wheels of progress. He wasn't entirely inexperienced at this since he had transformed Tesco into the monolith it is today, but there were some at Lord's who resented him. 'Trade, old boy,' they sneered, and he gracefully withdrew.

But he'd made the breakthrough. English international cricket had been steered out of its somnolence into aggressive thinking, the result of which is what we are witnessing in an Ashes Test cricket series which, if it continues like this, will be the most thrilling ever played.

With my enormous knowledge of this game I took many bets, convinced Australia would wipe us out. As a sportswriter I am pressured to be neutral, but little would please me more than to lose every last wager. C'mon England.

This Test series has been so compelling because it has been played with remorseless ferocity but without ill-feeling.

The umpires have been under enormous pressure and, yes, there have been a few brief black looks when a decision has probably been wrong. More than that would incur the loss of an entire match fee.

Compare that with footballers whose snarling ambushing of referees, under weak-kneed authority, would hardly lose them a week's wages – not that some of them would miss £100,000 anyway.

But this unashamed eulogy of cricket's thrilling renaissance in recent weeks is not aimed at denigrating the other misnomered 'beautiful' game, although in one respect it might.

Channel 4's outstanding coverage has including many inter-action reconstructions of great Ashes cricket dramas in the past and interviews of the highest quality. One was Mark Nicholas chatting up Prince Philip, the best was Michael Atherton talking to Sir Alex Ferguson, who'd dropped in from the other Old Trafford across the road.

Listening to Ferguson's stunted Caledonian grunts when hauled before the cameras after a football match – he won't speak to the BBC anyway – the uncommitted viewer may well dismiss him as a near-illiterate Scot.

His response to Atherton's fearless and intelligent interview was revealing. He was aware he was being questioned by a man who had given his all for his country and responded accordingly. It was the most coherent conversation I have ever heard Ferguson deliver and it showed his respect for a cricketer who had fought his insides out for England in sterner times.

The ECB have made a dreadful mistake in selling the rights of future international games exclusively to non-terrestrial television, but claim they need Rupert Murdoch's millions. So, terrestrial viewers, enjoy this colossal Test series while you can.

It is 50 years since spectators ringed Lord's at 7 a.m. to watch Denis Compton bat and more than 70 years since the City emptied at the news that Donald Bradman was entering the arena.

Those days are in cricket's valiant past. New ones are upon us if this glorious Test series can convince the nation that football is not the be-all and end-all of our existence.

This may be difficult. Cricket is a transitory game, badly managed at the highest international level in many ways. Many have learned from the past fortnight that it could regain its status here as the Englishman's heritage, once described by another lovely homespun poet, Hugh de Selincourt.

He naturally had no idea of what it felt like to have a Brett Lee bouncer drawing blood as it smashed into the left temple of his helmet, and so may seem out of sync.

This is cricket now. A violent confrontation, but as gripping a battle between our two countries as there has ever been.

I first watched England v. Australia as a short-trousered school-boy at The Oval in 1948 when Don Bradman required only four runs to average 100 in Test cricket. He was out second ball, for a duck.

Since then, long-trousered and representing this newspaper, I have reported many Test matches between the two countries, both there and here.

None has remotely compared with the present conflict. Ladies who spend their lives watching 'Coronation Street' have been phoning radio stations saying they have never been more trans-fixed.

The simple truth is that cricket must go on from here. It has the young lions to do so and a nation now behind them.

Breathless hushes in the cloistered closes will be no more.

RICHIE PITCHES IT JUST RIGHT

As a broadcaster as well as a newspaper journalist, IW was
well placed to recognize quality. He ranked his friend Richie
Benaud among the select few of great sports commentators,
alongside Longhurst, Arlott and Alliss.

S O IT is farewell, then, to the Master of Measured Words. Richie
Benaud will not be returning to England next summer to sustain
his pre-eminence as cricket's finest television commentator.

That is not merely my judgement. A recent poll by *The Wisden
Cricketer* magazine attracted an astonishing 12,000 votes.
Precisely 10,128 of them nominated Benaud as the best.

Fortunately, he does not leave us without a word or several
of advice to those who seek to emulate his success, particularly
retired players whose agents deem them instantly equipped to
pick up a microphone and irritate us with an effluent of Tower
of Babel verbiage.

He does so in a valedictory book to be published next month,
of which more later. It is an encyclopaedia of broadcasting
wisdom.

He names no names. He is too polite for that. Nor is there
a hint of the tetchiness that occasionally afflicts icons in their
pensionable years.

At 74, Benaud is still as fit as a flea, the result of a lifestyle
as measured as his commentating. Yes, there are rare occasions
when he will let down his hair with the rest of us, but when
serious business is afoot he will rise from an increasingly raucous
dinner party, check his watch that it is exactly 10 p.m. and
announce: 'Thank you very much. We're off.'

At sunrise next morning, he and Daphne, his elegant and unfailingly supportive English wife, will be striding out on their three-mile constitutional.

He is meticulous in all things. On TV commentary days even Daphne is not allowed to iron his shirts. He presses them himself. He is a food faddist, preparing his Test match lunch boxes at home to be certain of what he is eating. Once he took a week-long course in Italy to learn how to cook pasta to perfection.

His desks at his homes in London, south of France and Sydney are polished plateaux of precision, his reference-book shelves indexed for instant reach.

It is this unrelenting self-discipline, instilled by a schoolmaster and great club cricketer father and a lovely mother – there is a gorgeous picture of her celebrating her 100th birthday with Richie and his Test cricketer brother John in the book – that launched him into his dual career life.

The first, of course, was in cricket, where to haul oneself from school to club, to State, the Australian team and then its captaincy, was a classic climb. Benaud led his country in 28 of his 63 Tests and never lost a series. Such was his cunning as a wrist-spinner that his batsmanship was often overlooked.

In fact, he became the first, in an era when far fewer Tests were played, to scale the double of 200 wickets and 2,000 runs.

But what next? All of seven years before he retired from cricket, Benaud wondered if there could be a distant future in the communications industry. There was little doubt about that since he had been a young crime reporter on a Sydney newspaper, where sub-editors ruthlessly deleted from his copy any flowery phrases which he thought rather good but were irrelevant to the story. It was an important lesson.

Then a curious opportunity, which couldn't happen in today's schedules, presented itself. At the end of Australia's 1956 tour to England, all their players were given three weeks off to enjoy such fleshpots of relaxation as they could discover in the British Isles.

Benaud proceeded otherwise. At his own expense he moved from the Kensington Palace Hotel into a cramped lower ground room in the RAC club in Pall Mall and took a BBC television training course, watching alongside directors, commentators, even audiences, to learn how television worked.

He trailed Peter O'Sullevan at Newbury and he studied the commentating techniques of Henry Longhurst on golf and Dan Maskell on tennis. All three had their idiosyncrasies, but one thing they had in common.

O'Sullevan, voice rising to overdrive at the climax of a horse race, was circumspect about collateral chatter just as Longhurst and 'Oh I say' Maskell knew the value of golden silence. Indeed, one of Longhurst's silences was so long that his director asked over the private intercom: 'Excuse me, Henry, but are you still alive?'

Benaud now says: 'I didn't know if I had a future in broadcasting. If I hadn't done that BBC course my life would have been very different, even though I had to wait for seven years for my chance. The key feature it taught me was the economy of words. Never insult the viewers by telling them what they have seen perfectly clearly themselves. Only add to it if you had something pertinent to say.'

These days, if only.

Has he ever made a bloomer? Of course, like all of us, he has. On one celebrated occasion, handing over from a Test match for a news update from Moira Stuart, he called her Moira Shearer, the celebrated ballerina who had starred in an acclaimed film.

When Moira Stuart handed back he said: 'Thanks, Moira, our newsreader wearing Red Shoes.'

Many, who had not heard his initial blunder, wondered what on earth he was on about.

'At the time,' he recalls, 'I thought it was a pretty clever remark, but many tuning in at that moment had no idea what it meant. It taught me never to be such a smart-arse again.'

Laconic, economic, massively instructive and with a dry impartial wit about whoever is getting the upper hand in a Test match, I wonder if we shall ever hear his like again on television?

Many are called and surprisingly many are given the opportunity behind the microphone. Very few have served the slogging apprenticeship that makes a master cricket commentator.

NO FLOWERS PLEASE FOR GEORGE BEST

IW's sympathetic but clear-eyed farewell to George Best, is a tribute to a footballer whose genius he admired and whose flaws he recognized. He had liked Best since first meeting and writing about him 40 years earlier.

O NLY THE waning hours of a monarch or great statesman could have equalled this week's half-hourly news bulletins updating the nation on the fading life of a maverick footballer.

Indeed on Wednesday, Sky TV broke away from its prestigious Prime Minister's Questions coverage to take us to London's Cromwell Hospital for the latest statement from the lugubrious Professor Roger Williams who, throughout, has understood the demands of a voracious media and responded with an admirable lack of sentimentality.

By yesterday, some newspapers jumped the gun by publishing

ream upon ream of obituary notices even before poor George Best was dead.

Anticipating the inevitable may be considered a smart move in the current circulation wars but, frankly, I did find this rather callous and upsetting for his gathering family. Since I am about to do much the same – George was still tenuously clinging on to life as I began to write these words – I shall probably be accused of rank hypocrisy.

George, of course, wouldn't give a damn one way or the other. He lived much of his life in utter chaos, largely attributable to his fatal addiction to alcohol, even after he had been offered a reprieve by receiving a liver transplant. And may I say in passing how much I despise those ghastly puritans who wrote to newspapers saying he should never have been given a second chance.

The irony of his plight was that his last coherent message to the youth of Britain – 'Save yourselves, don't do as I have done' – coincided with our Government's appalling decision to extend drinking hours to twice round the clock.

Any regular drinker, as I have been all my adult life, knows the perils of that rather better than Ms Tessa Jowell, its defender, whose porcelain complexion suggests she has never experienced a full-scale bender when one drink inevitably leads to half a dozen more.

But how did George with his manifest fallibilities – appearing roaring drunk on television shows, failing to arrive at all at dinners staged in his honour and with a tangled love life involving wives, Miss Worlds, sundry mistresses and random one-night stands – attain the iconic status that sees him genuinely mourned by millions today?

Above all, obviously, was his glittering brilliance as a footballer, exercising his wonderful birthright of sheer balletic balance which, over 10 years, saw him making donkeys out of exasperated defenders who would willingly have chopped his legs off below the knees.

I don't claim to have known him half as well as some of his obituarists, a number of whom I note rely on newspaper cuttings rather than personal acquaintance, but I watched his mesmerizing talent many times playing for Manchester United in the 1960s when I was ghost-writing columns for their manager, Matt Busby.

Matt was a kindly, gentle man who occasionally confided, strictly for non-publication, the troubles he was having with his Northern Irish larrikin, who was drinking and fornicating his way around Manchester on the strength of his two other natural attributes: he was devastatingly handsome and highly intelligent. He was convivial with everyone unless some hanger-on attempted to lure away his latest inamorata, in which case there could be mighty trouble.

I suspect Alex Ferguson would have applied a far firmer hand but that is hindsight speculation. Their Celtic temperaments would certainly have clashed.

Was George the greatest attacking forward Britain, even the world, has ever known, as some have effusively claimed? Better than Pelé or Maradona?

I have watched all three, magnetised by their respective bewildering brilliance, but am too ignorant about the game to presume to offer a judgement which could only be subliminal anyway.

What I do know is that George Best beat both of them in his post-football life. Maradona turned into an obese pot of lard and Pelé went around the world boring everyone stiff with pontifical statements about the state of the game and a highly lucrative TV commercial concerning male erection problems.

Dear George, meanwhile, who had scant difficulty in that area until recent weeks, continued to attract headlines he mostly didn't want for his continued erratic behaviour. It made me curious how at least half the nation warmed to a maverick whose later

385

life was a two-fingered salute to even the outer margins of political correctness.

There was to be no long-term redemption. He died yesterday of his own folly. No flowers, please, from tiresome sentimentalists who pretended to know him but didn't. George, whether he is raising hell somewhere or eyeing up some heavenly virgins, would laugh at that.

KERRY PACKER – THE REBEL

IW had been the first to break the news of the defection of the Packer cricket rebels, on 9 May 1977.

THERE WERE no two ways with Kerry Packer. There was his way and no one else's, a ruthless characteristic directly responsible for detonating the deepest schism in cricket history.

Thwarted from winning the rights to add live television cricket coverage to his rapidly expanding media empire, Packer, who died yesterday aged 68, struck the game's unsuspecting establishment a paralysing blow beneath the belt.

With immense secrecy, he persuaded almost all the world's most exciting players to renege on their national contracts and join his World Series rebels in Australia by the simplest of expedients.

He offered them a wage commensurate with their immense talents, in some instances paying them up to 10 times more than they had earned only a month previously.

It was 1977. He was 39 at the time, in robust health and didn't give a damn that he was now a reviled figure in most corners of the conventional cricket world. Lifelong friendships were impaired and I regret to say that even now, 28 years later, there is residual suspicion of those prepared to give Packer a fair hearing at the time, of whom I happened to be one.

I argued in these pages that all Packer had done was pre-empt the inevitable. Top cricketers were so abominably paid that at some time there would be a revolution. Packer had merely precipitated the situation with an outrageous coup.

This stance had two repercussions. Such was the heat of the debate that certain colleagues accused me of treachery. But Packer and I struck up a strange affinity, far from the friendship it became years later. I had never met him before and detested the obsequiousness with which those of his inner circle fawned upon him to keep their jobs.

I wanted nothing from this massively rich media tycoon who, on an impulse, might offer one 10 times the salary I was receiving from the *Daily Mail*. No way would I want to work for a volatile powerhouse who was as likely to fire you the first time you ever wrinkled your brow in disagreement. He was a bully, no doubt about that, and ruled by intimidation, but there was another side to him which I was later to discover.

We got on rather well because I think he appreciated there was at least one English reporter who didn't condemn him out of hand. He gave me interviews which others couldn't get and amazingly agreed to co-operate for a full-length TV documentary, *Mr Packer and the Poms*, which Michael Begg and I produced for BBC2.

Eventually, of course, he won the day when he brought a High Court case against cricket's establishment in London. It lasted three weeks and cost a fortune but it was won on the grounds of restraint of trade on the opening morning by a brilliant speech by Robert, later Lord, Alexander, who died only a couple of months ago aged 69. Brilliantly they had won the issue.

In the years that followed I was privileged to see a side of

Kerry Packer that eluded so many of his detractors. There were certain things that I detested about him, particularly his insistence of addressing me as 'son'. Kerry was five years my junior but he would still say: 'Look, son, why don't we . . .?'

There was an afternoon in Sydney when I received one of these come-hither calls. Kerry was presiding over a post-lunch gathering of his editorial chiefs who were mostly drunk. Kerry wasn't. He was a compulsive smoker and swore like a dervish. But he didn't drink at all. But I was to be the butt of his latest gag, the Pom who was about to take my lovely, pristine wife on a 10,000-mile journey around the Australian Outback.

'What the f*** do you know about the Australian Outback,' he declared. 'How dare you take that girl out there when you know f*** all about it. It is very dangerous.' He was right: it is. His acolytes roared their approval. That evening I flew to Melbourne where on arrival a communication from Packer's PA awaited me. 'Kerry wishes to meet you at Sydney airport at 9 o'clock on Monday morning,' it stated.

Actually it didn't suit my itinerary but I went, waiting in a hut far from the terminals, where a man burst in and said: 'Come with me.' I did. A few minutes later I was sitting in Packer's private plane.

There were two pilots and a butler prepared to serve gin, vodka, scotch or beer. We were on the way to Elliston, Packer's country estate. On arrival there was a jeep waiting at the end of the runway. It whisked me to the main house where his estate manager, Tony Miles, gave me three hours of instructions about the perils of the Outback, many letters of introduction and showed me how to get a four-wheel drive out of bulldust. After lunch we went kangaroo shooting, which I hated.

On a flight home Packer, having devoted his entire day to this operation, said: 'Just look after that girl and remember to take a gun.' We did and never used it.

I have many memories of Kerry Packer. Many found him deplorable but without him cricket would not be the vibrant game it is today. A rapscallion, certainly, but a man who changed the world game. I have one particular fond memory. Late in life he became a polo addict and brought many of Argentina's great players to Britain.

One evening after a late match somewhere he was returning to his home in Sussex when he asked his secretary to phone the nearest local restaurant to prepare dinner for his team. They responded that they would be closing by that time.

She rang the next restaurant down the road where they said they would be very happy to stay open for him and they provided everything that was necessary.

He left a small tip on condition that they told the first restaurant what it amounted to. It was £10,000. That was Kerry Packer.

POSTSCRIPT

GOOD TIMES HAD BY ALL

ON A HOT March morning in 1982, wandering into the beautiful cricket ground in Port Elizabeth, South Africa, it occurred to me that it might be courteous to say hello to the local Secretary, whoever he might be. A young black man led me to an office next to the dressing rooms where a large, affable white man extended a huge right hand and introduced himself.

'Welcome,' he said. 'I'm Tom Dean.'

Well, it's some way back to 1948 but there was no mistaking

the man who on the County Ground, Southampton, had flattened my off stump and with it my unwarranted dreams of a career in professional sport.

'Good God,' I heard myself saying. 'You're the man who changed my life.'

'For the better, I hope.'

One had to admit that free tickets for the best seats everywhere with someone else footing the hotel and travel bills had certain compensatory factors. Driving back from our salutary reunion after 34 years I began to compile a mental list of what one would have missed. It was not all sport.

There were the awesome hues of an Indian Ocean sunset seen from the after-deck of the *Canberra* and the staggering pyrotechnics of the aurora borealis viewed from an Eskimo village on the rim of the Arctic. There was the radiant goodness that shone from the astounding face of Pope John XXIII as he passed within a yard in St Peter's Square, greeting Olympic athletes and confusing entrenched agnostics. There was lunch with Segovia, patron saint not only of the guitar but of wisdom. There were the many Spanish mornings in Pamplona, waiting for the bulls to lurch round Estefeta and present them with their last chance to reverse the normal outcome of a bullfight. There was the conversion to jazz in a night-long tour of New Orleans and also the joining of the never-ending queue that shuffles silently forward for the privilege of staring for a few brief seconds at the waxen face of Chairman Mao, the most influential man of our times, in his very public resting place in Peking. There was the bewildering hour watching Jimmy Grippo, aged 83 and the greatest card manipulator of any age, accepting a newly shuffled pack in Las Vegas and dealing the perfect poker hand 10 times out of 10. There was the halved birdie four with Gary Player at the Houghton course in Johannesburg, not to mention the nine at the next par three. There was the trans-Atlantic flight with the charming neighbour who left it until somewhere over Newfoundland before he revealed he was Sir Robert Watson-Watt, inventor of the radar that was homing us so safely into New York. There was the impromptu cricket match with West Bromwich Albion's footballers on the lawn in front of a hotel in Shanghai, watched by 4,000 bewildered Chinese Communists, on a Sunday afternoon. In London there were the dinners, in shimmering candlelight, with Brigadier Michael Hobbs and the Grenadiers guarding the Queen. There was the chat in a B29 flying high above Texas with the man who dropped the bomb on Hiroshima. There was the friendship with the late Vincent Mulchrone, the best writer of the decade in Fleet Street, and the companionship of Ron Atkinson, now manager of Manchester United, as we roared Cambridge Lad home to a terrific victory and lots of pocket-money in a bent race at the Happy Valley race-course in Hong Kong for the simple reason that Atkinson had once managed Cambridge United. There was the 10-lap drive in a charity race round Brands Hatch which induced a fear I have never known before or since. There have been afternoons looking at the Goyas in the Prado, Madrid, and evening listening to opera in that strange, hooded building in Sydney. There was also the morning when a Polish newspaper editor insisted I went with him to learn something about German culture and I suddenly found myself, outside Katowice, staring at the mind-rending horrors of the Auschwitz concentration camp. There have been rounds of golf in the Rocky Mountains, deep-sea fishing over the Atlantic Shelf off Bermuda, train journeys up the inside of the North Face of the Eiger and a glimpse of the peaks of both Everest and Kilimanjaro. There has been a visit down a South African gold mine, to Gandhi's ashram in Ahmadabad and to Beethoven's birthplace in Bonn. There has been money lost gambling on the pelota in Mexico City and money won at the roulette tables in Baden-Baden, home of the world's most beautiful casino. One of the most eerie experiences was simply drinking a glass of sherry at the home of the Terry family in Jerez, knowing that it had lain in the huge black cask since 1815. The only point to this list is that being condemned to write about sport instead of playing it has paid for, subsidized or provoked each experience.

There have been many great cricket innings which could be marked for elegance or splendour but the most memorable, for me, were both by Englishmen batting against West Indies to inspire their teams back into the fight. Ted Dexter's 70 at Lord's, in the bronchial dampness and cathedral gloom of Friday, 21 June 1963, was struck off 74 balls of venomous intent and was described by several who had watched 50 years' more cricket than I had as probably the greatest short innings ever played. It remains the greatest *any* innings I have ever seen, fractionally ahead in technique, though not in character, of Ken Barrington's essay in resolution in Trinidad in January 1968. Barrington's small problem, as he walked out to bat that day, was that two years earlier he had publicly declared that Charlie Griffith, of West Indies, was a cheat who wilfully threw a cricket ball instead of bowling it. Now, by force of wholly unpredictable circumstances and to a packed crowd baying for his blood, here was Barrington emerging to face a man of wrathful temperament who clearly believed he had been seriously slandered. Four times in the first nine balls he received, Barrington survived appalling injury only by hurling himself flat on the ground. The outcome of the affray was rather more dignified. Barrington scored 143 but I shall always believe the strain of it contributed to the heart attack which killed him.

So often it is the circumstance that heightens the achievement. It was so for Mary Peters, determined as she was to win an Olympic gold medal in Munich not only for herself but for the beleaguered city of Belfast. It was so for Sebastian Coe, coming back from a stinging defeat in the 800 metres at the Moscow Olympics to win the 1500 metres in a style that left so many of us that evening, crouched at typewriters in a frantic Press-room, wondering where the words would come from this time to do justice to a human being in his finest hour.

The danger lies with the wild superlatives. The fear is that you could underplay it. The object is to bring a million readers to your seat, and the rule is that when the presses roll several minutes later, your words will be beneath them. You wind a sheet of paper into the typewriter and, after such time as the deadline gave you, you reach for the telephone. It is a nervous business, every time, and when it is done you laugh again and have a drink. It is a strange way to go through life but, to Tom Dean and others, my eternal thanks.

FINAL WORD

MAX WOOLDRIDGE

IT WASN'T always a wise move introducing a girlfriend to my father. Invariably she fell instantly in love with him and it would be several days before I won her back. Then I'd constantly be badgered for another dinner date around his house. Ever the gentleman, Dad was good enough never to act upon their infatuation.

Like countless other people who met him, they adored Dad's wit and charisma. They loved his mix of old-world charm and understatement. He represented a simpler, gentler and easier time when Britain owned all the pink bits on the map. The good old uncomplicated days when wholesome folk who resembled Ian Carmichael ran the civil service and Terry-Thomas the country.

At dinner, he would hold court at the end of the table, always dressed in an immaculately pressed long-sleeved shirt. A dimpled tumbler of whisky was never more than an arm's length away as he enthralled guests with anecdote after entertaining anecdote. These stories were sometimes interrupted by novelty items, such as talking parrots or singing fish, hastily summoned from the mantelpiece.

In an age when gobby, shameless self-promotion is all the rage, my father remained endearingly unfashionable until the end. Even if he thought he was the best sportswriter of his generation – and wrote better than anybody else – he had the grace to keep it a secret.

The same charisma and quiet dignity saturated his newspaper columns, and, as a result, people who never met my father felt that they knew him. For many women with little or no interest in sport, my father was the only sportswriter they ever read.

I grew up in Ealing, west London, and on wintry Saturday afternoons when Dad wasn't on assignment abroad, our family home would be plunged into darkness. No bizarre black-magic sacrificial rituals here; this was how he watched the Five Nations rugby. Long before high-definition television sets were available he simply closed the curtains to ensure a clearer picture. If Dad wasn't at a match, he'd monitor it closely on TV, even if it meant the rest of us stumbled around the house.

It was a happy household in which to grow up, filled with my father's *joie de vivre*. He could extract humour out of ordinary circumstances. For instance, during the summer holidays one year, when I was about six, I was bored beyond belief. The clattering noise of a typewriter filled the top of the house – always a sure sign that Dad was home – but suddenly it stopped and my father called me up to his office. I ran up the stairs as quickly as I could and opened the door but couldn't see him anywhere. The room was so thick with cigarette smoke I needed a thermal imager to locate his whereabouts. Undeterred, I waded through the fog to find him sat behind his desk, still in his boxer shorts. On the desk, next to the typewriter, telephone and overflowing ashtray, stood an empty glass.

'Ah, my boy,' he said, 'be a star and fix me a gin and tonic?' I was delighted to be asked. He always brought me back presents from his travels, now this was my chance to do something for him. Anyway, it sure beat playing racing cars on the bedroom floor. I raced downstairs and filled a glass with two-thirds gin and a third tonic before bombing it with ice. The result was easily the worst gin and tonic ever made. By the time I carried the concoction back to the top of the house the ice had melted.

'Ah, splendid, Max,' Dad greeted me, before returning to his typewriter. As I left the room, the typing resumed, but it stopped just as quickly, to be followed by a cough and then a loud laugh, an infectious sound somewhere between a chuckle and a groan.

The foolishness of asking his youngest son to make him a drink had not been lost on him. Typically, he never mentioned the incident but it was many years before he asked me to fix him another drink.

Our house was often filled with sporting legends – Mary Peters, Ian Chappell, Sir Learie Constantine, Cliff Morgan, Geoff Boycott, Ted Dexter, John Arlott to name but a few. One evening, Richie Benaud, the former Australian wrist-spin bowler and television commentator, gave me a personal tutorial in the art of leg-breaks, googlies and flippers with an orange across the lounge floor.

My elder brothers, Kevin and Simon, and I would wait until guests were outside before we sidled up to them and asked for autographs – we were too nervous to ask when they were actually in the house. Many nights I fell asleep to a hubbub of warm laughter rising from the dinner table downstairs. In the morning, I scoured cereal packets for free stickers and breakfasted among the debris of empty Courvoisier bottles and full ashtrays. At school later, I boasted about our famous houseguests and felt gutted when none of my friends had heard of them.

I was immensely proud of my father and all his achievements, even if, as a youngster, I didn't always understand their true significance. Much to Dad's amusement, I told friends he'd been voted 'Communist of the Year'. It was, of course, Columnist of the Year – an award he won twice, as well as a stash of other prizes.

In my early 20s I told Dad I wanted to write. He responded by lending me his treasured copy of Evelyn Waugh's autobiography *A Little Learning*, saying, 'Read this.' After he died I learnt that he offered the same advice to every young journalist he met – except they never got to borrow the book.

I cherished our impromptu discussions about writing. Often it was like listening to a prophet speak. Sometimes, too embarrassed to take notes in front of him, I'd rush to the loo and scribble down everything he had said. Dad made writing look easy, effortless even, but only a privileged few saw the dedication it took to get it right.

Indirectly, he launched my own writing career. In the late 1980s, he took me to Pamplona one year to run with the bulls. I wrote about those heart-pumping minutes and won an *Observer* travel-writing competition. As a young writer it didn't help much having such a well-known wordsmith lurking in the background. It was hard to ignore the pressure to succeed and I often felt like a footnote to my father's life. But all that changed when confidence in my own writing blossomed. I loved being his son again, and felt proud as punch when others spoke about him.

Before serious illness took hold he'd unfailingly telephone me when I had a double-page travel feature published – often hideously early, just a few hours after I'd got in from partying. 'Well done, old boy!' he'd say in a hoarse voice. It's just not the same when I have something in the papers now. The silence deafens my heart.

Despite being desperately ill he worked tirelessly until the end. He continued to write his column until the week before he died. Fittingly, his last piece was a heart-rending charity appeal on behalf of the brain-damaged boxer Gerald McClellan. That was typical of our old man – he'd remember sport's fallen heroes or keep in touch if their circumstances changed. On a family holiday in Ireland in the 1970s we visited Danny Hearn, a former rugby international who had become a paraplegic after a crunching tackle.

Dad covered every major sporting event for the *Daily Mail*, including 10 Olympic Games. Even if the nature of sport had changed dramatically and it was no longer the noble pastime he grew up loving, Dad genuinely liked the sportsmen and women who embellished it. That said, he rarely disguised his contempt for the vultures who could surround them. I always thought he wrote brilliantly about boxing and one of my favourite passages is the following from the mid-1990s. Hilarious and incisive, even today I find this just as astounding a piece of writing as when I first read it. Like a boxer himself, Dad lines us up for a battering before he disarms us with a sucker punch:

> *As a preposterous little poseur, Chris Eubank has had no rival since Mussolini. He struts around like some tailor's dummy, Master of Foxhounds, monocled like the twittish disinherited drop-out of a terminally in-bred aristocratic family, and speaks total balderdash with the impenetrable conviction of Edward Heath. I will now tell you why I adore this extraordinary professional pugilist. Never mind the opponents he has beaten by the dodgiest of margins. He has beaten boxing at its own disreputable game.*

The last time I saw my father properly was in early February 2007, a few weeks before he passed away. It was the Saturday of the Calcutta Cup rugby clash and Jonny Wilkinson's triumphant return to the England side. Throughout the match Dad was in discomfort, often doubled over in pain that could be assuaged only by a cocktail of drugs and single malt.   I joked that I thought of suing him for wilfully squandering my inheritance on decades of booze and bad living. Through the pain, he chuckled, his response unrepeatable.

I thought then he had about a month left but he passed away a couple of days later. I wasn't ready for him to go. There were so many things we hadn't discussed, so many memories to summon up again; so many conversations we'd never have now. Touching obituaries followed. Rival sportswriters gave him a farewell fit for a reigning monarch and even his beloved *Guardian* published a send-off usually reserved for little-known Guatemalan poets or Mongolian land-rights campaigners. With

Dad's passing it was as though a chapter in Fleet Street's history had closed.

I spent a tearful Tuesday reading the tributes, my father's life suddenly laid out before me like a wall chart. Kind messages of condolence arrived but one email in particular provided some much-needed light relief. It came from a fellow travel-writer friend, Ian Belcher, who's clocked nearly as many adventurous escapades as the old man. He forwarded a message he'd received from a sarcastic friend called Fat Gareth:

'Oi, Belcher! I've just been reading the obituary of some really big journalist. He sparred with Idi Amin, trekked across Alaska with huskies, ran with the bulls in Pamplona, hurtled down the Cresta Run and flew upside down with the Red Arrows. Now, you useless bastard, what have you done in your bloody life?'

The old man would have loved that. But no laughter this time. Instead, he would have smiled quietly to himself and then poured a large Scotch.

INDEX